SHAPING THE PUBLIC GOOD

Shaping the Public Good

WOMEN MAKING HISTORY
IN THE PACIFIC NORTHWEST

||||||||||||||||||||||||||||||||||||||||||||||||||||||||||||||||||||||||||||

Sue Armitage

To Judy —
In celebration of women of
all times & places —

Sue Am

Oregon State University Press   Corvallis

The paper in this book meets the guidelines for permanence and durability of the Committee on Production Guidelines for Book Longevity of the Council on Library Resources and the minimum requirements of the American National Standard for Permanence of Paper for Printed Library Materials Z39.48-1984.

Library of Congress Cataloging-in-Publication Data

Armitage, Susan H. (Susan Hodge), author.
 Shaping the public good : women making history in the Pacific Northwest / Sue Armitage.
   pages cm
 Includes bibliographical references and index.
 ISBN 978-0-87071-816-8 (paperback) — ISBN 978-0-87071-817-5 (ebook)
1. Women—Northwest, Pacific—History. 2. Northwest, Pacific—History. I. Title.
 HQ1438.A19A76 2015
 305.409795—dc23
                                     2015030645

Oregon State University Press
121 The Valley Library
Corvallis OR 97331-4501
541-737-3166 • fax 541-737-3170
www.osupress.oregonstate.edu

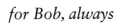

for Bob, always

Contents

Introduction

Preceding page: Tsagigla'lal, still watching from the banks of the Columbia River
(courtesy of Kristine Birch)

This book takes its inspiration from the story of Tsagigla'lal, She Who Watches, whose face is carved into a rock overlooking the Columbia River. The Wishram people tell her story this way:

A woman had a house where the village of [Wishram] was later built. . . . She was chief of all who lived in this region. That was long ago, before Coyote came up the river and changed things, and people were not yet real people.

After a time Coyote in his travels came to this place and asked the inhabitants if they were living well or ill. They sent him to their chief, who lived up in the rocks, where she could look down on the village and know all that was going on. Coyote climbed up to her home and asked: "What kind of living do you give these people? Do you treat them well, or are you one of those evil women?"—"I am teaching them how to live well and to build good houses," she said. "Soon the world is going to change," he told her, "and women will no longer be chiefs. You will be stopped from being a chief." Then he changed her into a rock, with the command, "You shall stay here and watch over the people who live at this place."

All the people know that she sees all things, for whenever they are looking up at her those large eyes are watching them.

Tsagigla'lal's continuing watchfulness epitomizes the ways in which women have always made history. Although, as the story tells us, after "people [became] real people" women were stopped from being chiefs, with Coyote's help Tsagigla'lal kept right on guiding her community and guarding its development. Today women hold a number of official leadership positions, but their mothers, grandmothers, and women before them followed Tsagigla'lal's way. Excluded from positions of public authority, women worked persistently and cooperatively with other women to protect their families and build their communities, and in so doing they made our regional history. Like She Who Watches, women have never been mere observers, but in fact have been watchful guardians and active shapers of the public good.

It is time for the history of the Greater Northwest—the Pacific Northwest and British Columbia—to reflect that reality. In the past several decades, there has been an outpouring of books, articles, films, and exhibits on women. Each one has added to our knowledge about individual women, but few have changed popular understanding, leaving the impression that women were only minor characters in the making of our regional history. I aim to change that with this book.

First, let me locate my boundaries. The region that environmental historian William Robbins has called "the Greater Pacific Northwest," which I have shortened to "Greater Northwest" for ease of reading, is the territory bordered by the Pacific Ocean on the west and the Continental Divide on the east and connected by the Columbia River and its tributaries. Today we call it the Pacific Northwest—the states of Washington, Oregon, Idaho, and the western part of Montana—and British Columbia. As Robbins points out, this territory shares north–south bioregional features that were reflected in the experience of the Native peoples who lived in the region for millennia before European contact. Although their Greater Northwest was divided in geographic ways that separated seagoing Coastal peoples from those on the Columbia Plateau, and from tribes in the arid Great Basin to the south, they were linked by long-established trade carried on well-traveled seaways and Columbia River routes. Later, fur traders and pioneers in the early nineteenth century described these same geographical boundaries as Oregon Country: the land north of Spanish California, south of Russian Alaska, and west of the mountains. Today, although an international boundary divides British Columbia from the Pacific Northwest states, both economies, and especially their natural resources, are similarly affected by global capitalism and world markets. On the other hand, they have different governments, British Columbia beginning as a colony in the British Empire and continuing today as a province of Canada, while the Pacific Northwest territories (later states) have been governed by the laws of the United States. Thus in spite of the geographic similarities, different governmental policies have affected women on each side of the border differently. And finally, the unifying concept of the Greater Northwest acknowledges the widespread popular sense of regional distinctiveness, of being, as the title of Jean Barman's history of British Columbia tells us, in *The West beyond the West*, no longer the very remote place it was in the past, but still pretty far out there.

Most of us know something about a few extraordinary women in Greater Northwest history. Sacagawea, the Shoshone woman of the Lewis and Clark expedition, usually heads the list, followed perhaps by missionary Narcissa Whitman, Mother Joseph of the Sisters of Providence, suffrage leader Abigail Scott Duniway, artist Emily Carr, and perhaps a contemporary female politician or two. Knowing something about these few women does not explain how women have made the history of the region. We need to look beyond them. There *were* extraordinary women (more than those listed), and there were even larger numbers of women whose daily activities and opinions were never recorded. But most women fell into a third group, the ones whose personal and community activities affected the development of the Greater Northwest. In these pages, I will show the ways that women shaped regional history in a narrative that encompasses the famous, the forgotten, and the women in between.

Why don't we know more about these women? Why aren't they in the history books? The reason is not hard to find: standard histories are about important national political, military, and economic events, and until very recently women have not been national leaders in these fields. That must mean, the reasoning goes, that women haven't done anything important. In fact, women were doing something *different*, namely family-based, domestic activities that were judged less important than the achievements of the male leaders who are the subjects of standard histories.

In contrast to great and important histories, so-called grassroots history explores the daily lives of ordinary men and women and members of racial/ethnic* groups who have generally been overlooked. This viewpoint is driven by the belief that *everyone*—man and woman alike—is an actor in history, shaping, to a greater or lesser extent, their own lives and those of the people closest to them. Cultural history has added the insight that every human group organizes and ranks itself according to cultural beliefs about race, class, and gender; as a result, some people have substantial power and others have little or none, while everyone, high and low, is affected by that ranking. This view of history insists on human agency and autonomy while at the same time recognizing the very real constraints— sometimes external, sometimes self-imposed—on people of differing sex, race, and economic status.

For Greater Northwest women as a whole, the greatest historical constraints have been deep-seated beliefs about women's family roles. Until very recently, most women have been wives and mothers who have regarded their family responsibilities as primary. These women were molded by the cultural beliefs and economic necessities of their time,

---

* I use the term racial/ethnic to denote all the groups that we used to call "minorities." Later in this study I also use the term "women of color" as well as specific names for individual groups.

and as best we can tell, most of them derived real satisfaction from their domestic lives and community activities. Those who were not satisfied, or who had wider aspirations, were usually deterred by economic circumstances and social attitudes. It was not until well into the twentieth century that women insisted on their right to participate in the political and economic world and assume visible leadership positions. A basic assumption made in the following pages is that, before then, most women worked quietly and informally to assure the stability and security of their own families and of the communities of which they were a part. Many older accounts of historical events discuss men's actions and opinions, assuming that they included those of women, but that was not necessarily true. Women had different perspectives based on their own priorities on which they often acted quietly and independently. They were not bystanders: they were actors in history whose beliefs and activities in building the Greater Northwest have not been fully visible.

This survey of women as history-makers tells the story, so far as possible, of women's activities and purposes from the earliest inhabitants to yesterday's newest migrant, told within the general contours of the growth and change of the Greater Northwest. It is based on over three hundred books and articles that have been written about regional women in the past thirty years. I am immensely grateful to the authors of each work; every chapter includes an extensive list of sources for readers who want to learn more about particular women and for teachers and students who want to analyze topics in depth. I have drawn on these books to create a continuous narrative about women's lives and activities in the Greater Northwest. This historical survey reveals patterns in the ways women's cooperative efforts have developed over time. Overall, my intent is to showcase the varieties of women's activities and values and what they have held in common. My purpose throughout has been to provide an ongoing context for women's lives and to demonstrate how their activities have made the history of the Greater Northwest.

One of the challenges of writing a survey history, I discovered, is that the available information varies considerably for different periods of time. Many topics have not been researched at all, and others only slightly. In particular, I could not tell the stories of racial/ethnic women as fully as I would have liked. Nor could I explore the history of women of the Greater Northwest since 1945 in the detail they deserve. In many cases, I could not find individual women's voices and have been forced to be generally descriptive rather than specific. In those cases, I wrote about events affecting an entire community and the women in it, even when I lacked individual names. Readers inevitably will disagree with some of my perspectives, my omissions, and my conclusions. Throughout, rather than limiting the story to notable women, I have tried to find representative voices and examples to illustrate the ways ordinary women have shaped our lives.

The first and most striking thing about the history of the Greater Northwest when viewed through women's eyes is how unsettled it has been. For over two centuries the Greater Northwest has been a site of constant change, for no sooner did groups of migrants make communities than newer groups remade them.

To use a harsher but perhaps more accurate word, the Greater Northwest has experienced multiple invasions. The most far-reaching was the European conquest at the turn of the nineteenth century that devastated long-lasting patterns of Native life. Then, in the 1840s, the invasion of American farmers swiftly ended the fur trade and the way of life associated with it. Next came more localized destruction and resettling caused by recurrent gold rushes, beginning with California in 1848 and continuing to that of the Yukon half a century later. In the next invasion, in the 1880s, corporate forces scrambled for control of the region's extractive industries, reshaping the economic and social lives of old and new residents and provoking protest and reform movements that lasted into the 1920s. Following in rapid succession were the dislocation of the Great Depression, massive wartime militarization, postwar suburbanization, Cold War pressures and fears, the sudden awareness of natural-resource limits, the impact of new waves of immigrants and the assertion of civil rights by other groups, and the economic shocks of the postindustrial globalized world.

Women led none of these invasions, but they were part of all of them, as either victims or victors. As you will read in the following pages, the work of women was integral to the survival of the First People,* Native women made the fur trade possible, pioneer women kept families fed and clothed and settled, women's domestic skills made life in gold camps tolerable, miners' wives built communities as their men built union solidarity, Indian women held their families together through repeated displacements, women's clubs worked diligently for community betterment. Add to this

---

* "First People" refers to Indigenous people before European contact; "Native" to those people in the contact era; "Indian" to the common and inaccurate term that Americans used to denote them. Thus language itself reflects the impact of conquest.

the increasingly assertive women working in temperance organizations, as missionaries and teachers on Indian reservations, as home economists and public school teachers, as urban reformers and "municipal housekeepers," as sustainers in the depths of depression and war at home and in internment camps, as suburban community-builders, as civil rights activists, as workers, lobbyists, politicians and labor organizers—women have always been there, always making history.

Threaded through this narrative of women's lives are three recurring themes. The first is the story of how Native women, over the course of two centuries, have found ways to save themselves and their communities from destruction. Their efforts are described in nearly every chapter, both as a reminder of the ongoing costs of the conquest and to draw attention to their remarkable record of survival.

A second theme is domesticity, an activity shared by women of all races and classes. Because it has been so closely linked with culturally shaped ideas about appropriate female behavior, domesticity has meant different things in different settings. Nothing shows that more dramatically than the shocked response of missionary women to the domesticity of their Native counterparts (chapters 2 and 5). Because domesticity has been such a variable concept, let me be specific about what I mean. First, I use domesticity as an economic term, denoting the skills necessary to gather, grow, and process the items essential to feed and clothe one's family, as in the lives of the First People (chapter 1) and the Oregon pioneers (chapter 3), or to manage the family budget in miners' families (chapter 6) and in the Great Depression (chapter 9), to give just a few examples. Closely related are women's relationship skills that nurture and maintain family networks and, by extension, build and maintain family-based communities (chapter 5). Late in the nineteenth century, proponents claimed that women's skills at "municipal housekeeping" would clean up urban politics and that the profession of home economics would "elevate" families (chapter 8). In the twentieth century, as the economy changed, women's household production was replaced by consumption, and the economic value of domesticity diminished while its nurturing aspect expanded, explaining why domesticity was so dominant a theme in postwar suburbs (chapter 10) and why its defense formed a major part of the backlash against the women's movement in the 1970s (chapter 11).

A third and final theme is women's work, at home and in the workforce. Historically, until modern times, the gender-based division of labor within the family made perfect sense: there was so much to do, and specialized skills were necessary (chapters 1 and 3). But in the workplace, gender assumptions trapped women in limited, low-paying jobs that were primarily domestic in nature owing to the economic primacy of male-dominated occupations (chapter 6). As women's jobs gradually expanded in number, they remained categorized as lower-paying "women's work" (chapters 7 and 8). The breakthrough during World War II (chapter 9) was temporary, and only since the 1970s have cracks in workplace gendering appeared for a few women (chapter 11). The current situation in which women, many of them mothers of small children, make up almost half the workforce is unprecedented and has not yet found an adequate political solution (chapter 11).

This book argues that the major activity of women of all races and all times in the Greater Northwest has been to build and rebuild families and communities. Even the most cursory survey reveals the absolute centrality of their efforts and of their methods. Cooperation was basic: women rarely acted alone. They worked with family members—male as well as female relatives—to establish their families and to build communities. As some communities crumbled, women worked to rebuild and to adapt or change them. This effort is as real and ongoing today as it was two centuries ago.

We have not fully understood the many ways in which women's family responsibilities have always reached far into their communities to shape, change or rebuild them. That is the major task of this book, to show how and why women have made—and are still making—the history of the Greater Northwest in personal and informal ways within their own families and communities as well as at a more visible level. It is a record that deserves to be widely known and recognized as an essential source of the making of the history of this region. I hope that this book contributes to that goal, and that we will all come to see that, just as Tsagigla'lal herself still watches above the Columbia River, women in the Greater Northwest have been continuing guardians and shapers of the public good.

SOURCES FOR THIS CHAPTER

This version of the Wishram story of She Who Watches is on the website of Warm Springs artist Lillian Pitt (www.lillianpitt.com/culture/native_legends.html), and in the print collection by Jarold Ramsey, *Coyote Was Going There: Indian Literature of the Oregon Country* (Seattle: University of Washington Press, 1977). Most well-known of the major regional histories is the old standard text by Dorothy O. Johansen and Charles M. Gates, *Empire of the Columbia: The Pacific Northwest* (New York: Harper and Bros., 1957). In the 1990s, it was largely replaced in the classroom by Carlos Schwantes, *The Pacific Northwest: An Interpretive History* (Lincoln: University of Nebraska Press, revised and enlarged edition, 1996); and Jean Barman's monumental *The West beyond the West: A History of British Columbia* (Toronto: University of Toronto Press, 3rd ed., 2007). There have been few recent efforts at overviews; the one I found most useful was William G. Robbins and Katrine Barber, *Nature's Northwest: The North Pacific Slope in the Twentieth Century* (Tucson: University of Arizona Press, 2011). For national women's history, I have used the textbook by Mari Jo Buhe, Teresa Murphy, and Jane Gerhard, *Women and the Making of America* (Upper Saddle River, NJ: Pearson Prentice Hall, 2009).

Chapter 1
First Women 10,000 BCE–1770s

As the long winter drew to a close, the families readied themselves to begin their seasonal journey to gather food for the coming year. They sharpened their digging tools, repaired holes in their carrying baskets, checked their bows, arrows, nets, and fish spears, and packed the essentials for travel, burying the rest of their belongings in baskets until their return. Still, they waited. They could not go until the grandmothers said so, for only they knew when the first roots would be ready to dig and when each subsequent root and berry they sought would be ripe this year. The survival of the entire group depended on their special knowledge. Very busy months of travel and work for all the family lay ahead as the women gathered and the men hunted and fished. But for now, everyone waited for the grandmothers to say "Go."

Throughout the Greater Northwest, the summer season was a time of urgent action, when the bulk of the winter's food was found and preserved. Precise details differed by geographic region—the above example comes from the Native group we now know as the Coeur d'Alene Indians—but the whole describes millennia of summers in the lives of the people of the Greater Northwest, who today are called Indians in the United States and known as First Nations in Canada.* And the seasonal round reveals the crucial role that Native women played in their people's survival. They and their kin were embedded in millennia-old work routines that assured everyone the ability to survive and cherish the bounty of their homelands.

The ancestors of these first peoples probably came from Asia, thirty thousand to ten thousand years ago, crossing a land bridge between present-day Siberia and Alaska or taking coastal routes now submerged in water. The precise time span is in doubt: archeological finds confirm that people have lived in the Greater Northwest for more than ten thousand years, but elsewhere in North America there is evidence of even earlier dates. In any case, as different groups migrated southward from present-day Alaska and spread across the continent, each settled in a distinct geographic area. Because they derived all their food and shelter from the land, their specific local environment was the most important fact of their lives.

Many Native people are unimpressed by scientific evidence of long-ago migration. "We have always lived here," they say, knowing their land in deep and multiple ways. Imagine knowing a place so thoroughly that

---

* In this book, I use the word "Native" as a general term throughout the narrative as well as the more common terms, "Indian" and "First Nations," when they come into general use.

21

you know every rock and meadow, every place where something edible can be found, the habits of every animal, and every possible variation in the weather as well. Because everything they had came from the land under their feet (or the sea at their doorstep), all Native children learned these things from adults and from accumulated knowledge contained in the stories about each place that had been passed on from generation to generation. This attentiveness to the land was the basic skill that hunting and gathering societies worldwide used to survive. Equally, they knew that they could never live alone. No single person had the variety of knowledge and skills necessary to survive, so one's kin group was essential to life itself. This knowledge of a particular place gained through direct experience and from collective stories gave Native peoples a connection to the land that was different from that of the Europeans who came later, if only because the European history in the region—a mere two hundred years—was so short in comparison. Nor has that deep sense of the land been forgotten by Native people today. As one member of the Colville Confederated Tribes voiced a shared belief, even in today's changed world, "land stands for existence, identity, a place of belonging."

For most Native people, living with the land demanded their full attention. Finding enough food to eat and to store for the long winters required constant labor. Anthropologists are agreed that hunting and gathering tribes like those in the Greater Northwest divided the work by gender. Women knew where and when to dig and gather the vast variety of roots and berries that made up more than half their diet. They knew how to fillet and dry salmon and other fish, and how to preserve and store food for long journeys and longer winters. Male hunters knew certain territories and the behavior of the animals that populated them, and fishermen knew the ways of the salmon that made their way up the rivers, and every ebb and eddy of those rivers, as seafaring fishermen knew the ocean currents. Each sex respected the expertise of the other because their skills were complementary and each was essential to the whole. In reality, every indigenous group made its own adjustments depending upon environment, circumstances, and individual personalities. As with every other human society, the precise skills each sex was assumed to possess varied from group to group, and there is no way to know how different the division of labor might have been in the millennia before European contact. But the basic gendered division of labor, and the expertise on which it was based, was vital to the survival of all.

The relationship that each group had with the land went beyond detailed geographic familiarity, for knowledge of place was cumulative. Each particular North American Native group identified itself and its place by telling stories about the powers associated with physical landmarks, animals, and other local phenomena. The Nez Perce of present-day northern Idaho still point to the rock they call "the heart of the monster" and tell the story of how Coyote bested him, while the Clallum people say that Mount St. Helens was once a beautiful woman named Loo-wit who was courted by two jealous chiefs, Wy'east, now Mount Hood, and Klickitat, who became Mount Adams. Even after they became mountains they continued to quarrel: "They caused sheets of flame to burst forth, and they hurled hot rocks at each other." (It seems that Loo-wit got the last word when she "blew her top" in 1980.) The seafaring Native groups who occupied the Pacific Ocean coast knew the water better than the land, so many of their stories read like sailor's warnings transmogrified into myth, as in the Tsimshian story about Getemnax, the huge monster with the head of a woman and the body of a man, who created a whirlpool that reached out to drown those who did not show proper respect.

Everyone knew the particular stories of their own place, and they also knew the appropriate circumstances in which to tell them. Grandmothers told some stories to their grandchildren, while men told or performed others at ceremonial gatherings. In this way the group history of the place was constantly remade as stories were passed from one generation to the next. Thus to Native people these places, and these stories, are alive with both collective and personal meanings. As Laguna Pueblo writer Leslie Marmon Silko points out, "one story is only the beginning of many stories and . . . stories never truly end." These stories—alive and renewable expressions of group and individual consciousness—were at the heart of indigenous life. They taught basic lessons in how humans should behave in the powerful and unpredictable natural world upon which their lives depended. Until recently, non-Native anthropologists and historians dismissed these oral traditions as merely "myths" and "legends," but it is becoming clear that the experts have overlooked an entire dimension of Native life.

Kin, place, connection, and continuity were the basic components of North American Native life for millennia before European contact. Terrains vary in what they can provide, and consequently different peoples adapted their societies to their locations. Although the gendered division of labor was true everywhere, Native women lived differently in different settings.

Anthropologists today distinguish three large groupings of Native peoples in the Greater Northwest: the Coastal peoples who lived off the bounty of the Pacific Ocean; the Plateau people who fished the Big River and its tributaries for salmon, gathered roots and berries, and hunted deer; and the Great Basin people who foraged and fished and, later, once some of them had horses, hunted the buffalo. Although today most groups are known by recent European names, in their own languages they all had names to identify themselves and where they lived. For example, the Nez Perce call themselves Ni-Mi-Puu, meaning "Our People" while the Tlingit on the coast of what is now southern Alaska call themselves Linget, the "People of the Tides." The Coeur d'Alene in present-day Idaho simply call themselves Schitsu'umsh, which means "the ones that were found here," underlining the bond between the people and the homeland.

The Native peoples who lived along the Northwest Coast—the Tlingit, Haida, and Tsimshian in what is now southeast Alaska; the Kwakiutl, Bella Coola, and others in what is now British Columbia; and the Nootka, Makah, and Quileute-Hoh, who lived on what is now the Washington coast—were all fortunate in their location. With the Pacific Ocean at their feet and densely forested mountains behind them, a summer's worth of fishing and gathering of coastal greens and berries was enough to provide year-round food, with a surplus left over for trade. Reflecting these patterns of activity, Coastal peoples sharply divided their year into secular and spiritual halves. In the summers, they moved away from their winter villages to temporary fish camps that were hives of activity as great runs of salmon and halibut were caught by the men and filleted and smoked by the women, as they dug shellfish and netted small fish (especially the prized eulachon that contained fat essential to the diet) and seaweed and gathered forest greens. In winter, people retreated from fierce coastal storms into the huge cedar-planked longhouses that housed several families and generations of the same kin group. Winter was for repairing or making hunting, craft, and ceremonial items, but above all for settling into the deep dark wombs of the longhouses where storytelling and ceremony were enacted by performers in elaborate masks and costumes.

One of the winter themes was the close but respectful kinship relationship between humans and animals. The Haida-Tlingit story of Ripsunt, the Bear Mother, is one example. Ripsunt, a spoiled young princess, complained loudly when she stepped in some bear scat by mistake while out picking berries, and for her disrespect was captured by the bears and forced to marry one of the sons of the Bear Chief. Ripsunt, at first unwilling, became resigned to living with her husband and came to love him, although she did find his claws painful during lovemaking. Equally painful was the experience of nursing her sons, the Bear Twins. After her husband was killed defending the twins from human hunters, Ripsunt returned to her own people, where she was honored as the mother of the legendary Bear Twins whose ursine heritage brought new strength and skill to her people.

Northwest Coastal Native societies were distinguished by their elaborate clan systems, represented by the famous totem poles that were lineage identifiers before the houses in each village. They were also stratified, with rigid ranking systems. Wealth brought prestige to the top-ranked families and, with it, the absolute obligation to give it away in great potlatch ceremonies held to mark important life events like a birth or a marriage, a son or daughter's coming of age, or accession to a leadership position. Early anthropologists were deeply impressed by the generosity expressed in this remarkable custom of potlatching and considered it one of the most distinctive features of Northwest Coastal groups. But before the giveaway came the acquisition, and the desire to accumulate wealth for the potlatch drove Coastal peoples into frequent hostile contacts with other tribes.

Wealth was acquired by trading and raiding. Much of the trade was with other Coastal societies, and was carried out over long distances in great seagoing canoes navigated with superb seamanship and knowledge of coastal waters. Tlingit women were famous traders, widely considered to be shrewder about getting and keeping wealth than their more flighty husbands. As a contemporary Tlingit woman said, "men are foolish about money," and it is up to women to protect their family's wealth. Among the Tlingit (although not in all Northwest Coastal peoples) clan lineage was matrilineal: newborn children belonged to their mother's kinship group. As in all ranked societies, power and wealth accrued to members of the elite regardless of gender. Women derived much of their personal power and prestige from their role as mothers. As anthropologist Laura Klein points out, grandmothers were the nurturers, while mothers were more socially active, protecting the family's clan status by the roles they played in politics, in potlatches, and in winter ceremonies. The most valuable thing a Tlingit mother could bequeath her children was her rank, which she could damage by a bad marriage. Hence the daughters of high-ranked families were secluded at puberty until they married, as they were trained by their mothers and grandmothers in manners and skills, including the accumulation of wealth. Primarily, however, this seclusion protected these young women from contact with inappropriate lower-ranked young men.

At the other end of the ranking order were slaves, usually women and children captured during raids on other Coastal people. They accounted for at least 15 percent of the population—sometimes much more—and their lot was fixed and unenviable. This slave system was unusually rigid: in most North American Native societies, slavery was common in the first captured generation but was rarely (except on the Northwest Coast) carried into subsequent generations. It was shameful to be a slave and few ever escaped from the status. Its widespread usage on the Northwest Coast clues us to the underside of the extensive trade network: the incessant intertribal warfare and raiding that was driven by the competitive desire to obtain wealth, even if the purpose was to give it away in potlatch ceremonies.

It seems that more is known about the extremes of Coastal societies—the nobility and the slaves—than of those of middling rank, who were surely the majority. This is slowly changing as members of some contemporary Native societies become more willing to share the meanings of their oral traditions while anthropologists and historians learn to understand them in new ways. Julie Cruikshank found, while conducting the life history interviews she published in *Life Lived Like a Story: Life Stories of Three Yukon Native Elders,* that it was impossible for Angela Sidney, Kitty Smith, and Annie Ned (each of partial Tlingit ancestry) to talk about their own past or about tribal history without telling traditional stories. Cruikshank wrote "the older women responded patiently to my [desire for customary historical evidence] . . . [but] they quite firmly shifted the emphasis to 'more important' accounts they wanted me to record—particularly events central to traditional [oral] narrative."

No personal biographies of Northwest Coastal Native women from the precontact period exist, but much more recent biographies give us a glimpse into the surviving values of women of these groups. The first remarkable thing to note is survival itself: all the Coastal peoples, like North

American Natives everywhere, were hit by the catastrophe of European conquest. Disease devastated tribes, cultural practices (such as the potlatch) were outlawed, and even those few groups who did not lose their homelands were unable to fully continue their traditional fishing-based economy. Yet however changed they are, members of Northwest Coastal tribes have survived and some, like Agnes Alfred, a Kwakwaka'wakw (formerly called Kwakiutl) woman of northern Vancouver Island, have led vibrant, creative lives. Alfred's life shows the commitment to ancient tradition combined with modern adaptation that is characteristic of successful North American Native lives today.

In the mid-nineteenth century, the Kwakwaka'wakw suffered the double blows of a Bella Coola slave-raiding party that destroyed their main village followed by a smallpox epidemic that killed all but 10 percent of the remaining population. Nearly as devastating was the impact of Christianity in the 1880s that destroyed some aspects of traditional culture and drove others underground. During her lifetime, for example, Agnes was arrested several times for participating in potlatches, which provincial authorities said were illegal and Christian missionaries taught were immoral.

Agnes was born into this changed world in the 1890s. Daughter of a noble family, she went through the traditional puberty ceremony and seclusion and was married even before her first menstruation to an older man, Moses Alfred, whose noble family had won out, after spirited bidding for her (she had no say in the matter). What made this young girl so appealing was her wealth, in the form of titles, positions within the outlawed potlatch network, and ceremonial privileges such as ownership of certain winter dances and the masks associated with them. As part of her dowry, Agnes gave Moses her inherited Peace Dance headdress as well as a much-prized Copper, a beaten-metal plaque of great value.

Moses Alfred was the first successful Kwakwaka'wakw seineboat fisherman. He owned his own boat and made enough money to build a large European-style three-story house in Alert Bay to which he moved Agnes, who had always lived in a traditional "big house." One of their children remembers: "He also put all modern appliances in this house. At first she refused to use them, but later on she got to use them. We have many funny memories of how she adjusted to each one."

Agnes gave birth to thirteen children, seven of whom were still alive at the time of her death in 1992. This is many more children than she would have had in precontact times; for Native women, this dramatic increase in the birthrate was surely one of the most significant changes in their lives. The reasons for the increase were complex, but one obvious cause was Christianity, for missionaries sternly disapproved of traditional Native methods that prevented or limited births. In addition to caring for her children, doing occasional work in canneries, and volunteering for the Native Sisterhood of British Columbia, Agnes was a revered storyteller who devoted her life to remembering and passing on her language and oral traditions, rituals, and the complicated histories of lineages that contained, for her, history itself. Her life history, in the volume *Paddling to Where I Stand*, is a repository of stories and genealogies of her people, thus expressing the extent to which her identity was collective rather than individual. Her stories stretch from "myth times" before European contact to events of the 1980s and, along with illuminating her life, demonstrate the living vitality of oral tradition.

Far to the south of Vancouver Island, Klickitat women today draw on a long Columbia River artistic tradition as they create the baskets for which they are famous. As Mary Dodds Schlick points out in her generously illustrated book, *Columbia River Basketry*, today women make baskets for museums or for the tourist trade, but long ago they were made for use. Everything they dug and gathered, hunted and fished, went into the right kind of container: tightly coiled cedar-root bowls to hold water, large cedar-root baskets for storage, round root-digging bags of twined hemp, flat twined bags for collection and storage, folded cedar-bark carrying cases. These highly functional baskets woven by women were beautifully decorated with figures of fish, birds, animals, and people, as well as more abstract designs representing mountains, trees, and water. In other words, they were scenes from daily life. This is an example of the way in which what we call "art" was part of the practical, everyday fabric of life among North American Native peoples.

The Klickitat and the others known as the Plateau peoples—the Wishram, the Wasco, the Yakama, the Umatilla, the Cayuse, the Nez Perce, the Coeur d'Alene, the Flathead, the Okanogan, and others—inhabit the Columbia Plateau in what is now central and eastern Washington and parts of Oregon, inland British Columbia, northern Idaho, and western Montana. The Plateau peoples, like those of the Northwest Coast, were people of the salmon, but they equally derived much of their food and culture from gathering roots and hunting. They fished for salmon in the Columbia River and its tributaries, sometimes from precarious-looking scaffolding erected at Celilo Falls and other sites where the men netted salmon making their arduous upriver journey to their spawning grounds. Male fishing was dramatic and dangerous, but the underlying reality was that the daily catch was always limited to the amount that the women could fillet and dry on the racks that surrounded the fishing sites. Subsequently women spent hours grinding dried salmon to a powder that they mixed with berries and grease to make an easily carried high-energy food ideal for people on the move. Tribal survival over the long cold winter depended on these cooperative efforts of men and women during the salmon runs and during the rest of the year too.

Except during the winter, the seasonal round kept Plateau peoples on the move, often as much as three hundred miles per season, as they located different items in their food supply. In these journeys the basic division of labor prevailed: men hunted, fished, and protected the tribe while women dug roots and picked berries (estimated to have provided between 50 and 70 percent of the diet), preserved and stored all the gathered and hunted food, made clothing and baskets, and put up and took down the family's teepee or tule mat lodge as they organized the family's move from one place to the next.

Anthropologist Eugene Hunn's detailed account of the seasonal round on the mid-Columbia River emphasizes the complex planning necessary to account for the ripening of roots and berries and the best places to find them, while also allowing time to catch and process the results of the huge salmon runs for which the river is famous. In the spring, long before the Chinook salmon run, families were already moving to nearby spots on tributary rivers, where the men caught spawning runs of lamprey while the women dug bitterroot and lomatium roots, dried them, and hauled them back to their winter villages for storage. When the salmon runs began, families moved to the "Big River," and the men caught and the women cleaned and dried the fish. Then, in late May, they began to move to the higher-lying camas meadows where they prepared to dig, roast, and store this favorite crop, which was so abundant that hundreds gathered to dig, socialize, gamble, and race their horses. For each woman, equipped with her digging stick and woven basket, camas was both a joy and a challenge, for the roots grew so close together that digging an intact bulb required experience, skill, and strength. Men dug the great pits in which the roots were roasted, after which they still had to be transported to the winter villages. Because a typical crop of dried roots might weigh as much as fifteen hundred pounds, this was a job for which the advent of the horse made a real difference. In early July, the summer run of steelhead and Chinook salmon occurred, and families again moved to the river, where the women, as the runs waxed and waned, took time to gather golden currants, serviceberries, and chokecherries. But a high point, in both elevation and anticipation, was the move to the huckleberry fields of the high Cascades in mid-August. James Selam (Hunn's collaborator and coauthor), described these huckleberry fields as "Indian Heaven," where the combination of cool nights and abundant berries tempted families to remain until October, a sojourn broken only by the major fall salmon run. The men fished, and then, as Selam recalled it, they hauled their catch back up to the huckleberry fields for the women to process. Fall was also the time to hunt deer and elk. By late October, driven out of the high country by cold and snow, families reoccupied their winter villages and brought another seasonal round to its end.

As ethnographer Rodney Frey says, it was necessary for Plateau peoples "to travel the landscape fully" to feed themselves, and it is not fanciful to see not just practical but psychological satisfactions in this yearly activity. These migrations, as we have seen, were highly patterned and predictable, depending as they did on careful attentiveness to the yearly cycle of the natural world and on skills and work routines that the older generation taught the young. And, after centuries of practice, the seasonal round became a deep tradition that was nothing less than a guide to life. One poetic reimagining of a Nez Perce grandmother telling a group of young children about their travels in the year ahead, and imparting a sense of each child's place in collective and natural life, goes like this:

> We work by the seasons. Men hunt deer and fish for salmon.
> January is blizzard season, and February, the time of the white
>   snow. Buttercup time.
> March Lah-te-tahl, time of flowers beginning to bloom.
> And April, the time of leaf budding and unfolding.
> May and June, the time of high water, bitterroot, and sunflowers.
>   We travel on horseback to dig Mu-shnih and Mehktut and
>   camas.
> July: Serviceberries and flowers in the high country.

August: Time for wild cherries and chokecherries. The Chinook
    salmon come into the headwaters to spawn.
September: We pick huckleberries, wild raspberries and
    thimbleberries. It is also salmon spawning time.
In November, the leaves yellow. For the winter, we dry the deer,
    elk, antelope and bear meat too and store it in pits lined with
    grass. Our people move to their winter homes.
December, the beginning of snowfalls, and the long winter. The
    deer embryo begins to form.

There were many routes for the passing on of tradition. Grandmothers bore the responsibility for teaching children both through storytelling and by making sure that daughters and granddaughters learned the specific knowledge necessary to guide the seasonal round of root and berry gathering. And as elders, they received well-deserved respect. For example, Klickitat elder Virginia Beavert says that tradition dictates that when a young girl makes her first basket, she gives it to the oldest women, just as she gives the first roots she digs and the berries she picks to her elders. Thus she learns to honor those who teach her the basic female survival skills, just as young boys are taught to offer their first bows and arrows to the senior male hunter who taught them in turn.

While the elders taught collective lessons, Plateau people also practiced the vision quest, which was in one sense very individual. In the quest, the young, pre-puberty girl or boy fasted alone in a remote spot and waited for a vision of their specific spirit power in animal form to give them a particular skill, perhaps in hunting, in basket weaving, in ability to find roots, in gambling, or as shamans. These skills were not simply individual but were understood to be for the benefit of the tribe. Thus in an important sense, individual skills were also collective, as in the yearly ceremonies where the first roots and the first salmon are honored, not the individual who dug or caught them.

Most people were comfortable in their traditional gendered roles and gender-specific powers, but a gifted person could "break ranks" and have nontraditional powers: women could be hunters or warriors and men excel at female skills like preserving or weaving. It just didn't happen very often. And Native peoples would have been puzzled by our modern emphasis on equality between the sexes. In their eyes, everyone worked together doing traditional tasks for the good of the tribe, but that did not eliminate the opportunity for exhibiting one's special skills, as, for example, the hours of work some especially talented women spent in basket weaving, leatherwork, and beading. The traditions continue today, in events like powwows, where elaborate and beautiful dance regalia challenge the skill and ingenuity of the women who make them and enhance the pride of their kin who wear them.

Two groups on the western edge of the Columbia Plateau, the Chinook and the Coast Salish, are classified by anthropologists as belonging to the Coastal grouping. But because they had so much interaction with Plateau people, and because, as it happened, they bore the brunt of early white contact, they need to be mentioned here.

The Chinook and the closely related Clatsop occupied the mouth of the Columbia River, a crucial trading location. They were the middlemen, controlling the trade between the Coastal groups north and south of them, and the peoples of the Columbia River to the east. As a result, like all middlemen, they were viewed with suspicion by other tribes. They were rich, and like similarly well-endowed Coastal tribes, they had a stratified society with a very high proportion of slaves. In fact, the Chinook became very rich from the profits they made in the slave trade. Because their location made them so vulnerable to raiding, high-status Chinook took the precaution of flattening the foreheads of their babies, so that they would never be mistaken for round-headed slaves.

Fifty different groups now classified as Southern Coast Salish lived in the Puget Sound area, among them such familiar names as the Skagit, the Duwamish, the Puyallup, and the Nisqually. They too were "people of the salmon," feeding well off the fish and shellfish of Puget Sound, supplemented by hunting and extensive gathering. Some groups practiced slavery, but not to the extent of the Chinook to the south or some of the northern Coastal tribes. Nor did they show the same rigid stratification or competitive intensity. What most characterized the Southern Coast Salish was the density of population and their intermingling. Intermarriage was common, and the network of kin relations between different tribes was complex.

On the eastern edge of the Plateau, in what is now Idaho and western Montana, lived another cluster of interrelated groups, the Coeur d'Alene, the Flathead, the Spokan, and the Kalispel, who combined the hunting/gathering customs of Plateau tribes with more watery pursuits. They built lightweight cedar, birch, and white-pine bark canoes to navigate the many rivers and lakes of the region and from which they fished with hooks and dip nets. Rodney Frey estimates that a third of the diet of the Coeur d'Alene came from fishing, a third from hunting deer and elk for which the men of the tribe were well-known, and a third from gathering.

Compared with the two groups above, the Great Basin peoples of today's Central Oregon and present-day Idaho lived on much sparser, more arid lands that challenged their ingenuity to survive. Like the Plateau peoples, the Shoshone, Bannock, and North Paiute peoples were hunter-gatherers. Primarily they trapped smaller game like rabbits, squirrels, and sage rats, dug for roots, collected pinyon nuts and seeds, and hunted antelope and deer when they could. These food-gathering activities were similar to those of the Plateau people, but because of the sparse forage in their high-desert homelands, Great Basin peoples had to travel in very small kin groups that were all a given location could support at one time. Their dogged and highly mobile activities, all in a markedly inhospitable terrain, were supplemented by occasional catches of freshwater fish, and especially of salmon in the Snake River. Although not as numerous as in the Columbia River to the north, salmon were abundant enough for spearfishing and netting during the spring spawning run. During that time the small bands got together in larger groups, but they had no time to develop the rich ceremonial life of say, the Tlingit of the Northwest Coast. It is clear that, most of the time, simply getting enough to eat was their overwhelming pre-occupation, and that food gathering was the constant, collective concern. Two groups on the western edge of the arid Great Basin illustrate the crucial importance of terrain: the Modoc, like other Basin tribes, subsisted by hunting and by gathering wild seeds, while the Klamath, favored by a well-watered location, were fishing people, catching suckers, salmon, and trout with dip nets, gill nets, harpoons, and spears, often at night from canoes lit by torchlight. Klamath women dug roots in the meadows and marshes and gathered mussels at lakes' edge and mosses and wild celery in the marshes. A special event in early August, the ripening of acres of pond-lily seeds in the Klamath Marsh, was the occasion for bands of Klamath, Modoc, and Paiute to meet while harvesting the abundant crop, which was gathered by women, who poled their way through the marshes in small dugout canoes.

Recently, women's historians and anthropologists have tried to identify the precise status of women in traditional Native societies. Were they, as Indian scholars insisted, equal? Or were they subordinate to men, as has

10,000 year-old sandals, Fort Rock OR
(Fort Rock sandals, Oregon Historical
Society, #bb003980)

seemed to be true of women all over the world and throughout history? The scholars who have studied the Native groups of the Pacific Northwest are pretty generally agreed that equality, or more accurately, complementarity, was the rule. In the hunter-gatherer-fisher groups of the Plateau and Central Basin—subsistence economies, in anthropologist's terms—the work of everyone was needed to provide food, shelter, and spiritual sustenance for the group. All of this work was divided by gender, as we have seen, but it all mattered, and women's expertise in the gathering of roots and berries was as valuable as that of the most skilled male hunters. It is also true that tremendous variation existed between the many Native societies in the Greater Northwest. The hardscrabble life of the small Great Basin bands was drastically simple. In subsistence hunter-gatherer societies such as these, anthropologists agree, everyone had to work together simply to survive. At the other extreme, in the rich, highly stratified Coastal tribes, gender was very much an issue, shaping in different ways the lives of high-status and slave women alike. But in those societies the most basic inequality was one of rank, not of gender.

Most Native peoples spent their lives within their homelands, which, because it denoted where they had kin, could be extensive for Puget Sound and Plateau peoples in particular, who had so much contact on their seasonal rounds, meeting as they dug roots or picked huckleberries, or at Celilo Falls and other sites for salmon fishing. Indeed, in each group, there was so much intermarriage over time that one anthropologist has described the Plateau as "one vast kinship web," and the same was true for Puget Sound people as well.

Trading and raiding provided other forms of contact, but not always peaceful ones. Coastal peoples traveled far to trade with others and to raid for captives to augment their supply of slaves. Women were prominent in both activities: as sharp and shrewd traders, and as the most likely captives of male raiding parties. But even among Plateau and Great Basin peoples on their customary seasonal rounds of gathering and hunting, as they came into contact with other groups the decision "friend or foe?" had to be made. Some groups, like the Chinook and the Nez Perce and the Shoshone and the Yakama, were recognized enemies, but even those animosities could be suspended on occasion, such as at recognized trade rendezvous points, the greatest of which was the annual meeting at The Dalles, near Celilo Falls on the Columbia River, drawing peoples and goods from far along the Pacific Coast and as much as one thousand miles inland. This trade fair, timed to coincide with the great Columbia River salmon runs, was the occasion not only for trade but also for gambling, horse racing, and romance.

Nor were the relationships among different groups unchanging. The lives of the easternmost Plateau tribes, and of the closely related Great Basin Shoshone, Bannock, and Paiute, were changed by the coming of horses. Extinct in North America, horses were reintroduced by the Spanish when they invaded what is now Mexico in 1519. Horses were gradually traded and stolen north until they reached the Pacific Northwest in the mid-eighteenth century. Everywhere they appeared, horses increased the ability to travel easily, but for the Native groups living in buffalo country, the change was fundamental. Mounted, they could hunt buffalo much more successfully than before. Some of the Flathead, the Shoshone, the Bannock, and the Northern Paiute shifted their basic subsistence patterns and became mobile, buffalo-hunting people. But because the prime buffalo grounds were fiercely protected by the Blackfeet and the Crow farther to the east, hunting parties had to be heavily armed, even though they also included women to butcher and preserve the meat. Inevitably, the balance of authority in these newly mounted Native groups shifted to men, for they bore the new responsibilities for hunting and fighting in these changed circumstances. Slowly, the importance of women's activities in food provision decreased as the time they spent in support activities, especially in the curing and tanning of buffalo hides, increased.

The Nez Perce, on the edge of buffalo country, are an interesting example of the effect of the changes in gender expectations. Too far away to take up buffalo hunting full time, the Nez Perce compromised by sending yearly hunting parties eastward. In the meantime, they acquired herds of horses, the effect of which was to raise the general standard of living considerably. One could travel farther and carry more of the traditional subsistence foods than before. Everyone rode, but the herds were owned by the men. Their huge herds bred competition, ceremony, and a new source of prestige and wealth. But they also bred warfare, as far-ranging Nez Perce became involved in the continuing conflicts of buffalo country. The voices of hunter-warriors began to carry more weight within the tribe, while more women were widowed. Paradoxically, women's gathering activities were easier and food more abundant because of the use of horses but less valued in the overall tribal economy.

Throughout the Greater Northwest, Europeans began changing things long before they arrived in person. The addition of the horse was the first and most benign of the changes. Then, in the 1770s, came the first smallpox epidemic, probably carried by Spanish explorers on the northern coast. This was closely followed by a wave of catastrophic deaths among the peoples of the Plateau and the Columbia River, apparently caused by contact with infected Crow people encountered on buffalo hunts. Subsequent attacks of smallpox, malaria, and other European diseases attacked Native bodies that had no biological protection, sowing fear and social confusion. As tribe after tribe in the Greater Northwest was devastated, the close-knit kinship networks of the Native world were torn to shreds. And as if these incomprehensible losses were not enough, the changes now came in person, first in the form of seaborne fur traders, with whom the Coastal peoples bore the first brunt of contact. Given these events, it is perhaps not surprising that few regional tribes made much of the arrival from the other direction, in 1805–1806, of a small, poorly equipped group of European men who claimed to be exploring territory well-known to the Natives. Only the fact that one member of the expedition was a woman with her baby (Sacagawea and her son, "Pomp") saved them from being treated as a war party. Thus an event that looms large in US national history, the Lewis and Clark expedition, takes on a different meaning when viewed from the perspective of Natives of the Greater Northwest already in the grip of calamitous change.

These losses would have been overwhelming at any time, but what is most striking is their speed. In the space of fifty years, the changes roared through a Native world based on millennia of observation, practice, and minutely detailed rituals, beliefs, and traditions. Who could possibly have imagined that such an ancient and apparently durable way of life, in which the lives and work of women and men were so embedded in kinship networks, could be so fragile? And yet today, Native people and their core beliefs survive in spite of the fact that much of the land itself is changed out of all recognition and the former ways of living with the land are no longer possible. Today Native people say, with justifiable pride, "We are still here," and have won the attention and respect of environmentalists for their determination to preserve and rebuild as much of the Native relationship with nature as they can. The struggle of the Native women of the Greater Northwest to save their communities started at first contact with Europeans in the 1790s and, many would argue, still continues today.

SOURCES FOR THIS CHAPTER

It is difficult to recapture the full spirit of the people who lived so long ago and in such a different world. I've tried to pay special attention to the Native relationship with the land, which seemed essential as the starting point for a regional history. I found an extraordinary example of Native knowledge and attentiveness to natural detail in Hugh Brody's account of hunters in present-day British Columbia, *Maps & Dreams: Indians and the British Columbia Frontier* (Vancouver, BC: Waveland Press, 1977). For the spiritual dimension, Bruce Chatwin's 1987 classic, *The Songlines* (New York: Penguin Press, 1987), is deeply evocative, but it is not about the Greater Northwest. For a fuller understanding of the historical, collective, and spiritual importance of oral tradition, I turned to Native stories, especially to those documented by Jerold Ramsey, *Coyote Was Going There: Indian Literature of the Oregon Country* (Seattle: University of Washington Press, 1977); to Leslie Marmon Silko, *Yellow Woman and a Beauty of Spirit* (New York: Simon and Schuster, 1996); and to their sensitive use in Jonathan Raban's *Passage to Juneau: A Sea and Its Meanings* (New York: Random House, 1999).

I found another way to explain the Native relationship to the land in descriptions of the seasonal round. For this, Rodney Frey's study in collaboration with the Schitsu'umsh, *Landscape Traveled by Coyote and*

Crane: The World of the Schitsu'umsh (Coeur d'Alene Indians) (Seattle: University of Washington Press, 2001), and the clear descriptions of Eugene S. Hunn with James Selam and Family in *Nch'i-Wána, "The Big River": Mid-Columbia Indians and Their Land* (Seattle: University of Washington Press, 1990) were invaluable. Gail Miller's poetic rendering of the Nez Perce round in "As We Were: Onstage with Washington Women" (Pullman, WA: Women's Studies Program, 1981) is evocative.

For basic information about social organization, work patterns, and beliefs in the Greater Northwest, the standard source is the comprehensive multivolume William C. Sturtevant, ed., *Handbook of North American Indians* (Washington, DC: Smithsonian Institution, 1990), especially volumes 7 (Northwest Coast), 11 (Great Basin), and 12 (Plateau). Richard D. Daugherty provided a unifying overview in "People of the Salmon," in Alvin Josephy, ed., *America in 1492: The World of the Indian Peoples before the Arrival of Columbus* (New York: Random House, 1991). For the Plateau tribes, I found Elizabeth Vibert, *Traders' Tales: Narratives of Cultural Encounters in the Columbia Plateau 1807–1846* (Norman: University of Oklahoma Press, 1997), insightful. Theodore Stern, *The Klamath Tribe: A People and Their Reservation* (Seattle: University of Washington Press, 1965) was useful.

For a closer look at women I turned first to the work of Lillian Ackerman, especially *A Necessary Balance: Gender and Power among Indians of the Columbia Plateau* (Norman: University of Oklahoma Press, 2003). More specialized studies include Julie Cruikshank, *Life Lived Like a Story: Life Stories of Three Yukon Native Elders* (Lincoln: University of Nebraska Press, 1990); Martine J. Reid, ed., *Paddling to Where I Stand: Agnes Alfred, Qwiqwasutinuxw Noblewoman* (Vancouver: University of British Columbia Press, 2004); Mary Dodds Schlick's beautiful *Columbia River Basketry: Gift of the Ancestors, Gift of the Earth* (Seattle: University of Washington Press, 1992); and the profusely illustrated anthology edited by Lillian A. Ackerman, *A Song to the Creator: Traditional Arts of Native American Women of the Plateau* (Norman: University of Oklahoma Press, 1996), especially Virginia Beavert, "Origin of Basket Weaving."

Controversy over questions of equality or subordination of Native women emerged in the 1980s, as women's anthropologists and historians began to realize how complicated and difficult it was to compare the status of women in different societies worldwide. In North America this led many scholars to abandon the generic term "Indian" and to begin to look seriously at cultural distinctions between tribal groups. For the Greater Northwest, I found the most useful books for thinking about the status of women in Native societies were Laura F. Klein and Lillian A. Ackerman, *Women and Power in Native North America* (Norman: University of Oklahoma Press, 1995); and Patricia Albers and Beatrice Medicine, *The Hidden Half: Studies of Plains Indian Women* (Lanham, MD: University Press of America, 1983), which was particularly useful for understanding the ways in which the introduction of horses affected gendered work patterns, especially on the plains. More general and widely known books such as Theda Purdue's *Sifters: Native American Women's Lives* (New York: Oxford, 2001) and Nancy Shoemaker, ed., *Negotiators of Change: Historical Perspectives on Native American Women* (New York: Routledge, 1995), do not cover the precontact past nor pay particular attention to Native women of the Greater Northwest.

The field of anthropology developed in the late nineteenth century in response to fears that "primitive" societies (as they were then known) might soon disappear completely. Information about women was at first sparse, because the majority of European observers and scholars were male and often had limited access to them. This lack of access was so serious that the first women anthropologists were recruited specifically to interview Native women. However, when their findings conflicted with existing accounts, their work was often discounted. Overcoming this bias has been a struggle for women anthropologists and historians, as Shirley Leckie and Nancy Parezo point out in their edited volume, *Their Own Frontier: Women Intellectuals Re-visioning the American West* (Lincoln: University of Nebraska Press, 2008).

Chapter 2
Between Worlds
MÉTIS AND MISSIONARY WOMEN, 1780s–1840s

Preceding page: Fort Vancouver, 1845 (Oregon Historical Society, #bb010522)

In 1836, two American women, Narcissa Whitman and Eliza Spalding, and their missionary husbands made the overland trip from St. Louis to the Columbia River in the remote northwest. The route they traveled later gained renown as the Oregon Trail, but in 1837 it was still a primitive, difficult track, which the women accomplished on horseback, riding sidesaddle, the accepted mode for European women at the time.

The party's first destination was Fort Vancouver, on the Columbia River, which had been the Hudson's Bay Company (HBC) headquarters in the Greater Northwest for more than a decade. Greeted first by HBC chief factor Dr. John McLoughlin, the ladies were promptly introduced to his wife Marguerite McLoughlin, a métis (from the French word for "mixed") whose mother was Cree and whose father was a Swiss trader. It is a moment worth pondering: the two American women, tired and threadbare from their long journey, greeted graciously by the French-speaking silk-clad hostess of the fort—who was a "half-breed" (Narcissa's word). In a later letter, musing on the fact that all the HBC men had Indian or métis wives, Narcissa wrote, "Some [of the wives] are half-breeds and are so white than you can scarcely tell the difference."

This meeting between the first American missionary women and the métis wife of the HBC chief factor was symbolic of two very different kinds of early European contact with the Natives of the Greater Northwest. The missionaries had come to convert the Natives to Christianity, while the men of the world's foremost fur trading company married them. These two kinds of contact meant very different consequences for women on both sides of the exchange, although they shared one thing: the status of being between European and Native worlds and not fully part of either. In a place where the transition from first contact to conquest occurred with stunning rapidity, women of all races and faiths occupied pivotal locations from which to affect outcomes. Native women actively acted as bridges between fur traders and their own societies; missionary women, in contrast, failed to play the part they envisaged in leading Native peoples to Christianity.

The first face-to-face encounters between Natives and Europeans in the Greater Northwest occurred in the 1780s, as British and American trading ships eagerly solicited the cooperation of coastal Natives to trap the fabulously profitable sea otter pelts that they then sold in China. Clearly, first encounters between peoples were a shock to both sides, as described in this story, told by the Clatsop people:

An old woman was walking along the beach mourning the death of her son, when she saw something in the ocean that she thought at first was a whale, but when she came near she saw two spruce trees standing upright on it. She thought: "Behold! It is no whale. It is a monster!" She reached the thing that lay there. Now she saw that its outer side was all covered by copper. Ropes were tied to those spruce trees, and it was full of iron. Then a bear came out of it. He stood on the thing that lay there. He looked just like a bear, but his face was that of a human being. Then she went home. She thought of her son and cried, saying, "Oh my son is dead and the thing about which we have heard in tales is on shore!"

Hearing her news, the Clatsop plundered the ship for its valuable treasures of copper, brass, and iron, and took the two strange "bears" captive, one to one village, one to another. There is no surviving record of what happened to the two European men who were mistaken for bears.

Already accustomed to keen trading among themselves, Coastal tribes quickly learned to anticipate yearly visits from seaborne traders and to bargain hard for the iron, copper, blankets, tobacco, and guns they wanted. Familiarity with the maritime trade was one reason why the Chinook, at the mouth of the Columbia River, were uninterested in the Lewis and Clark expedition that wintered there in 1806: compared with the yearly bounty of seaborne trade goods, the overlanders had nothing to offer them.

Until very recently, historians' understanding of the early years of contact was based almost entirely on the written records of explorers like James Cook and from seaborne and land-based fur traders. The Native perspective, and especially that of Native women, was missing, an oversight that pioneering scholars Gray Whaley and Mary Wright are just now beginning to correct. Like the Clatsop story of first contact, the Native accounts offer new insights.

If, at the first local sighting, the grandmother saw a bear with a human face, what did the British and American men of the seaborne fur trade see when they looked back? They saw an all-but-naked woman wearing a short apron of twined cedar bark, the customary Coastal female garment, with earrings and nose ornaments of shells and feathers. European men reacted to Native women dressed such as this with a mixture of shock and desire, disturbed by their differences from the women they knew at home but aroused by their unaccustomed nakedness. Or perhaps, more mundanely, since they were sailors on a long voyage, they simply hoped that some women might be available for sex. In at least some of the coastal trading encounters, the answer was yes. Sexual intercourse between Native women and European men began with the seaborne fur trade in the 1790s. Rapidly the Coastal tribes realized that the eagerness of sailors for sex made it an item of sale or barter like any other. However, contrary to European assumptions, not all Native women were prostituted, but only slave women, who had themselves been captured from other tribes. Native women *were* deeply implicated, however, in the sense that high-status women owned the slaves who were offered to Europeans. It seems reasonable to assume that using slave women to satisfy European offers to pay for sex turned it, in Native eyes, into simply another commercial exchange, not a transaction that had any bearing on their own status or sexuality. So far as we know, the concept of female sexuality as an item available for purchase did not exist in Native North America prior to European contact. Thus the concept of prostitution, like the introduction of disease, can be directly attributed to European contact.

It was not so much the sex trade that bothered some widely quoted early European commentators, but differences from the European cultural norms of proper dress and behavior for women. Chinook women behaved appropriately for their own society, but members of the Lewis and Clark expedition in 1805 were taken aback by the fact that they were comfortable with their own nudity, bathing openly and even, as William Clark noted, "sport[ing] openly with our men." Perhaps as disconcerting to Europeans was the fact that high-status Chinook trader women were much more assertive than they expected women to be. Some European men were offended, among them fur trader Alexander Ross who scornfully (and inaccurately) commented that "chastity is not considered a virtue by Chinook women and their amorous propensities know no bounds. All classes from the highest to the lowest, indulge in coarse sensuality and shameless profligacy."

Ross was simply wrong, but why was he so certain of his opinion? Feminist scholars have shown that, worldwide, European male conquerors and colonizers projected their own sexual desires onto scantily clad Native women, who were then described as shameless and provocative. In recent years, we have come to call this hypocritical attitude "blaming the victim," as, for example, when women's choice of clothing (or the lack of it) is blamed for rape. At the time, European men did not accept the idea that anything but European definitions of "male" and "female" were correct, or that their own behavior was an example of imperialist attitudes. Unfortunately, there are no accounts by Native women of what these brief sexual encounters looked like from their side. What we do know is that they paid a heavy price in mortality from venereal disease, and that for a long time to come, reputedly "degraded" female sexuality among the Natives of the Greater Northwest was considered by many more men than Alexander Ross as a sign of cultural inferiority that justified European conquest. But most fur traders disagreed. The fleeting sexual encounters of the maritime trade and the scornful attitudes of some explorers toward Native women bore little relationship to the more permanent sexual unions of the land-based fur trade. In fact, the land-based trade could not have survived without the willingness of Native women to form sexual unions with Europeans.

The centuries-old land-based fur trade in beaver skins found a permanent home on the Pacific Coast in 1825 when Dr. John McLoughlin of the Hudson's Bay Company established Fort Vancouver on the Columbia River, near present-day Portland. For the next twenty-five years, Fort Vancouver, which an admiring Narcissa Whitman called "the New York of the Pacific," functioned as the hub of the Greater Northwest. From Fort Vancouver, McLoughlin directed fur brigades that operated from San Francisco Bay north to the border of Russian Alaska as well as far inland. In other words, all of the Greater Northwest was in his purview.

For hundreds of years the fur trade was the primary point of contact between Europeans and Native peoples in North America. Begun by the French in the sixteenth century, the fur trade gradually moved deeper and deeper into the continent via the Great Lakes and the rivers farther west; in the process of searching for furs, Europeans explored what was to them an unknown continent. By the 1760s the fur trade was dominated by the British, who took over French western networks, employing many French Canadian trappers and voyageurs as "servants," while the officers were Scots and English.

The European men who worked in the fur trade were traders, not settlers. They brought no European women with them. From the very beginning it was obvious that the trade would not succeed without the cooperation of Native peoples. This meant that the Europeans had to meet the Natives on their own terms and act in ways acceptable to them. The customary Native way to cement relationships of trust was to become kin by marrying into the tribe; traders did the same. Marriage "according to the custom of the country"—that is, stable but not church-sanctified unions—were common in the fur trade. So it was that Native women who married Europeans became bridges between worlds: they facilitated the acceptance of their husbands by their own tribal group, while on the other hand they provided sexual companionship, local knowledge, and essential work skills such as curing hides, preserving food, and sewing moccasins for their European husbands.

By entering into marriage alliances on Native terms, the traders accommodated themselves to indigenous cultures and customs, not the other way around. Historian Sylvia Van Kirk insists that this type of marriage, "after the fashion of the country," was *the fundamental social relationship through which a fur trade society developed* (emphasis original), thereby providing a striking example of a gendered cross-racial connection that persisted over time because it served the needs of both parties. These unions of Native women and European traders were the engine of the North American fur trade for over 150 years. Over that time, these unions created and sustained a new people, the mixed-race (Métis) people of western Canada. Beginning as children of the fur trade, the Métis claimed and built their own communities centered in the Red River of western Canada (now Winnipeg), where the way of life they developed was a mixture of buffalo-hunting Plains Indian life and French Canadian Catholicism and culture. Their sense of distinctiveness was so strong that they demanded their own province when the region became part of the Canadian Confederation in 1870. When their demand was refused, the Métis, led by Louis Riel, rose in rebellion in 1869 and achieved a degree of autonomy. But in the second rebellion in 1885, their demand for sovereignty led to defeat and Riel's own execution. Because, in contrast, the land-based fur trade lasted fewer than fifty years in the Greater Northwest, the mixed-race children of the region never coalesced into a distinct identity group, and scholars use the lower-case métis to distinguish them from the distinctive "big M" identity group in Canada.

From the perspective of the European man, the benefits of intermarriage were obvious. There were cases of abandonment, of men with "a wife in every fur trade post," and cases of Native wives passed on from one man to the next, but many men, Dr. John McLoughlin among them, took their "country marriages" very seriously. But from the Native viewpoint, why would a woman want to marry an unskilled, sexually demanding, and hairy white man, someone who appeared so alien to Native life that he could be mistaken for a bear? The customary answer has been that women were attracted by western trade goods, physical comfort, and security, as well as the benefits of the alliance to their kin group. But the fact remains, as historian Jacqueline Peterson has pointed out, this would have been an extraordinary step that only a few Native women would initially want to make. Only young women willing to break with tradition, for example those whose vision quests had yielded them unusual dreams, would be likely to favor such a choice. Native women looking for more powerful, nontraditional roles, Peterson suggests, were the ones who chose to marry whites, not their more traditional sisters.

In the Greater Northwest, there may have been another reason that Native women agreed to marry white men: disease. Even before Fort Vancouver was built, the Chinook had experienced smallpox epidemics of such ferocity that entire villages were left deserted. Nor was that devastation unique: in the epidemic of 1824 and 1825, Chinook chief Concomly, for example, lost eight members of his own family. Native women may have hoped that relationships with fur traders would serve as a refuge from the consequent wave of social disorganization, but disease dogged them. Fort Vancouver itself was a locus of malaria attacks from 1830 to 1834, the first of which was so severe that HBC chief factor McLoughlin reported that it was causing "dreadful havoc among the natives." For the appalling fact was that while malaria debilitated whites, it killed Natives outright, including Concomly himself, who died in 1830. Recurring attacks of malaria, each as devastating as the first, led McLoughlin to report in 1834 that three-quarters of the Native population had died, a figure that modern estimates have raised to nearly 90 percent. Subsequent epidemics of dysentery in 1844 and measles in 1847 caused still more Native deaths. Thus at least some of the Native women who took fur trader husbands might have been the orphan survivors of their original kin groups.

Just as Native women initially linked European traders and Native peoples together in the practical matter of trapping furs, so in a different way the special case of the mixed-race daughters of fur trade officials revealed the persistence of European values at the higher level of the trade. Because the Hudson's Bay Company barred white women until 1832, a man in the trade either remained single or found a Native wife. So, in an extraordinary example of cultural dominance, an elite group of women "between worlds" was created that served the needs of the fur trade officer class—biologically mixed-race, but trained to act as "white" as possible. An ambitious young man just arrived from England or Scotland might begin his career in the fur trade as a clerk, but if he aspired to move up the officer ranks, perhaps eventually to command a fur trade post, he needed to please his superior officers. How better than to marry the métis daughter of a high company official? These fathers, on their side, made great efforts to educate their métis daughters and sons in the European way. Sons were often sent to Quebec or to Europe to be educated; daughters were kept closer to home but were taught to dress and act in acceptable European ways.

All the women at Fort Vancouver were Native or métis. By 1845, most of the approximately two hundred male HBC servants, themselves a mixture of Native, French Canadian, Métis, and Hawaiian, were married "after the fashion of the country" to Native women. All of them, with the exception of officers and their wives, lived outside the gates of Fort Vancouver in the sprawling Kanaka (Hawaiian) Village when they were not trapping and traveling. Sometimes as many as six hundred men, women, and children crowded into the thirty to forty longhouse-like log huts which, with HBC precision, were laid out in rows with broad lanes or streets between. The majority of the women were coastal Chinook (a number of whom brought their slaves with them), while the rest were from other Coastal or Plateau tribes. The predominance of Chinookan women was explained by proximity, and by the importance of the Chinook's vital trading position at the mouth of the Columbia River, as was shown by the 1811 marriage of Pacific Fur Company leader Duncan McDougall with Illchee, the daughter of Chinook chief Concomly. High-status marriages such as these were generally arranged by the men, with the women acting as diplomatic bridges between worlds. The couples appeared to have communicated with each other either in French (the language of most of the men) or in the trade language, Chinook jargon.

High-status women quickly adopted European standards of body decoration and clothing, as the men made clear the necessity of covering themselves and conforming to European custom. But, according to historian Mary Wright, the women did not fully adopt European behavior and values. Several points of contention with their European husbands remained. Perhaps the most difficult was the Chinookan custom of flattening the forehead in infancy to denote high status, a practice most Europeans definitely did not want inflicted upon their own children. The second was ownership of slaves, another mark of status in Chinook society to which some Europeans objected, especially when one of the most common uses of female slaves was prostitution with white men. Here compromise and evasion were prevalent: no women freed their slaves, but they sometimes transferred ownership to a kin member. A more pervasive worry among European men was that their Native wives brought to their marriages an unaccustomed degree of autonomy. Although they may have been given in marriage to Europeans for political reasons, Native women expected to exercise their customary right to divorce. They thereby demonstrated a sexual freedom that European men did not expect from women. White women, brought up in a patriarchal system, were much easier to control. Details of the lives of most of the Chinookan women at Fort Vancouver remain invisible in the records that have come down to us, but the very frequency of intermarriage indicates that whatever the cultural difficulties, the men of Fort Vancouver, both elite and servant, found their Native partners to be hard workers, excellent traders, and useful interpreters and interlocutors with Natives of other tribes, and the women found enough satisfactions to remain in their new circumstances.

In one quite striking exception to the general anonymity, historian David Peterson del Mar has recovered the story of Celiast Smith, a Clatsop woman. Her life stands as an example of the ways in which some Native women were able to use the possibilities of intermarriage to seize powerful roles as bridges between worlds. Celiast's father, Coboway, a respected Clatsop leader, probably arranged her marriage to French Canadian Basile Poirier in 1821, when she was about eighteen or nineteen. Coboway clearly wished to cement relations with the HBC, as Celiast's older sister also married an HBC man. Celiast's husband, Poirier, a baker at Fort Vancouver, was apparently a drunk and abusive, and she tried to escape the marriage in 1829 by getting another HBC employee to marry her, only to have the chief factor himself refuse the request.

Four years later, however, Celiast did escape, improbably, by running off with American Solomon Smith, who was himself something of an anomaly. Smith, a member of the failed fur trade venture of Bostonian Nathaniel Wyeth, decided to stay in the Greater Northwest and became the schoolteacher at Fort Vancouver in 1832. Somehow this rootless, unconnected foreigner (the American overland migration to Oregon did not begin for another decade) crossed paths with Celiast, a Native married woman nine years his senior, and they eloped to join her sister and her French Canadian husband at French Prairie in the Willamette Valley. In 1840, Celiast, Solomon, and their children moved to Clatsop Plains, her original home, where she served as an interpreter and assistant to the area's first Methodist mission. She also owned and directed the labor of a number of slaves, a high-status prerogative, and became the spokesperson and advocate for Clatsops as the area filled with white settlers after the American migration to Oregon in the 1840s. Solomon Smith himself thrived as a local farmer, a sawmill and store owner, and eventually as a state senator. In effect, like the fur traders "marriage according to the custom of the country," Solomon's marriage to Celiast won him the approval of the Clatsops and a level of cooperation they did not extend to other white settlers.

Rapidly, however, the Clatsop population dwindled, ravaged by malaria, measles, and venereal disease, and by damage to traditional foods such as roots and berries caused by settlers' pigs and other livestock. By 1855, less than a quarter of the 1840 Clatsop population remained. Over the years, the relationship between Celiast and Solomon must have changed also, as white disapproval of "squaw men" (white men who married Native women) came to prevail. Solomon remained loyal to Celiast and did not leave her, but it is telling that when he died in 1876, his obituary mentioned neither Celiast nor their three children. Of them, "half-breed" Silas became a respected lawyer and local historian, but his much-married sisters Charlotte and Josephine complained bitterly of prejudice against them.

Celiast was a full-blood Clatsop, but the elite women at Fort Vancouver were métis, an important distinction in the fur trade. Both Marguerite McLoughlin, who greeted Narcissa Whitman and Eliza Spalding so graciously at Fort Vancouver, and Amelia Douglas, wife of the assistant to the chief factor, James Douglas, were the offspring of European fur trade officials and their Native wives. The lives of these women, and of their female children, although luxurious by local standards, were much more restricted than those of the Native women who clustered around Fort Vancouver. The male-dominated fur trade was organized in military fashion, with strict discipline and status, studded with male rituals, a prime example of which was the all-male officers' mess. A 1839 visitor, Thomas Farnham, has left us a vivid word portrait of McLoughlin standing at the twenty-foot table in the Big House "directing the gentlemen and guests to their places according to rank" while his wife and children, who also lived in the house, remained secluded. Indeed, Marguerite McLoughlin, Amelia Douglas, and their female children seem to have spent most of their time in seclusion, except for horseback riding, at which both women excelled.

Within the fur trade, métis wives of this class were treated with respect and deference, but by the time of the Fort Vancouver meeting with the missionary women in 1837, other viewpoints were gaining ground. In Narcissa Whitman's eyes, métis women, however white they appeared, were still "half-breeds," and the British missionary Reverend Herbert Beaver, just arrived by ship from England, was scandalized to discover that the McLoughlins were only married "according to the custom of the country" and accused them of living in sin (in response, the dignified John McLoughlin beat him up). Clearly, the hazards of living "between worlds" for métis and Native women were heightened as the fur trade dwindled and the American presence in the Pacific Northwest increased, as the following history of an all-but-forgotten métis community illustrates.

In the 1820s, some French Canadian trappers and voyageurs retired from the HBC and with their Native wives began to farm the region later known as French Prairie on the Willamette River near present-day Newberg, Oregon. Most of them located near existing villages of the native Kalapooyans, with whom they had developed trade or kinship ties. In 1831 the Kalapooyans and the French-Indian settlers were struck by the first of the series of malaria epidemics. For the Kalapooyans, the result was devastating—at a conservative estimate, 75 percent died, and many Native wives and their mixed-race children at French Prairie died as well. Most of the French Canadian men remarried, often to younger métis wives. By 1841, the French-Indian population in the Willamette Valley totaled 322, composed of seventy-five men, sixty-seven women, and 180 children in sixty-four families.

Thus when the American pioneers began to arrive in the 1840s, they found an existing agricultural settlement that was mixed-race, Catholic, French-speaking, and Canadian. It is difficult to say which—the race, the religion, the language, or the nationality—was more shocking to these migrants from the United States of the 1840s, which was gripped by the most serious wave of anti-immigrant, anti-Catholic feeling the nation had ever experienced.

Because the American migration was so large, the history of this small French-Indian community at French Prairie has remained largely overlooked. Recently, however, historian Melinda Jetté has restored a small bit of that history by carefully tracing three generations of her own family beginning with Joseph Rochbrune, a HBC voyageur (canoeman) from Quebec, who first came to Fort Vancouver in 1827. He married a Native woman, Lisette Walla Walla (the tribal affiliations of Native wives were commonly denoted by their last names), and they had seven children, four of whom survived to adulthood.

Joseph and his family retired in 1839 to French Prairie, where in 1849 their young métis daughter Celeste Rochbrune became the second wife of a considerably older widower, Tanis Liard, another French Canadian voyageur whose first Native wife had died in the measles epidemic of 1847–1848. The Liards took up a 540-acre Donation Land Act claim (explained fully in the next chapter), and their only child, Marguerite, was born on the claim in 1851. When Tanis died in 1852, Celeste married another French Canadian, Honoré Picard, and they and their children lived on the claim through the 1870s. Trying to hold onto the claim, they took out a mortgage in 1876, but when Celeste died in 1877, during her twelfth childbirth, the family couldn't keep up the payments and lost the claim. All but one of the Picard siblings later settled on the Umatilla Reservation in eastern Oregon, where they successfully reclaimed their Native heritage (presumably through their Walla Walla grandmother).

Marguerite Liard's own petition for land from the Umatillas, however, was denied, according to the family story because her Picard siblings denied her Native ancestry, although they shared the same métis mother. At that point, Marguerite Liard had no choice but to try to make it in the white world. She had married Adolphe Jetté in 1871. Born in Quebec, Jetté had first come to Oregon in the early 1850s, going first to the goldfields in southern Oregon, where he married a Native woman, Julie Rogue, and had two daughters with her. They moved to French Prairie to escape the violence of the Rogue River Indian war of 1855–1856. When Julie died of tuberculosis, Adolphe married Marguerite. After they lost their farmland, they moved to the town of Champoeg on French Prairie and lived there for thirty years, successively owning a saloon, a general store, and a grain elevator. The Jetté family was successful enough in Champoeg to send four sons to Mt. Angel College and five girls to Mt. Angel Normal School, but by 1910 they had moved to Portland, where Marguerite ran a boardinghouse for laborers in the shipyards and lumber mills. Adolphe died 1917 at the age of ninety-one, Marguerite at eighty in 1931. Their children scattered, and so did their family memories, until their descendant Melinda Jetté regathered them.

This brief recital of the Jetté family heritage is a tangle of death, hard choices, and survival, complicated by changing definitions of race. It is impossible to say how typical it was of early western settlers, métis or otherwise. How much of this story can be attributed to the American prejudice against "half-breeds," which was undoubtedly prevalent after the 1840s, and how much is really a common story of western hardship?

Adding weight to the importance of changing ideas about race is another multigeneration story of an elite métis family, that of HBC chief factor John McLoughlin and his métis wife Marguerite. Their two daughters, Maria Elizabeth (Eliza) and Maria Eloisa (Eloise), both married white men before their father retired from Fort Vancouver in 1845. Their oldest son, John, was killed at the age of twenty-nine under mysterious circumstances at the fur trade post of Fort Stikine. McLoughlin then sent his youngest son, David, to France for training as an engineer with the prospect of employment with the East India Company. Instead, David returned from France to Fort Vancouver and, after working briefly as a clerk, rebelled and, as his great-granddaughter wrote, "just saddled up his horse and rode away." The great-granddaughter was Janet Campbell Hale, a well-known Indian author, who wrote about her family's fortunes in *Bloodlines: Odyssey of a Native Daughter.*

David McLoughlin married a full-blood Kootenay woman, Annie Grizzly, in 1866 and lived with her and her people on what became the Idaho-Montana border, where he may have had a trading post. An unsympathetic source (not Hale) reported that although David inherited money from his father, he "had squandered it all by 1901 and had to be given a fare and clothing just to attend a celebration in Portland in honor of his father." Most of David's daughters and granddaughters married white men, but one granddaughter, Maggie Sullivan, daughter of an Irish railroad worker and a Kootenay-métis mother, married a man of the Coeur d'Alene tribe. Her children, among them her daughter Janet, were shunned by her "white" sisters and cousins because they looked like Indians. Thus in four generations, the world in which McLoughlin's descendants lived had changed so dramatically from the métis world of the fur trade that Hale's relatives rejected her because of the color of her skin and her teachers in school simply did not believe her when she told them that McLoughlin was her great-great-grandfather.

The métis women (and occasional Native women such as Celiast Smith) described above lived at a moment of transition, from the inclusiveness of the fur trade to the more restrictive racial notions of incoming American and British settlers. After the transition, these women were no longer a bridge between worlds but "half-breeds," in the pejorative language of the time, and no longer acceptable as marriage partners for respectable white men. Looking at this from a utilitarian perspective, once the fur trade was over, Native women were no longer useful. In the calculus of conquest, peaceful trade and the need for cooperation with Natives had ended and the next phase, occupation, could begin.

Missionary women were the harbinger of the transition. Their "in-between" status may need some explanation, because we are accustomed to thinking positively about their activities. But in fact the American missionary women brought with them an alien set of values that had no meaning to the Native cultures on which they sought to impose them. Contrary to what missionaries believed, most Native people did not wish to be "saved." Nearly all the Native peoples who had contact with missionaries initially rejected their teachings, acquiescing only when they were enforced by the full weight of the state. When missionary women found no welcome among the Native women they sought to convert, they found themselves stranded between worlds.

The attitudes of early missionaries were characteristic of the American settlement of the Pacific Northwest that was to come. The best-known missionaries are the two couples who arrived in 1837: Marcus and Narcissa Whitman, who established a mission to the Cayuse at Waiilatpu (near present-day Walla Walla), and Henry and Eliza Spalding, who ministered to the Nez Perce at Lapwai (near present-day Lewiston, Idaho). The Whitmans, in particular, were deeply involved in fostering American settlement. This was one factor, along with the devastating effects of a measles epidemic that killed many Cayuse but spared white lives, that led, in 1847, to the uprising known as the Whitman Massacre, in which Marcus, Narcissa, and eleven others were killed. In the aftermath, the other Protestant missions were quickly evacuated, and the first Protestant missionary effort in the Pacific Northwest came to an abrupt end.

Historian Julie Jeffrey reminds us that the 1830s were a time of deep religious ferment and fervor in American society. Famous preachers like Charles G. Finney mounted revival campaigns in New York state, lasting for a month or more, that attracted widespread public attention. Fostering an individualistic, emotional hope of personal salvation, evangelical religion changed the lives of many, and not least those who chose to devote themselves to dangerous foreign missions such as the one in the Pacific Northwest. Motivated by a sincere desire to bring salvation to "heathen" Natives, missionaries were at the same time dogmatic, rigid, and unsympathetic to Native culture, which they were determined to change. For example, the Whitmans insisted that the Cayuse abandon their traditional seasonal round of fishing, digging roots, and gathering berries, on which they depended for sustenance. Instead, the Whitmans wanted them to settle down and become farmers, an occupation previously unknown among the Plateau tribes, so that they would always be available for religious instruction. Firm in his faith, Marcus Whitman had such high standards that he was unable to find one Cayuse Indian ready for conversion in the ten years he ministered at Waiilatpu. At Lapwai, Henry Spalding had a higher conversion rate, but some of his brother missionaries whispered among themselves that his standards were too lax. In any case, the lives of these early Protestant missionary men were difficult. They served on isolated posts in conditions of some physical hardship, ministering to Native peoples whom they did not understand and who, as time went on, were increasingly hostile to them and to their religious message.

Difficult as the situation was for the missionary men, it was much worse for their wives. The women were not ministers themselves, for no major religion ordained women in the early nineteenth century. But they were women of deep faith and considerable daring. In the religion of the day, women were supposed to be faithful members of the congregation, to raise money and work actively for charitable purposes, to support the (male) minister, and to be content with their subordinate status. But Narcissa Whitman actively sought mission work, even though she knew that a single woman was not allowed to go on a mission on her own. Pursuing her missionary goal, Narcissa married a man she barely knew and spent her honeymoon on the journey westward. She and other missionary wives were daring in the sense that, by moving beyond the customary female role, they hoped for an active role in what they called a "wider sphere of usefulness" in the Pacific Northwest. In this hope, Narcissa and the other missionary wives were disappointed.

Narcissa Whitman was a tall, commanding, and outspoken woman. She lived for ten years at the Waiilatpu mission, where she suffered the tragic loss of her only child by drowning. Perhaps in compensation for that loss, she established a school for the mixed-race children of American fur trappers and warmly welcomed the Oregon Trail pioneers who rested at Waiilatpu before continuing on down the Columbia River. Over the years, she wrote increasingly urgent and plaintive letters to her parents, imploring them to travel west to join her. Clearly, she was desperately lonely. She neither understood nor liked the Natives with whom she came into contact. In her early years at the mission, she taught Bible classes to Cayuse women and children, largely with pictures. But she found the Cayuse women uninterested in learning the basic European female domestic skills of spinning, weaving, and knitting.

At Lapwai, Eliza Spalding had more luck teaching Nez Perce women in domestic skills. Whether that was because of differences between the Cayuse and Nez Perce or between Whitman and Spalding is not clear. Because Eliza Spalding kept no diary and left no papers, historians have perhaps inevitably drawn unfavorable comparisons between her and the ill-fated Narcissa. Eliza worked to learn the Nez Perce language; she took eight Native children into her home as family members, not as servants; she did not object to the constant presence of Native observers as she went about her domestic routine; and she especially endeared herself by welcoming Native women to join her in tending her four babies when they came. In short, she seemed to be the anti-Narcissa—warm, welcoming, culturally sensitive. Was she? There is no way to know, nor can we assume that her apparently open attitude toward the Nez Perce was shared by the other missionary women. The available evidence suggests that Eliza was unusual and that Narcissa's sharp opinions were more typical.

About Native women, Narcissa wrote to her parents: "Feel to pity the poor Indian women who are continually traveling . . . during their lives and know no other comfort. They do all the work, such as getting the wood, preparing the food, pitching their lodges, packing and driving their animals, the complete slaves of their husbands." This is, of course, a complete misunderstanding of the importance of the female activities and skills essential to the seasonal rounds of the Plateau peoples described in the previous chapter, and it stands as vivid proof that belief in European sex roles blinded European women, as well as men, from seeing Native women clearly. Some of the reasons for Narcissa's misunderstanding of Native ways were simple differences in domestic practice. After living in small, cold, and crowded quarters for three years, the Whitmans built a larger house, which they designed with a special room for Indians. Narcissa wrote to her mother:

Could dear mother know how I have been situated the two winters past . . . I know she would pity me. . . . The greatest trial to a woman's feelings is to have her cooking and eating room always filled with four or five or more Indians—men. . . . When we get into the other house we have a room there we devote to them especially, and shall not permit them to go into the other part of the house at all. They are so filthy they make a great deal of cleaning wherever they go, and this wears out a woman very fast. We must clean after them, for we have come to elevate them and not to suffer ourselves to sink down to their standard.

All of Narcissa's deep training in domesticity and cleanliness—the constant battle against dirt, grease and lice—was in conflict with the personal habits of the Natives she was pledged to save. In true nineteenth-century fashion, she could not separate Christian belief from "civilized" behavior like washing and dressing properly and adopting European sex roles and occupations. Other missionary women, such as Mary Richardson Walker among the Spokans, would not entrust their children to Native nursemaids because they disapproved of their lack of cleanliness and feared that their social attitudes might affect their children. Women like Walker, who had envisaged an active missionary role for herself, found themselves increasingly confined to domestic activities as they tried to protect their growing numbers of children from the bad influence of the very people they had come to save.

Widely separated geographically, Narcissa Whitman, Eliza Spalding, Mary Walker, and the handful of other Protestant missionary women nevertheless looked to each other for support. In September of 1838 they formed the Columbia Maternal Association, the first white women's group in the Greater Northwest, as a tangible symbol of that support. At the time, throughout the United States, groups of mothers came together in churches to help each other in the Christian education of their children. The Columbia Maternal Association was certainly the westernmost group, and among the most creative. Because they could not meet together in person, the women decided that they would devote specific biweekly hours in the assurance that the other women would join them in prayer at that time. As missionary Mary Gray wrote, "notwithstanding we are thus separated I trust our hearts are united in this great work and that no one has at the hour for United Maternal prayer forgotten to present her petition [for her children] before the mercy seat."

Although confinement to domestic activities disappointed the women, it was just what the Mission Board had in mind when it allowed married couples to undertake missionary work. Fearing that a single man might succumb to the temptations of Native women, the Mission Board expected that good missionary wives would realize that they could best serve God by serving their husbands. In fact, it is unlikely that the Mission Board even realized that some women harbored greater hopes. Ironically, in their desire to move beyond the customary female domestic and religious role, missionary women found themselves even more confined by domestic responsibility than if they had stayed at home and not ventured west.

Another, less-noticed group of missionary women had greater success than the Protestant missionary wives. Catholic women religious, either French or of French descent, made an early appearance in the Pacific Northwest. Six sisters of Notre Dame de Namur from Quebec were summoned to St. Paul's Mission in the Willamette Valley by Franciscan father Norbert Blanchet in 1844, to teach the children of the French-Indian settlement at French Prairie. Although the students paid to attend school, they usually paid in kind—flour, meat, eggs, salt, and occasionally tea. To augment this, the sisters milked the mission cows and sold butter, a classic female way to raise money. By the 1850s, the French-Indian community they served had all but disappeared after suffering a typhoid epidemic and the "gold fever" that drew many to California. The Sisters of Notre Dame de Namur relocated to San Jose, California, in 1853.

Undeterred, Father Blanchet, now Bishop of Nisqually, sent for more nuns. This time five sisters of Charity of Providence from Montreal answered the call. Among them was Mother Joseph of the Sacred Heart, who devoted the next forty-six years of her life and impressive talents to service in the Pacific Northwest. Mother Joseph founded, built, staffed, and ran schools, hospitals, orphanages, and homes for the aged throughout the region. Her design and supervision of one particular building, Providence Academy in Vancouver, Washington, in 1873, prompted the American Institute of Architects to award her the retrospective title of "First architect of the Pacific Northwest." All this activity required money, and Mother Joseph unblushingly organized yearly "begging trips," as she called them, to the mining camps of Idaho, British Columbia, and Montana. For her astounding record of achievement, she is recognized with a place in Statuary Hall in the US Congress.

Catholic women religious had some advantages the Protestant missionary women lacked, above all the fact that they had each other for company. They were also, relatively speaking, more culturally tolerant than Protestants. Catholic missions had a better record of conversion, and of somewhat more equal treatment of white, mixed-race, and Native children, than did the early Protestant missions. But the nuns suffered their own varieties of subordination, sometimes as relatively subtle as always being second in line behind priests for funding, or as blatant as the insistence of the Jesuits of St. Ignatius Mission in western Montana that the Sisters of Providence wash their clothes, make their beds, and cook for them. Even a whirlwind visit from the formidable Mother Joseph herself could not free the sisters from the burden of the brothers' housework.

The amazing record of achievement of these pioneering women religious deserves to be much better known than it is today. The reasons for our ignorance are not hard to find: these were French-speaking nuns ministering to a small Catholic population in a region that was about to be overwhelmed by English-speaking American Protestants. This changing demography made Mother Joseph and her sisters transitional figures. Mother Joseph's Providence Academy still stands today, but perhaps the nuns' most lasting impact was their work as teachers and nurses on Indian reservations, where they ministered to the health of Native people while at the same time devotedly working to destroy traditional ways of life so that the Natives might be rescued from their status as "heathens."

Many women, both Native and white, bridged the new boundary line between worlds that marked these decades of initial contact between European and Native peoples in the Greater Northwest. While the fur trade remained dominant, the active participation of Native and métis women was crucial, for they formed the bridge between worlds upon which the trade depended. But bridges are only as strong as their supports. As once-strong Native societies were devastated by disease and fur traders were replaced by farmers, the bridge collapsed and, in white eyes, the usefulness of Native women came to an abrupt end. In contrast, the hopes of missionary women to play active roles collapsed almost immediately, as they confronted a world they did not understand and could not change. Nevertheless, the arrival of these first missionary women in 1837 presaged the dramatic change of terms that was to occur in the 1840s with American settlement. Now the bridge between cultures was posted by a "One Way" sign as the handful of Native women who survived recurrent epidemics watched as their world was replaced by a settled Christian and European one.

SOURCES FOR THIS CHAPTER

This chapter relies heavily on Sylvia Van Kirk's pathbreaking *Many Tender Ties: Women in Fur-Trade Society, 1670–1870* (Winnipeg, MN: Watson and Dwyer, 1980; Norman: University of Oklahoma Press, 1983); Van Kirk, using the same fur trade sources that other historians had, paid attention to the Native women that they had overlooked.

Because the history of Native and métis women in the early-contact and fur trade years of the Greater Northwest is so little known, I have deliberately devoted more space to them in this chapter than to the better-known missionary women. I have relied very heavily on Mary Wright, "The Circle, Broken: Gender, Family, and Difference in the Pacific Northwest, 1811–1850" (PhD dissertation, Rutgers University, 1996); and Gray Whaley, *Oregon and the Collapse of Illahee* (Chapel Hill: University of North Carolina Press, 2010), and his article, "'Complete Liberty'?: Gender, Sexuality, Race and Social Change on the Lower Columbia River, 1805–1838," in *Ethnohistory* 54:4 (Fall 2007), pp. 668–695.

My account of the earliest European-Native contact and perceptions of gender has been deeply influenced by feminist scholars of gender relations in imperialism worldwide. The centrality of sexual relationships was first demonstrated in the Dutch East Indies by Ann Stoler, *Carnal Knowledge and Imperial Power: Race and the Intimate in Colonial Rule* (Berkeley: University of California Press, 2002); the imperialist distortions of gender perceptions in India by Antoinette Burton, *Burdens of History: British Feminists, Indian Women, and Imperial Culture, 1865–1915* (Chapel Hill: University of North Carolina, 1994); and racist sexual attitudes in Africa by Jennifer L. Morgan, "Male Travelers, Female Bodies, and the Gendering of Racial Ideology, 1500–1770," in Tony Ballantyne and Antoinette Burton, eds., *Bodies in Contact: Rethinking Colonial Encounters in World History* (Durham: Duke University Press, 2005). These studies have demonstrated the centrality of gender in European-Native contact. Juliana Barr, in *Peace Came in the Form of a Woman* (Chapel Hill: University of North Carolina

Press, 2007), shows in a North American case that gender affected much more than assumptions about sexuality. As one example, the inclusion of a woman like Sacajawea in a group of strangers was a sign to observers that it was not a war party.

For Native women in the Greater Northwest fur trade, see David Peterson del Mar's fascinating account, "Intermarriage and Agency: A Chinookan Case Study," *Ethnohistory* 42:1 (Winter 1995); John A. Hussey, "The Women of Fort Vancouver," *Oregon Historical Quarterly* 92:3 (Fall 1991); Emma Milliken, "Choosing between Corsets and Freedom: Native, Mixed-Blood, and White Wives of Laborers at Fort Nisqually, 1833–1860," *Pacific Northwest Quarterly* 96:2 (Spring 2005), pp. 95–101; Jacqueline Peterson, "Women Dreaming: The Religio-Psychology of Indian-White Marriage in the Western Great Lakes Fur Trade," in Lillian Schlissel, Vicki Ruiz, and Jan Monk, eds., *Western Women: Their Land, Their Lives* (Albuquerque: University of New Mexico Press, 1988); and Melinda Marie Jetté, "Betwixt and Between the Official Story: Tracing the History and Memory of a Family of French-Indian Ancestry in the Pacific Northwest," *Oregon Historical Quarterly* 111: 2 (Summer 2010), and her *At the Hearth of the Crossed Races: A French-Indian Community in Nineteenth-Century Oregon, 1812–1859* (Corvallis: Oregon State University Press, 2015). Finally, see Janet Campbell Hale's powerful family history, *Bloodlines: Odyssey of a Native Daughter* (New York: Random House, 1993), for a personal account of the changing status of elite mixed-race fur trade families.

For Protestant missionary women, the standard source until recently has been Clifford Drury, *The First White Women Over the Rocky Mountains,* 3 vols. (Glendale: Arthur H. Clark Company, 1963–1966), which remain valuable because they contain, among other things, the verbatim diaries of Narcissa Whitman and Mary Richardson Walker, as well as those of other lesser-known women. See also Deborah Dawson Bonde, "Missionary Ways in the Wilderness: Eliza Hart Spalding, Maternal Associations, and the Nez Perce Indians," *American Presbyterians* 69:4 (Winter 1991), pp. 271–282. For more recent critical biographies, see Julie Roy Jeffrey, *Converting the West: A Biography of Narcissa Whitman* (Norman: University of Oklahoma Press, 1991); and Patricia V. Horner "Mary Richardson Walker: The Shattered Dreams of a Missionary Woman," *Montana: The Magazine of Western History* 32:3 (Summer 1982), pp. 20–31.

In spite of the fame of Mother Joseph, the information on Catholic women religious in the Pacific Northwest is scanty. See Sister Mary Dominica, *Willamette Interlude* (Palo Alto, CA: Pacific Books, 1959), on the Sisters of Notre Dame de Namur; Carl P. Schlicke, "Nun in Statuary Hall," *Pacific Northwesterner* 24 (3), pp. 41–45; and Sister Mary McCrossen, *The Bell and the River* (Seattle: Health Printers, 1957), on Mother Joseph and the Sisters of Providence. Anne Butler's recent *Across God's Frontiers: Catholic Sisters in the American West, 1830–1920* (Chapel Hill: University of North Carolina Press, 2012), provides the comprehensive understanding that smaller and more focused studies have not. Unfortunately, Jean Barman's comprehensive and richly detailed *French Canadians, Furs, and Indigenous Women in the Making of the Pacific Northwest* (Vancouver: UBC Press, 2014) appeared too late for me to incorporate into this chapter.

Chapter 3
A Shared Venture 1840s–1860s

In the spring of 1842, one hundred people in eighteen covered wagons rolled out of Independence, Missouri, bound for Oregon Country, two thousand miles away. In the following year, more than nine hundred people started west in more than one hundred wagons. By 1860, fifty-three thousand people had followed the Oregon Trail west. The Oregon pioneers quickly became a national symbol of the inevitable rightness of American westward expansion, and of American courage in setting forth into the unknown to claim new land in the name of democracy.

The epic journey over the two-thousand-mile-long Oregon Trail has been described, analyzed, and explained at length by many historians, but few of them have paid much attention to women. The vast preponderance of surviving trail diaries were written by men, especially those who "rushed" to California for gold in 1849; earlier historians assumed that women's diaries could shed little additional light on male accounts of the journey. Initially, women were depicted as reluctant pioneers, too delicate for the rough trip, and their apparent lack of activity made them seem little more than baggage on the overland journey. Since then, however, historians have recognized that there was a female pioneer experience that differed in important respects from that of men, and that their support was essential to the enterprise.

The differences begin with the decision to go west. In the 1840s, it was accepted that husbands made the big economic decisions and it was the wife's duty to follow. Tempted by glowing accounts of rich farmland in Oregon's Willamette Valley, few men in the early years fully realized that they were committing themselves and their families to a slow, tedious, exhausting, and often fatal journey. Doubtless some wives refused outright or delayed until the "Oregon fever" that gripped their men abated; there is no way of knowing how many women moved west out of duty, or how many others were as eager for the adventure as their husbands, but we know that the journey and the settlement that followed was a shared venture. It had to be, for it called upon the specific work skills and courage of both genders. And in the earliest years, when men really *were* facing unknown dangers on an uncertain trail, they needed all the domestic and emotional support they could get.

The diary of Elizabeth Dixon Smith (later Geer), is a vivid record of the 1847 journey that she, her husband, and seven children undertook. In it, she captures the pleasures and difficulties of the trip, and the fortitude and effort required.

Beginning in a train of twenty-two wagons that left St. Joseph on the Missouri River in early June, Smith believed she was well prepared for the long journey. She wrote: "No one should travel this road without medicine, for they are almost sure to have the summer complaint [diarrhea, often fatal for young children]. Each family should have a box of physicking pills, a quart of castor oil, a quart of the best rum, and a large vial of peppermint essence." She was pleased by the good spirits in their train: "Every night we encamp we locate quite a village, but take it up next day. We have plenty of music with the flute and violin and some dancing." She learned to cook with new fuel: "We see thousands of buffalo and have to use their dung for fuel. A man will gather a bushel in a minute: three bushels makes a good fire. We call the stuff 'buffalo chips.'" The Smiths were fortunate in the first phase of their journey, during which travelers in other years encountered spring rains and consequent muddy trails and swollen rivers. One 1852 traveler recorded that these conditions caused such "great discouragement" that ninety-six of one hundred wagons in their initial party turned back. But in less than a month the Smith's luck turned: they and other members of the train lost many of their oxen and were unable to find them. Some members of the train had to "hire, borrow, buy" new oxen to pull their wagons.

During the search for the oxen one man accidentally shot himself, leaving a wife and six children. "The distress of his wife I cannot describe." Further unhappiness was to come. By mid-July dysentery was common among them and they continued to lose cattle, some to Indian theft and some to sickness. As they traveled westward, Smith lamented that she had so little time to observe the landscape, or to write in her diary. "I could have written a great deal more if I had the opportunity. Sometimes I would not get the chance to write for two or three days, and then would have to rise in the night when my babe and all hands were asleep, light a candle and write."

As the trip wore on, Smith complained (as did everyone) about the dusty trail along the Snake River in present-day southern Idaho. "You in 'The States' know nothing about dust. It will fly so that you can hardly see the horns of your tongue yoke of oxen. It often seems that the cattle must die for want of breath, and then in our wagons, such a spectacle—beds, clothes, victuals, and children, all completely covered." The Snake River was dangerous: two men in their train drowned swimming stock across, while Smith's husband stood watching and could do nothing. By now it was early September, and there was increasing difficulty. Two other people in the party died as they made their way slowly through eastern Oregon and over the steep and difficult Blue Mountains. By early October, both Smith and her husband were sick with the summer complaint. By the end of October they were traveling along the Columbia River in the rain among Indians who were "as thick as hops here, and not very friendly. Anybody in preparing to come to this country should make up some calico shirts to trade to the Indians in cases of necessity [trading for fresh food, crossing rivers, etc.]. . . . Against we got here, my folks were about stripped of shirts, jackets and "wammuses [jackets]." The Smiths built rafts to float down the river but were delayed for more than two weeks by wind, bad weather, and cold. Portages were necessary: "I carry my babe and lead, or rather carry, another through snow, mud and water, almost to my knees. . . . My children gave out with cold and fatigue and could not travel, and the boys had to unhitch the oxen and bring them and carry the children on to camp," where they joined hundreds waiting for boats to take them down the Columbia.

The family finally arrived in Portland at the end of November, but Smith's troubles were not over. Her husband, seriously ill since early November, never recovered and died on February 1: "This day my dear husband, my last remaining friend, died," leaving Smith a widow with seven children. She was, she wrote, "as poor as a snake." She persisted and married again (to Mr. Geer) in 1849, which was the only realistic choice for a widow with small children. Fortunately, her new marriage was a happy one.

In his 1977 book, *Women and Men on the Overland Trail*, John Mack Faragher was the first to describe in detail what women actually did on the Oregon Trail. They did the most mundane and essential domestic work: cooking, washing, keeping things orderly, doctoring small ailments and injuries, and tending to children. They had done the same things at home, but each of these activities was much more difficult on the trail because of limited supplies, limited space, constant motion, weather, exhaustion, and relentless time pressure. In the morning, women hurriedly prepared breakfast and a cold lunch as the men gathered stock and hitched up oxen. Then women rode in wagons or, more usually, walked, for about twenty miles, keeping track of the children, while the men were occupied with scouting the route, driving oxen, and occasionally hunting. Finally at night, once the men had found a good stopping place with enough grass and water, women cooked the evening meal, got children to bed, and made preparations for the next day.

In spite of this settled routine, danger could strike at any time. Children died under wagon wheels, were burned in campfires, wandered off and were never found. Men died of gun accidents in camp or of drowning while crossing rivers, leaving widows with small children. Babies were born and not all of them lived, but being pregnant was no reason for a woman not to join the westward migration. In bad years, adults and children died, sometimes overnight of cholera or more slowly of other ailments. Indian attacks, which everyone feared, were rare, but horse stealing was common, causing constant anxiety. Tempers flared and wagon trains broke apart; sometimes families broke apart as well. In one case, half of an extended family went to Oregon, the other half to California. It was more than a year before each located the other again. From these facts, Faragher extrapolates some gendered differences in attitude:

> For men the trip West was an active test of competition, strength, and manliness. It meant measuring themselves against the already romanticized images of their heroic pioneer fathers and grandfathers traversing the Wilderness Road and the Cumberland Gap. For women the trip West was a test of their inner strength . . . of self-denial, a kind of active passivity and endurance.

And he adds: "Women on the trail were a source of great strength to the parties," precisely because they acted in customary ways and thereby affirmed the family partnership.

For however dangerous the journey might prove to be, the striking fact is how conservatively everyone acted. Women did the same work they did at home, and they invested it with accustomed meanings. Although they often "helped out" with male tasks like driving wagons, few aspired to assume male tasks. They had more than enough responsibilities and purposes of their own. In her acclaimed study, *Women's Diaries of the Westward Journey*, Lillian Schlissel observes, "In their accommodation to the life of the road, the women tried to weave a fabric of accustomed design, a semblance of their usual domestic circle." As they had on the farms from which they came, women did their domestic part of a customary cooperative venture.

Schlissel notes that the greatest differences in women's trail experience were age-related. Young girls were generally unaware of the dangers of the trail and were unencumbered with the worries that burdened their parents.

Mary Ellen Todd was nine years old when her parents decided to leave Arkansas for Oregon in 1852. She was thrilled with the news and eager to depart. When her grandmother expressed sorrow that they were moving so far away, Mary Ellen blithely said, "Oh! . . . you'll soon be going to Oregon [too]." In fact, she never saw her grandmother again. Adolescent girls were not as carefree as their younger siblings. Expected to do their full share of work, they also used up a lot of diary space lamenting the friends and family they left behind. Agnes Stewart was twenty-one and unmarried in 1853 when she traveled west in a large party with her parents, siblings, and marriage-related kin. She felt the pangs of parting from close friends very keenly and wrote about them lengthily and melodramatically in her diary. "O Martha, my heart yearns for thee my only friend. . . . I will never forget thee. . . . I know I can never enjoy the blessed privilege of communing with thee yet look for the loss of one I will never see on earth. . . . I cannot bear it." And so on. Adult women with several children bore the heaviest burden of work and worry on the Oregon Trail. They had full responsibility for feeding their families, keeping track of children, and, in the background, worrying about the choices their men were making about the route and rate of travel without themselves having a voice in the decisions—and, at least in some cases, privately helping their husbands deal with the anxieties that they could not voice in public.

The Oregon migration was a family migration with the most traditional of goals: land for the family for several generations to come. Often three generations came westward together: middle-aged parents, their adult children, and young grandchildren, with other relatives joining them in subsequent years. They rapidly spread out and claimed large tracts of land in the Willamette Valley, thereby fulfilling the aim of keeping the family together by having enough land for sons to farm their own lands next to parents and grandparents, with the senior man or men in charge of directing and coordinating the whole. Thus, although the thought would have surprised and offended them, for the pioneers the importance of the basic connection between land and kinship was the same as for the "savage" Native peoples they displaced.

William Bowen's demographic study of early settlement, *The Willamette Valley*, found that at least 45 percent of Willamette Valley households had blood ties in 1850 and that these early settlers clustered in rural neighborhoods by kinship, place of origin, or other social ties—religious, fraternal, business. His estimate is almost certainly an undercount, because there is no way, using the census data alone, to recognize the kinship ties between sisters who took different last names when they married. From all of this data, Bowen extracted a striking picture of a rural frontier characterized by dense networks or clans of farmers initially from the South but most recently from the southern parts of the Midwest, having already made one or more moves before the great move to Oregon. Perhaps, at least initially, they envisaged the overland journey as simply a longer version of a customary uprooting. It was *much* longer, and more challenging.

According to historian Dean May, who in *Three Frontiers* studied an early farming community in Oregon, the vision of enough land to keep the family together originated in the South in colonial times and had been one of the main impulses behind migration since then. In the South, the warping effect of slavery caused plantation owners and small farmers alike to act in intensely patriarchal ways, with men determined to assert their own independence and absolute control over their own households, black and white, male and female. But in Oregon, May claims, women as well as men were committed to establishing the family farm for subsequent generations. He thus prefers the term "familial" to patriarchal, although it is clear that men had much more freedom of action than women, as well as having all the legal rights.

Members of Oregon's well-known Applegate clan were typical early migrants, as one descendant, Shannon Applegate, describes in her family chronicle, *Skookum*. A trio of Applegate brothers—Charles, Lindsay, and Jesse—were originally from Kentucky. They were already in their early thirties when they and their wives, Melinda, Elizabeth, and Cynthia, and their children, migrated to Oregon in 1843. Settled on adjoining claims at Salt Creek (near present-day Salem, Oregon) the three Applegate women cultivated large gardens and planted fruit trees from seedlings. The trio of Applegate males planted wheat and Jesse built a grist mill. They also tended the cattle they had trailed west, and Cynthia Applegate, who had insisted on bringing milch cows, saw them burgeon into a herd of forty, from whose milk she made quantities of butter and cheese. So also did their own families continue to burgeon. Charles and Melinda had nine children before the move to Oregon in 1843 and six subsequently; Lindsay and Elizabeth came with six children, lost one to drowning on the journey, and later had six more; Jesse and Cynthia also came with six and lost one to drowning, and later had four more. The Applegates quickly became known for their generosity to exhausted migrants who arrived too late every fall to begin farming on their own. The Applegates and other earlier migrants helped tide them over.

It was fortunate that they were accustomed by reasons of kinship and neighborliness to help each other, for the early years were extremely difficult for everyone. Many of the migrants of the early 1840s initially owed their survival to the Hudson's Bay Company. Chief Factor John McLoughlin began the yearly practice of sending rescue parties back along the trail to help those in desperate condition, furnishing boats and crews for the dangerous trip down the Columbia River from The Dalles to Fort Vancouver, and providing food, medical treatment, and temporary employment once they arrived safely. Later, these same early migrants, like the Applegates, provided assistance to subsequent migrants, who often arrived as destitute as they had themselves and who needed help to "winter over" until they could plant crops in the spring (two thousand migrants arrived in 1845, another thousand in 1846, and over three thousand in 1847). Few migrants, either female or male, kept up their diaries once they arrived in Oregon, and although early political activities are fairly well documented, there are few records of the coping strategies that these pioneers used in their daily lives. Thus the following account is pieced together from the available scraps of evidence. From the evidence we can see that, if anything, the challenges for women increased once the journey was ended. Now stability and continuity were more necessary than ever, for men faced unaccustomed soil and climate conditions, and women had to figure out how to feed their families until new crops came in.

Contrary to western myth, the Oregon frontier did not foster innovation or adventure. Faced with strangeness, scarcity, and isolation, both men and women fell back into their most basic and traditional roles. As the men were struggling to establish cash crops, their wives were "making do" with what was available. Meat was scarce and expensive, and sometimes so was flour. Milk and potatoes, with butter, which depended on women's dairying skills, was common fare. Clothing posed another problem. One early pioneer, Martha Morrison Minto, remembered that in 1844 "there was but one bolt of calico in Oregon that we could hear of," and many Oregon housewives sacrificed their sheets to make shirts for their husbands or one-piece garments for their children. Everyone wore buckskins and moccasins or patched together clothing from wagon covers, blankets, and whatever else was available. In winter, buckskin clothing was clammy and damp, an

unpleasant reminder to the pioneers that they were little better off than
the few dispirited Kalapooya Indians who had survived the devastation of
the series of malaria attacks in the 1830s. (Except that the Kalapooyans,
unlike tribes further inland, wore clothing made of cedar, not buckskin,
precisely because of its clamminess in the wet climate.) In desperation,
Melinda Applegate spun yarn from wolfhair and knitted it into a sweater.
It was circumstances like these that prompted diarist Elizabeth Smith Geer
to describe herself as "as poor as a snake."

As newcomers to the region, farm men confronted a good deal of
novelty. They had to learn, either by experimentation or by observing a
neighbor, what crops would grow well in unfamiliar soils. In his environmental history of the Willamette Valley, historian Peter Boag describes
the challenges they faced. One early surprise was to discover that corn, a
Midwest staple, did not grow well in the Willamette Valley. Fortunately for
the American newcomers, there were two sources from which they could
learn: the huge commercial farms that Chief Factor John McLoughlin
had established north of the Columbia River, from which the Hudson's
Bay Company sold produce that fed the Russian American Company in
Alaska, and the much smaller and nearer farms of the French-Indian settlement at French Prairie. From both of these "foreign" sources the intensely
nationalistic American farmers learned, albeit grudgingly.

However new the soil and weather conditions might have been,
the American migrants, like the Natives who lived there before them,
depended on the basic and traditional division of labor that they brought
with them. Historian Nancy Grey Osterud describes, in her study *Bonds of
Community,* the basic American agricultural division of labor that all farm
families followed: "Men were responsible for plowing and planting the
fields, cultivating and harvesting the field crops, and preparing the hay and
grain for use as animal and human food. [They were also] responsible for
the construction and maintenance of the house, barn, and outbuildings, for
the provision of fuel for heat and cooking, and for the repair of farm and
household equipment." Osterud continues: "Women were responsible for
tending the vegetable garden, processing and preserving the year's supply
of vegetables and fruits, and preparing meals." In addition to daily meals,
they did laundry and household cleaning, sewed and mended clothing, and
gave birth to children and nurtured them.

Although many of these tasks were carried out separately, farmwork
required a high degree of coordination. "Farm processes often began in

men's domain and culminated in women's: many farm products had to pass through women's hands before they could be used or sold." And some events, like harvesting, took precedence over everything else. For example, women often dropped their household work temporarily to help with haying or harvesting. Thus, although they would have been surprised to hear it, the Oregon pioneer farming venture, like that of the Indians they were displacing, was a mutual dependency based on complementary gendered work activities. Or, as John Faragher put it, "women and men [in farm families] achieved common goals by doing different jobs."

Many farm women, over the years, have described their farms as hardworking partnerships devoted to passing on a successful enterprise to the children. But in law and in custom, the farm belonged solely to the man, and the father was the acknowledged head of the household, decision-maker, and patriarch. Any man who chose to abuse his authority was free to do so. Although the work of farm women was essential, and the women knew it, many farm men took the hard work of farm women for granted, or at least never publicly acknowledged it.

Unusually, on the Oregon frontier, one woman spoke up to remind them. Abigail Scott Duniway vividly remembered her workload during those years when she was a young farmwife:

> To bear two children in two and a half years from my marriage day, to make thousands of pounds of butter every year for the market, not including what was used . . . at home; to sew and cook, and wash and iron; to bake and clean and stew and fry; to be, in short, a general pioneer drudge, with never a penny of my own was not pleasant business for an erstwhile school teacher, who had earned a salary that had not gone before marriage, as did her butter and eggs and chickens afterward, for groceries, and to pay taxes or keep up the wear and tear of horseshoeing, plow-sharpening and harness-mending.

Duniway, who began writing a column called "The Farmer's Wife" for the *Oregon Farmer* in 1860, chided farmers for the many ways in which they took their wives' work for granted. Pointing out that many newly arrived farmers actually derived most of their income from women's work—"dried and preserved fruit, butter and eggs, soap and candles, pigs, pickles, vegetables and chickens"—Duniway daringly suggested that farm women needed hired help even more than their husbands. And even more daring, she suggested to the men that they were not following the rules of good horse breeding in respect to their own wives. If their wives were pregnant less often, Duniway indelicately suggested, their health and that of their children would be better.

For the most striking fact about these early migrant women was how many children they had. Demographers have long known that the female fertility rate was high on frontiers due to a combination of the early age of marriage and rural values that fostered fecundity. On a farm, each baby was considered an addition to the farm workforce, not, as urban couples were finding in the 1840s, an expensive dependent who could not earn wages for a number of years. Many early Oregon women, like the Applegate women, had ten to fourteen children each. As a result, compared with a national average fertility rate per woman of 1.31, Oregon led the nation with a fertility rate of 2.10. Clearly the first generation of Oregon migrants took the injunction to "go forth and multiply" to heart.

The consequences for women were considerable, entailing for the most fertile at least twenty years of constant pregnancy and nursing with the almost certain result, as Duniway so bluntly pointed out, of physical debilitation if not actual injury. Childbirth was usually in the hands of experienced midwives, but medical help for unusual birth situations was unavailable. Surgical procedures such as Caesarian sections were not performed anywhere in America in the 1840s, much less on the frontier. As a result, Oregon mothers suffered the same deaths and birth-related injuries as women in the East: tearing of the perineum in labor caused prolapsed uteruses, urine leakage, constant back pain, fatigue, and fears of further damage in subsequent childbirths. In this physical sense, being a woman on the frontier was no different from being one elsewhere, except for the pressing need to continue to work hard to get the farm established.

And perhaps there was another difference. In the East, prominent women such as the educational reformer Catharine Beecher spoke out publicly (if euphemistically) about women's reproductive health, but Dr. Ada Weed ran into a storm of criticism when she discussed the subject in Oregon in the 1850s. Weed and her husband were hydropathic doctors who shunned all medicines and recommended a strict diet of cold water, vegetables and graham crackers, fresh air, and unrestrictive clothing. Weed was also an outspoken advocate of women's rights, speaking in favor of votes for women, dress reform, and temperance. Weed would not have been at all unusual among East Coast reformers such as Elizabeth Cady Stanton, the Grimke sisters of abolitionist fame, or Amelia Bloomer, but she was too radical for Oregon. Unable to gain a foothold, the Weeds moved to California in 1860.

Why did Oregon women shun Weed and Duniway in spite of the fact that they raised what must have been common concerns about women's reproductive health? Partly, perhaps, because these were understood to be matters to be discussed only privately among women. Perhaps women did not care to be reminded of their own helplessness, for there was no sure or acceptable way, except abstinence, to avoid pregnancy. Contraceptives were not only unavailable but also considered immoral (only prostitutes used them), and unless one's husband agreed to limit his traditional marital rights, there was no way to refuse intercourse. But in a wider sense, out-spoken advocacy of women's rights represented a threat to their entire way of life. The familial settlement pattern so eagerly implemented by Oregon's early pioneers rested on the unspoken agreement that men held positions of control and authority within the family and clan by providing security for their women and children. This was the traditional farmer's bargain; thanks to Oregon's fertile and healthy land, families were closer to realizing their goal than ever before. Surrounded by a network of kin, following completely traditional work routines, most women were grateful for their security and cherished the belief that their traveling days were over and they were well and truly settled.

Duniway was correct to point out that, on new farms, it was women's work that brought in the cash income. The 1850 census figures bear her out, reporting a yearly total of 29,686 pounds of wool and 640 pounds of flax, as well as 36,980 pounds of cheese and a staggering 211,464 pounds of butter. The first two, wool and flax, were produced by the cooperative and complementary work of men and women, but the making of butter and cheese were female enterprises. Butter-making was a long and compli-cated process, involving many tasks from milking the cow to cleaning the equipment to churning, shaping, chilling, and marketing. Women doubt-less divided the many tasks among their children if they were old enough, but a woman with young babies, as Duniway was, had to do all the work herself. As she herself pointed out, her husband was working just as hard as she was, but on male tasks, not in ways that lightened her workload. Occasionally we read of men "helping out" when a woman was recovering from childbirth, but it was much more common for her to turn to female relatives or neighbors for help, just as her husband turned to male relatives or neighbors when he needed help in the fields. Even in the very favorable geographic and weather conditions of the Willamette Valley, everyone had to work very hard to adjust to new conditions.

Natives were not the problem that many migrants had expected. The Kalapooya, a hunting and gathering people native to the Willamette Valley, had been all but wiped out in the early 1830s by successive waves of malaria contracted after contact with seaborne traders and passed from tribe to tribe. Modern estimates are that fewer than one thousand Kalapooya were left to face cultural devastation as well as invasive white migrants who claimed land regardless of traditional hunting and gathering routes. As Peter Boag points out, white migrants, accustomed to intensive methods of farming, simply did not understand the contrasting Native methods of foraging and hunting over a wide expanse of land and therefore concluded that they had nothing to learn from them. Some migrants learned a few words of Chinook jargon, the trade language—*skookum, kloochman, til-licum*—but they regarded the remaining Kalapooyans as inconsequential. The much greater problem, in the migrants' eyes, were the wild animals also native to the valley, panthers and wolves, which ate not only chickens and pigs, but also threatened unwary small children.

The need to agree on steps for wolf protection was one of the reasons that male Oregon pioneers first met and set up a provisional government. The very fact that the Hudson's Bay Company was the strongest economic and political force in the region made the assertion of American interests imperative, or so many men believed. At the first large political gathering of male settlers in 1843, a governmental structure modeled on that of American territories was adopted, with elections and voting rights open to "every free male descendant of a white man of the age of 21 years and upwards." This definition of citizenship excluded Indian and Hawaiian men employed by the HBC, but reached out to the French Canadians who were retired HBC employees already settled in Oregon, and to the mixed-race sons of white men and Native women. The meeting also voted to ban slavery from the territory and to exclude all black people, slave or free. At the time, such action was not unusual: Ohio, Indiana, and Illinois enacted similar laws, which they repealed after the Civil War. Oregon, however, incorporated the exclusion measure in the 1857 state constitution. Although never enforced, it remained in the constitution until repudiated by voters in 1926.

The eventual fate of the jointly held Oregon Country—its division at the forty-ninth parallel—was settled far from the Columbia River by British and American diplomats in 1846, but the fact that by 1845 there were 2,110 Americans living south of the Columbia River surely influenced the final decision.

Women played no open part in these political decisions, but their importance was recognized in a major piece of legislation. The 1850 Donation Land Claim Act (DLCA), confirming the land use policies informally in use since the early 1840s, provided 320 acres of land to every white male citizen over the age of eighteen who had arrived in Oregon before December 1, 1851 (later extended to 1855); in addition (note the wording) he could claim another 320 acres in his wife's name. The DLCA, which preceded the better-known Homestead Act by twelve years, was the first US law to offer settlers free land and the only law ever to offer land to married women. (The later Homestead Act allowed single women and widows to file claims, but not married women.) Historians have favored the sentimental explanation that lawmakers wished to acknowledge the role women had played in the Oregon migration, but the truth is much simpler. The sheer size of the claim made it obvious that the aim was to have enough land to assure the family's future for several generations to come. Viewed in that light, the fact that the DLCA allowed wives, but not single women, to claim land underlined the fact that the purpose was not to reward women individually but to serve future family needs. Furthermore, while married women were granted the land, they could not sell or mortgage it without their husband's permission, for US law, following British common law, allocated all of a single woman's property to her husband when she married. (Laws to allow married women to retain property rights were not passed in Oregon and Montana until 1873; Idaho and Washington included a measure in their state constitutions at the time of statehood in 1889, by which time nearly all states had passed such legislation.) In that sense, the law was the quintessential "family claim."

The Donation Land Claim Act also reinforced American control by directly linking legally recognized marriage with land ownership. It excluded all marriages that were "according to the custom of the country" and also looser forms of sexual relationship between European men and Native women that had been the norm in the continental fur trade for almost two hundred years. The law made the American definition of marriage, as between two white people of opposite sexes, the norm in

Oregon as well. Thus it was a crucial tool in "Americanizing" the Oregon frontier. In a positive sense, the unusual inclusion of women in the DLCA served to underline the fact that pioneering in Oregon was a shared venture. However, its impact on young unmarried women seems to have been negative. It is said to have caused a spate of marriages between much older males and girls as young as twelve or thirteen, not a circumstance likely to foster female autonomy.

The American linkage of marriage with land stood in sharp contrast to the society north of the new border, in the fur trade region known as New Caledonia. There, in 1850, following the US-British border treaty, the Hudson's Bay Company reconstituted its headquarters at the new Fort Victoria on Vancouver Island. Under the direction of Chief Factor James Douglas, the HBC assumed control over the island, reestablished its agricultural enterprises, and provided a locus around which retired company workers could settle, all the while continuing to direct the fur brigades that pursued their trade in the entire northern region. The census of 1855 showed the success of these efforts, recording two hundred non-Native inhabitants of the fort and village of Victoria, 350 on nearby farms, and another 150 in the coal-mining settlement of Nanaimo. Aside from a handful of British immigrants, this entire population was either employed by or retired from the HBC. Aside from a few occupants of HBC fur forts, there were no Europeans on the mainland of what is today British Columbia; there were however, between three hundred thousand to four hundred thousand Native inhabitants.* This was the customary fur trade situation: vastly outnumbered by the Native population, HBC officials limited their contact with them to trade, and did not interfere in tribal affairs. Personal behavior common to the fur trade continued: European men continued the practice of making marriages with Native women "according to the custom of the country."

The "society" that grew up around Fort Victoria was led by a fur trade elite made up of European men and their métis wives and children, as had been true at Fort Vancouver. But now, in the 1850s, the vocal presence of a handful of British missionaries and other "civilizers" injected a new note of race consciousness: elite métis children became subject to special scrutiny,

---

* A change of terminology: I continue the use of the word "Native" for people north of the border, but because Americans uniformly used the word "Indian," I will use that term for people in the United States in future chapters.

and a marked gender difference emerged. All four daughters of Chief Factor James Douglas (later governor) and his métis wife Amelia married high-status British men, but the one surviving son, James Jr., failed to do well academically and socially in England, where Douglas had sent him to acquire education and "polish," nor was he a success when he returned to Fort Victoria where his father could keep an eye on him. He married a respectable white woman but continued without distinction until his early death at age thirty-two in 1883. Another HBC family, the eight girls and two boys of John Work and his métis wife Josette, showed a similar pattern. Again, the daughters all married white men, but the sons failed, and died unmarried at the ages of forty-nine and thirty-two. The gender disparity led a colleague, John Tod, to comment: "It is rather remarkable that so numerous a family of daughters should have turned out so well, their exemplary good conduct having gained the universal esteem and respect of their Neighbours, and the only two Sons, who survived their father, should have displayed characters the very reverse!"

What accounts for this pattern of assimilation of métis women and the rejection of sons? Certainly the scarcity of white women fostered the marriages of métis women and contributed to their brothers' failure to marry, but there are other explanations. The difference conforms to a worldwide colonial practice discerned by feminist scholars. As anthropologist Ann Stoler explains, it was not the presence of mixed-race offspring themselves that was problematic, but the possibility that mixed-race sons might claim the wealth and power of their white fathers. This concern over control ripped away the appearance of tolerance and reciprocity in the fur trade and marked the beginnings of a turn toward full-blown colonialism, as soon became obvious at Fort Victoria. As historian Adele Perry explains, so long as European and Native populations were joined in marriage or in shorter sexual liaisons, "imperial visions of orderly, white communities buttressed by distant and quiescent [Native] populations" were impossible. As the HBC continued the interracial patterns of marriage and sexual unions "according to the custom of the country" that had existed throughout the entire Greater Northwest before the arrival of the Oregon pioneers, new British immigrants began to object. Annie Deans wrote home to her brother and sister in 1854 to disparage former HBC chief factor, now governor, Douglas, who, Deans claimed "has spent all his life among the North American Indians and has got one of them for a wife so can it be expected that he can know anything at all about Governing one of England's last

Colonies in North America?" As the fur trade era came to a close, how could a handful of white people, vastly outnumbered by Natives, create a proper British colony? That was the question for the future.

For their part, the Oregon pioneers at first paid scant attention to Indians, because they did not have to: the tribes that occupied the Willamette Valley had been so devastated by disease that they did not resist white occupation. Delighted with their success at "twisting the [British] lion's tail," and banishing the HBC to Canada, the pioneers expected to continue their shared commitment to settlement-making unopposed. But the larger and stronger tribes east of the Cascade mountains—the Cayuse, the Yakama, the Nez Perce—were increasingly alarmed at the size of the annual Oregon Trail migrations. These fears, coupled with their anger over the differential effects of disease (whites sickened but survived, while Indians died), exploded in the killing of the Whitmans and eleven others at the Waiilatpu mission by Cayuse Indians in 1847. That action, and the white retaliation that followed, changed the terms of white settlement.

We are accustomed to thinking of pioneers as innovators and trailblazers. Viewed in these terms, the domestic activities of Oregon's female pioneers seem very conventional—and they were. On the Oregon Trail and in later settlement, women used their domestic skills to feed and care for their families in circumstances that often required both ingenuity and fortitude. The very predictability of their activities sustained their families both physically and emotionally in ways that were so customary that they were frequently taken for granted. White pioneer women successfully worked to reestablish by their domestic activities the values of stability and continuity that were so important to them and to their families. But the era of unopposed settlement was over. Women in Oregon, as well as those at Fort Victoria, sensed that they faced an uncertain future even before the dramatic changes of gold discoveries rushed in upon them.

SOURCES FOR THIS CHAPTER

The two books that changed the interpretation of women on the Oregon Trail (and initially provoked heated controversy among western historians) are John Mack Faragher, *Women and Men on the Overland Trail* (New Haven: Yale University Press, 1979), and Lillian Schlissel, *Women's Diaries of the Westward Journey* (New York: Schocken Books, 1982). Today they are the standard references. The most comprehensive diary collection is Kenneth Holmes, ed., *Covered Wagon Women: Diaries and Letters from the Western Trails, 1840–1890* (Glendale, CA: A.H. Clark Co., 1984, 11 vols.; reprinted, Bison Books, Lincoln: University of Nebraska Press, 1996). Specific diaries mentioned here are Adrietta Applegate Hixon, *On to Oregon* (Fairfield, WA: Ye Galleon Press, 1977), and "Diary of Mrs. Elizabeth Dixon Smith Geer," Transactions of the 35th Annual Reunion of the Oregon Pioneer Association, No. 35 (1908). A recent fictional account of the journey that seems to me to be true to the psychological reality is Karen Fisher, *A Sudden Country* (New York: Random House, 2005).

Patterns of early settlement were first explored by William A. Bowen, *The Willamette Valley: Migration and Settlement on the Oregon Frontier* (Seattle: University of Washington Press, 1978). Other important works are Dean May, *Three Frontiers: Family, Land, and Society in the American West, 1850–1900* (New York: Cambridge University Press, 1994); Shannon Applegate, *Skookum: An Oregon Pioneer Family's History and Lore* (New York: William Morrow, 1988); Cynthia Culver Prescott, *Gender and Generation on the Far Western Frontier* (Tucson: University of Arizona Press, 2007); Peter Boag, *Environment and Experience: Settlement Culture in Nineteenth-Century Oregon* (Berkeley: University of California Press, 1992); and Paul Bourke and Donald DeBats, *Washington County: Politics and Community in Antebellum America* (Baltimore: Johns Hopkins University Press, 1995). For basic farm routines and the division of labor, I found Nancy Grey Osterud, *Bonds of Community: The Lives of Farm Women in Nineteenth-Century New York* (Ithaca: Cornell University Press, 1991), to be especially useful, as were early chapters of Faragher. Biographies of notable women include Abigail Scott Duniway, *Path Breaking: An Autobiographical History of the Equal Suffrage Movement in Pacific Coast States* (Portland, OR: James, Kerns & Abbott Co., 1914; reprint New York: Schocken Books, 1971); Ruth Barnes Moynihan, *Rebel for Rights: Abigail Scott Duniway* (New Haven: Yale University Press, 1983); and G. Thomas Edwards, "Dr. Ada Weed, Northwest Reformer," in G. Thomas Edwards and Carlos A. Schwantes, eds., *Experiences in a Promised Land: Essays in Pacific Northwest History* (Seattle: University of Washington Press, 1986), pp. 159–178. For less famous women, there is a grab bag of interviews by newspaperman Fred Lockley from the early twentieth century, compiled by Mike Helm, *Conversations with Pioneer Women* (Eugene, OR: Rainy Day Press, 1981).

Information on Oregon's black exclusion law is in R. Gregory Nokes, *Breaking Chains: Slavery on Trial in the Oregon Territory* (Corvallis: Oregon State University Press, 2013).

Most accounts of the Donation Land Claim Act fail to consider the implications for married women, in spite of its unusual inclusion of them. This is a not uncommon oversight that women's historians frequently encounter, and we have all learned how to ferret out the obscure sources we need. In this case an article by Richard Chused, "The Oregon Donation Act of 1850 and Nineteenth-Century Federal Married Women's Property Law," *Law and History Review* 2:1 (Spring 1984), pp. 44–78, answered most of my questions.

This chapter introduces a major source, Jean Barman's impressively comprehensive *The West beyond the West: A History of British Columbia*, now in its third edition (Toronto: University of Toronto Press, 2007). I have relied on her heavily in this chapter and chapters to come.

For the transition from fur trade society to British colony, see Sylvia Van Kirk, "Tracing the Fortunes of Five Founding Families of Victoria," *BC Studies* 115/116 (1997-98), pp. 148–179, and her "A Transborder Family in the Pacific North West: Reflecting on Race and Gender in Women's History," in Elizabeth Jameson and Sheila McManus, eds., *One Step Over the Line* (Edmonton: University of Alberta Press and Athabasca University, 2008); also Adele Perry, *On the Edge of Empire: Gender, Race, and the Making of British Columbia, 1849–1871* (Toronto: University of Toronto Press, 2001); and Ann Laura Stoler, "Rethinking Colonial Categories: European Communities and the Boundaries of Rule," *Society for Comparative Study of Society and History* 31:1 (1989), p. 148.

Chapter 4
Invaders 1850s–1880s

Preceding page: Barkerville, a Fraser River gold rush town (Image E-06573, courtesy of the Royal BC Museum, BC Archives)

The Oregon pioneers have cast a long shadow over the subsequent history of the Greater Northwest. The stories of the pioneer farm families who peacefully claimed the Willamette Valley as a place of permanent settlement led many subsequent migrants to expect the same. In fact, outside of the Willamette Valley, the costs in death and disruption caused by conquest affected women of all races everywhere. The gold rushes were a disaster for Native women and seriously disrupted the stable settlements that white women had hoped to achieve.

Like the Willamette Valley pioneers, migrants who settled elsewhere in the region assumed that the land was theirs for the claiming and that any remaining Indians would soon be removed. This confident civilian attitude toward conquest was what Americans called peaceful expansion. These assumptions were first tested north of the Columbia River in the Puget Sound area, where the first handful of white settlers, looking for gold, encountered dense forests of evergreen trees and more Indians than most Americans had ever seen. The area was thickly settled by Natives of more than fifty distinct Salish-speaking groups tied together in wider kinship networks. The handful of pioneers was vastly outnumbered by Indians. Historian Alexandra Harmon estimates that by 1853, there were two thousand whites living among twelve thousand Indians.

Among that two thousand were Phoebe Judson and her husband, who crossed the plains in 1853 to take up a claim near her parents in Grand Mound, near Olympia, Washington. Phoebe counted only eleven other settler families within an eight-mile radius. Although eager to be friendly, the Judsons watched anxiously as the Indians continued to follow their accustomed seasonal rounds. Phoebe recorded that a "little old Indian chief" accompanied by his three wives ("Nika kloochmen," wrote Phoebe, showing off her Chinook jargon) built his "wigwam" near the springs on the Judson property. The Judson's reaction was partly sympathetic—"How could they realize they were trespassing our rights, when no doubt this spring had been one of their favorite camping places and hunting grounds?"—and partly possessive, as they decided to tolerate the "trespass" until the government formally dispossessed the Indians of their lands.

More worrisome was what looked to the Judsons like random transiency. "We were afraid of the Indians who were constantly roaming over the prairies on their ponies. Bands of them frequently crowded into our little cabin, where, squatted on their feet, they would sit for hours enjoying our open fire, as well as our 'pire sublil' (bread), which, though so expensive, I always gave them on demand—because I was afraid to refuse them; while I, baby in arms, with Annie clinging to my side, stood near the door, which I kept wide open, in order to allow the odor from their filthy garments to escape, as well as an avenue of escape myself with the children, should they offer to molest us." Other women doubtless shared Phoebe's sense of themselves as brave pioneers, who, she wrote, "each . . . bearing the privations incident to a pioneer's life, and doing his part in helping to develop a new country" thought of themselves as living peacefully if somewhat anxiously among the Indians, learning some Chinook jargon, observing Indian customs and seasonal rounds in a puzzled way, and hiring Indian help for farm and domestic work, while throughout continuing to pity "the poor, unenlightened Indian." Certainly it never crossed Phoebe's mind to think of herself as an invader, but the settlers' occupation of the land, coupled with the scourges of disease and alcohol, devastated Indian life in the Puget Sound region. And, although Phoebe would doubtless have been horrified by the comparison, the American settlers shared the same colonialist assumption about their unquestioned right to occupy the land as their British counterparts to the north, although they clothed it in the language of democracy, not of empire.

Seattle began as one of the settlements among the Indians. When the twenty-four migrants stepped off a lumber schooner onto Alki Point on a rainy November day in 1851 to face a welcoming party of Duwamish Indians, all the women were in tears, and one of the men. Arthur Denny suddenly realized what he had done: "It was not until I became aware that my wife and helpless children were exposed to the murderous attacks of hostile savages that it dawned on me that I had made a desperate venture." In fact the Natives were not at all murderous, simply curious. Within a few weeks, over one thousand Indians—Muckleshoot and Suquamish as well as Duwamish—moved to surround the settlers and study every aspect of their strange and different lives. Interaction was constant, and so were misunderstandings and irritations as Indians intruded into all aspects of the whites' lives. Much of the curiosity focused on the routines of domestic life, so familiar and yet so different from their own. White women complained that they were interrupted while cooking, or were expected to feed hordes of Indians out of their meager supplies. There were positive and crucial interactions as well: the Indians supplied both food and labor and taught the newcomers the skills they needed to survive. At least initially, the Natives appear to have assumed that whites would assimilate to Indian ways. Emily Denny, one of the first white children born in Seattle, recalled being told, "You were born in our country and are our people. You eat the same food, grow up here, belong to us."

The Seattle settlement grew and took root along the shore of Elliott Bay, where Henry Yesler located a sawmill and where he employed Indian as well as white workers. Still, not everyone was comfortable in this rough accommodation of cultures. Catherine Blaine, the wife of a minister, complained of the presence of "miserable indian shanties scattered all about," occupied by "coarse, filthy and debased natives" who were impossible to avoid. The Americans had unwittingly chosen to settle on the site of a Duwamish fishing camp, so the Indians were already there, although their numbers fluctuated between one hundred and five hundred depending on the season. Nevertheless, historian Coll-Peter Thrush argues in *Native Seattle* that the dependence of early Seattleans on Indian labor in the sawmills and the fisheries, in construction, and even for food itself was nearly absolute, especially when the California and Fraser River gold rushes emptied the town of most white men. Most of the settlers realized this interdependence and learned to accommodate to the customs of local Natives (the Blaines moved to Portland, which they regarded as more civilized, i.e., with fewer Indians), but as the 1850s wore on, the number of violent episodes increased, usually provoked by what Henry Yesler called "some worthless white man" who invited Indian retaliation. As a result, Seattle's initial success as a biracial community deteriorated.

In 1854 Isaac Stevens, governor of the newly created Washington Territory, moved to remedy the situation according to the standard government policy toward Indians. He briskly concluded three treaties with Puget Sound Indian groups and a fourth with Chief Seeathl (for whom the settlement was named) and other leaders in 1855 and then moved east of the Cascades to conclude treaties there. Stevens's intent, which was to remove all Indians to reserves or at least segregate them from settlers, provoked an immediate protest from the Indians throughout the Puget Sound region. One dramatic response was the so-called Battle of Seattle of January 26, 1856, in which the guns of the navy sloop *Decatur* were trained not on the local Indians but on about one thousand other Salish Indians who came from south Puget Sound. Elsewhere in western Washington there were sporadic clashes between Indian protesters and the militia. Some rural settlers, and a much larger number of Indians, were killed, provoking intense fear

on both sides and prompting many whites to cluster together in stockades, some for as long as sixteen months. These "Indian Wars" in Puget
Sound caused many settlers, the Judsons among them, to abandon their
claims. They gave up farming altogether and moved to Olympia, where
Mr. Judson opened a general store. They were far from the last to have
their initial expectations disrupted.

The Puget Sound Indian Wars were mild compared with what happened
elsewhere. Throughout the entire Greater Northwest, the notion of peace-
able, family-centered settlement was upended by the gold rushes that
violently disrupted the lives of Native peoples. The destructive rushes to
new sites throughout the region to claim gold paved the way for the later
claiming and development of the land by peaceful farm families. To ignore
the fact of the series of violent white invasions and to focus only on settlement is to distort the complex reality of how the Greater Northwest was
actually occupied.

The California gold rush was the first to jolt the Greater Northwest.
The immediate effect, in 1848, was to drain the territory of men. Oregon
pioneer Peter Burnett later claimed that two-thirds of the male population
headed to California that summer and fall, hoping to "strike it rich" before
news of the gold reached the East Coast. "Gold fever" was so intense that,
for example, the Hudson's Bay Company officers at Fort Victoria suspended fur trapping and granted all its employees a six-month leave of
absence so that they might travel to California. What men saw as opportunity, women often experienced as desertion, for they were left behind to
do all the work of keeping households and farms together—in effect, to
do double work. Some of it didn't get done, and wheat and other crops
were left standing in the fields for lack of harvesters. Slowly men returned,
some with gold to show for it; a considerable number, generally young
men, never came back, leaving their families to wonder whether they had
survived. The story of the Malick family illustrates the disruption. Oregon
Trail migrant Abigail Malick at first wrote home exuberantly in 1850 to
relatives in Illinois: "We have got Abutiful Claim near fourt vancover on
the Coulumbia River. A whol sexsion of land, and theare is ships asail-
ing every day on the greate Coumbia right befoure our dore." Already,
however, husband George and his oldest son Charles had been lured to
California by gold, returning much richer in just a few months. Charles,
who was nineteen, returned home with $5,000 in gold dust and promptly

went south again to get more. He never returned. At the time, the family heard different stories: that he had brain fever, that he had been robbed on his way home. He was simply gone.

The California gold rush established Portland, founded in the 1840s, as the major shipping center for the produce of Willamette Valley farmers, who rushed to supply food for the California miners. But in the short run, the effect on Portland's gender balance was dramatic. A contemporary reported, "Men abandoned homes, jobs, and ships. In midsummer 1849, only three men remained in Portland. . . . There were only women and children to serve stores and commission houses when settlers' wives and children drove their oxen or rowed their boats into town to trade." Some women, impoverished by their husbands' absence, developed strategies to cope. One Portland woman went daily to the ships to collect washing from sailors and soon, thanks to gold rush trade, had earned enough money to open a boardinghouse. A more universal strategy adopted by town and countrywomen alike was to spin wool yarn and knit socks, of which miners apparently needed an inexhaustible supply, for socks were soon so common that they were accepted as equivalent to cash, fifty cents a pair.

The next gold rush came in 1858, when gold was discovered along the Fraser River. It transformed Victoria, on the southern tip of Vancouver Island, from a fur trade outpost to a bustling city. Easily reached via a short sea voyage from San Francisco, Victoria was flooded with gold-seekers from all over the world, and it became the major supply point for them all. Companies sprang up to supply miners with everything from picks to clothing to food. Some of the institutions of civilization soon followed. First came schools: four nuns of the Sisters of Saint Ann opened a Catholic school for girls, Anglican schools followed, and finally city-financed common schools. By 1860, two years after the rush had begun, there were four churches and a hospital. The first city directory also listed a Ladies' Benevolent Society and a Hebrew Victoria Benevolent Society. The same directory listed, as was common at the time, the names and occupations of over one hundred leading men, most of whom seem to have been married and have families, though no details are given. By 1863, the population of the Victoria area was estimated at six thousand. This was a solid, thriving community, but as the Fraser River gold rush declined, so did Victoria, although it remained the provincial capital. Attention shifted from Victoria to the mainland.

By 1859 the mainland population, heretofore almost completely composed of Natives, swelled to thirty thousand people, largely American men. The impact of the Fraser River gold rush reverberated throughout the entire region. Large armed parties of men traveling overland through parts of what is now eastern Washington and British Columbia on their way to the goldfields invaded the Native societies they encountered along the way, stealing food and raping women, thereby provoking the Yakima war of 1858 in Washington Territory and the miner-Native skirmishes known as the Fraser River War of the same year. The Fraser River rush, and the smaller subsequent rush to the Cariboo region, farther up the Fraser River, in 1861, permanently disrupted the Native-white equilibrium of fur trade society that the Hudson's Bay Company at Fort Victoria had established and forced the authorities to consider other ways to make the territory viable. Alive to the real possibility of American annexation, the British government moved quickly to create the British colony of British Columbia, uniting Vancouver Island and the mainland under the governorship of James Douglas, who retired from the HBC to take the position. Thus, in a political sense, the European inhabitants of the new British Columbia found their initial regional identity in a determination to not be American.

The Fraser River and Cariboo gold rushes were far from the only ones. Gold was found in Oregon's Rogue River region in 1850–1851, in the Clearwater region of Idaho in 1860, in the Boise Basin in 1862, and in Bannack, Virginia City, and Helena, Montana, between 1862 and 1864. In every case the result was the same as in the Fraser River rush: large numbers of miners flocked to the site in total disregard of the Native population, causing skirmishes that often rose to the level of "wars" (as in the Rogue River Wars of 1851 to 1855, the Washington Indian wars of the 1850s, the Shoshone War of 1866 to 1868, and the Modoc War of 1864 to 1873). It was gold-seekers, not peaceful farm families, that disrupted Native societies so completely that they were forced to acquiesce to the reservation system, thus opening large parts of the Greater Northwest to what later settlers mistakenly thought was unoccupied land.

Typically we think of gold rushers as male, and mining camps as rough spots completely lacking in domestic comforts. Yet at the time, the few women in mining towns were immensely valued precisely because their domestic skills were so rare. Because mining camps were temporary and transient places, most men never considered bringing their wives with them.

In consequence, mining camps posed unique challenges to the handful of women who made their way there. On the one hand, a woman who could cook, sew, or do laundry (as most women could) garnered high prices for the domestic skills most nineteenth-century men did not possess. These women, almost always wives who refused to be left behind, were often more successful than their miner husbands. In the early days of a gold rush, the woman who opened a boardinghouse or restaurant (even if it was just a plank placed over two barrels) made good money, because her skills were in such great demand. For women, these gold rush opportunities offered a new role: suddenly they were not private housewives but businesswomen selling their domestic skills on the public market.

The women who participated in the Cariboo gold rush of the 1860s had "an impact on society out of all proportion to their numbers," Sylvia Van Kirk suggests. Janet Morris (also known as Scotch Jennie) began as a boardinghouse keeper but later branched out into hotels at the sites of new gold strikes in the district. Fanny Bendixen operated a well-known saloon, sometimes with her husband, sometimes alone. Another woman, listed in the local paper only as Miss A. Hickman, began with a simple lunchroom that blossomed into the New Dominion Dining Rooms. Even women of more lowly occupations, such as the two washerwomen, Madame Coulon and Rebecca Gibbs, made good money at their trade. Mining camps thus provided one rare occasion when women received not only pay but also admiration for the domestic work that was taken for granted elsewhere.

On the other hand, the domestic "skill" most in demand in these male-dominated camps was sex work. Prostitutes were a different class of women entirely, literally described in one mining town ordinance not as "women" but as "lewd and dissolute female persons." Respectable women had to take care that they dressed and behaved appropriately and avoided locations (like saloons) that might lead men to confuse the two. In a nineteenth-century version of "blaming the victim," a woman who was crudely accosted by a man must have failed to make clear that she was a private, not a public, woman.

Prostitutes were public women because they were available to all men who could afford to pay them for sex. In spite of the tone of titillation that characterizes much of the writing about western prostitution, it was a sordid and dangerous trade that few women willingly chose. To begin with, few prostitutes set their own terms: they worked for a madam or a pimp, and they did as they were told. Just as respectable women were restricted to certain parts of town, so were prostitutes, who were rarely tolerated outside the red-light district. Most significantly, prostitution was stratified by race. At the top of the trade were a few women, perhaps Frenchwomen (or claiming to be), who owned their own homes and could choose their own clients, or who had a single wealthy lover. Much more common were the Chinese, Indian, Mexican, and other racialized women who worked out of tiny "cribs" (a room with a bed) lining the streets of red-light districts and solicited multiple customers for a pittance. These "everynight workingmen's whores," as they were later known in Butte, typically had short lifespans, succumbing to alcohol, drugs, violence, or multiple abortions while still in their twenties. In between these extremes were the women who worked in tacky brothels with few pretensions to glamour, and who had to be ready to move on to the next town when the mines began to "play out."

Prostitution in the Cariboo, according to Van Kirk, both confirmed and confounded this profile. A big part of the organized sex trade involved dance-hall girls, also known as hurdy-gurdy girls, groups of whom were imported by saloon-keepers. "Hurdies," as they were known, danced with miners for a dollar a dance in rowdy, energetic, and sometimes indecent waltzes and galops. Hurdies were always willing to dance with a man for pay, but not to have sex with him, or so they claimed. Several Cariboo hurdies married merchants, but because they had been public, not private, women, their morals henceforth were always a subject for gossip.

The apparently limited extent of prostitution in Cariboo and its racial boundaries seems unusual, but perhaps this is more a failure of our assumptions than of historical fact. On the other hand, we have horrifying accounts of the degradation of prostitution elsewhere, like this account from Victoria's Chinatown in the 1880s:

The "cribs," each of which held up to six women, were slatted crates, often located out of doors, measuring approximately 12 feet by 14 feet with a curtain, pallet, wash basin, mirror and usually two chairs. A woman forced into crib prostitution would work for six to eight years; at the end of her usefulness, when she was ravaged by disease, physical abuse or starvation, she was allowed to escape to the Salvation Army, the hospital, or the gutter.

In contrast, the gold rush town of Helena, Montana, attracted a wealthier and more independent class of prostitutes. Of the approximately sixty women engaged in the sex trade there in 1870, Paula Petrik found that more than a third of them owned their own homes. These "proprietor prostitutes," as Petrik calls them, were white, native-born, and accustomed to independence. Only in the 1880s, when Helena was an old town by mining camp standards, did brothels controlled by madams supplant the enterprising proprietors of earlier years.

Another characteristic of the Cariboo gold rush, surprising to many, was the large number of Chinese miners and the handful of Chinese women who came with them. The presence of Chinese in mining towns is most fully documented by Liping Zhu, whose book, *A Chinaman's Chance,* describes Idaho's Boise Basin gold rush of 1863, when word of the gold discoveries in Idaho City briefly made it the largest city in the entire Greater Northwest.

In 1870, of the fifteen thousand people living in Idaho Territory, almost 30 percent were Chinese. This was the highest proportion in the country, far higher than any population ever reached in California. At first, the reaction to the Chinese, as elsewhere, was hostile, but as white miners wanted to move on to newer gold strikes in Montana, they were happy to sell their claims to Chinese miners who were already well known, on account of their thoroughness and cooperation (they worked in groups of ten to fifteen), for extracting substantial amounts of gold from apparently "played-out" claims. In addition to mining, Chinese men soon moved into supply occupations as truck farmers, peddlers, and laundrymen. In this last occupation, considered by most Americans as "women's work," Chinese men competed directly with poor white women, undercutting their prices and driving them out of the trade to such an extent that for most people "Chinese" and "laundry" became synonymous.

In 1870, Chinese were nearly half the inhabitants of the Boise Basin (45.7 percent). Among them were two doctors, six merchants, and fifty-five women, of whom thirty-five were prostitutes, sixteen worked at other occupations, and only four were listed by the census taker as "at home." Almost certainly these four were the wives of merchants, and some of the sixteen other women their servants. By 1880, the number of Chinese was counted as 1,225, of whom eighteen were merchants, all of whom had brought their wives from China and begun to have American-born children. Seventeen children were counted in 1880; when they were old enough, they went to public schools along with children of other races, in contrast to the segregated school system in California at the time.

We have no firsthand accounts of Chinese merchant wives in Idaho, but historian Judy Yung's description of their counterparts in early San Francisco in *Unbound Feet* gives a sense of their lives. As in China itself, elite Chinese women lived cloistered lives. Their mobility was constrained by their bound feet (an upper-class custom) and even more by social convention: they simply did not appear in public. Elite wives might occasionally visit each other, but mostly they lived within the household with their servants (some of whom, as bound servants, or *mui tsai*, might be second wives or concubines to the merchant himself). Limited as this life was, a Chinese merchant's wife experienced freedom from the absolute control of her mother-in-law that she would have endured in China, and as her children (and especially her sons) grew, she gained authority by running the household and raising the children. Furthermore, because so few men could afford to bring their wives, she was a valued status symbol for her husband.

In San Francisco, Protestant missionary women targeted these merchant wives, hoping to convert them to Christianity. In this they rarely succeeded, but Yung suggests that some wives did agree to educate their daughters, refuse to bind their feet, and even venture outside the household to church. Whether the small Chinese communities in the Boise Basin encouraged the same widening of horizons as San Francisco's Chinatown is unknown.

Twenty-seven Chinese prostitutes were counted in the 1880 census of the Boise Basin. They were among the most reviled and stereotyped figures in American society. Famous missionary enterprises like the one in San Francisco trumpeted tales of innocent victims rescued from miserable slavery, but at the same time, lurid images of seductive and exotic women epitomized the fear and fascination with which many Americans regarded the Chinese. In the Boise Basin (as in most mining towns), attitudes toward prostitutes were more matter-of-fact. Prostitutes often made more money than miners. Most owned property: a town lot and a house, which they might share with two or three other women. They served both Chinese and white men alike. At least one enterprising prostitute in Placerville offered her services on credit; when she had trouble collecting, legend has it that she went to the town square and shouted out the names of the delinquents behind in their payments. Today we know the names of none of these women, but perhaps their enterprise is epitomized by another more well-known Chinese woman, Lalu Natoy, more commonly known as Polly Bemis. Polly was sold by her family in China, sold again in San Francisco, and sent to the mining town of Warren in the northern part of the state, where she was the concubine of a Chinese tavern owner. Eventually she married a white man, Charles Bemis, and lived with him on his claim along the Salmon River. Living on, well after the other Chinese had left, the diminutive and engaging Polly was transformed in local opinion from threatening alien to local celebrity, and she is touted today as "the first Chinese woman in Idaho," which she certainly was not. Her circumstances were simply much more fortunate.

Impermanence was the fate of all but a very few mining towns. In the Pacific Northwest, only Butte (copper) and the silver-mining towns of Wallace and Kellogg in the Coeur d'Alenes (not discovered until the 1890s) lasted into the twentieth century. At the end of the nineteenth century, the Klondike gold rush briefly evoked the same enthusiasm as had the strikes in midcentury. More women participated in the Klondike rush of 1897, and we know more about them than in previous rushes, at least in part because of the growth of popular newspapers and the enterprising reporters who traveled the world to find good stories. The women who made the long hard climb over Chilkoot Pass into Canada's Yukon basin made good stories, or at least some of them did.

As in all previous gold rushes, women filled the domestic niche with restaurants, hotels, boardinghouses, and prostitution, but several reached beyond that base. Restaurateur Belinda Mulrooney, born in Ireland, opened two hotels, a telephone company, and a water company in Dawson while investing in mining claims. Harriet Pullen started out cooking for construction crews in Skagway, started a freighting business over White Pass, and finally established a notable restaurant that she proudly named Pullen House. Nellie Cashman opened a restaurant in Dawson in 1897, but only as a source for the funds she needed to prospect on her own for gold, an occupation she followed all over the West (and a good part of the North) from 1873 to 1925. Ellen Gibson followed her husband Joe to Dawson in 1898, where, as Joe had predicted, her work as a seamstress and laundress brought in more money than he did, enough to stake several gold claims and to purchase a steam laundry of her own. But Dawsonites, like other miners, had itchy feet, and when gold was discovered in Nome, on the Bering Sea, a reported eight thousand people left Dawson in one week for the new strike. Ellen resisted that move, but by 1902, when another strike was announced in Tanana (later Fairbanks), Ellen was ready to go, and to leave Joe behind. Inspired by Belinda Mulrooney's success as a hotelier in Dawson, Ellen planned to establish a similar establishment in Fairbanks, but that gold rush soon petered out, and Ellen never did get to build her grand hotel.

Another notable aspect of the Klondike gold rush was the presence of Native people. Tlingit women as well as men earned good wages packing supplies over Chilkoot and White Passes, and a Tagish woman, Kate Carmack (Shaaw Tláa), is credited with the initial discovery of gold. Unlike many mining towns, today Dawson still exists as a viable city, although the present population of about one thousand is a long way down from the gold rush high of fifty times that number.

Although gold rushes were usually brief, their impact on Native peoples was permanent. Any change to their traditional and embedded way of life would have threatened the lives of Indian women and their kin, but these blows were massive. The invasion of gold-seekers disrupted the subsistence rounds of every Native group, often violently. Native women were particular targets, as rape and stealing of food were the most common offenses. The invaders also brought disease and alcohol, further debilitating Native cultures.

When gold rushers invaded Indian lands, violence frequently erupted, and the US military or the local militia was called upon to restore peace. Sometimes the military action was horrific. In 1863, called upon to protect the route across Shoshone territory that was used by Montana-bound gold-seekers and Idaho-bound Mormon settlers, a column of California volunteers attacked a Shoshone winter camp at Bear River. In the four-hour battle that followed, 224 Shoshone men, women, and children died and 164 women and children were taken prisoner, making Bear River one of the worst slaughters in the history of western Indian wars. In a more typical but equally devastating case, the vigorous Indian resistance to gold miners in the Rogue River region of southern Oregon led to five years of vicious killings and counter-killings. In the end, the debilitated Indian survivors (two thousand out of an estimated ninety-five hundred) were harried out of the hills by militia and permanently removed from their homelands to the Grande Ronde and Siletz Reservations in northwestern Oregon. Even tribes that successfully resisted removal still experienced devastation by disease. Favored by geography, the Haida in the Queen Charlotte Islands successfully repelled American gold prospectors by force in the 1850s, only to succumb to smallpox, which reduced the population by three-quarters (from eight thousand to two thousand) in the subsequent thirty years.

In these circumstances, retreat to reservations may have seemed to Indian women to be the best available protection against continuing violence. We have no firsthand accounts from the first generation of Indian and Native women forced to adjust to reservation life in the Greater Northwest, but we can assume that they saw their first tasks as preserving as much of their traditional kinship web as they could and continuing their provider role by following the seasonal round, but that activity itself often led to further conflict. The treaties that Governor Isaac Stevens of Washington Territory conducted in 1854 and 1855 guaranteed each tribe the right to travel to their "usual and accustomed places" to dig roots, pick berries, and fish. But reservation boundaries were porous or inexact, and soon settlers were objecting to what they regarded as trespassing on their own private land. In contrast, in British Columbia, the British Crown claimed all the land by right of conquest, and local officials granted Natives only enough land for band villages, but agreed that they could continue their seasonal rounds without interference, which was easy at first because the white population of the British Columbia mainland was so small.

The disruptions of the gold rushes also caused a very large seasonal migration of Native peoples. Beginning in the 1850s, Coastal peoples from as far north as the Tlingit in the Alaskan panhandle to those on Vancouver Island and the adjacent mainland began the practice of annual migrations to Victoria, the Fraser Valley (including Cariboo), and Puget Sound. They went for a reason new to them: wagework—the men in the woods and sawmills, the women as traders or domestic servants, sometimes cohabiting with white men for the summer and then returning to their homelands in the fall. While wagework might have been new to Native people, its purpose was traditional: they worked to gather wealth to continue their customary potlatches in an effort to preserve an essential part of their cultures. There were many individual reasons why a Native woman might find a temporary sexual union with a white man the best of her very limited options, but because of European beliefs about female sexuality, all Native women became stereotyped and treated as sexually available. Thus, as historian Jean Barman has shown, the men who flooded the streets of Victoria on their way to the Fraser gold rush regarded all Native women on the streets of Victoria as prostitutes, even if in fact they were married to HBC employees, or were domestic servants or street hawkers selling beans or clams. At a time when newspapers like the *British Colonist* could assert, without apparent challenge, that "[all the Indian] men to-day are a horde of thieves and cut-throats, and the women a community of prostitutes," there was little a Native woman could do to protect herself, and the constant denigrations and temptations, in particular liquor and dance halls, were hard to resist. The very fact of being on the streets was enough to condemn her.

By 1885 as many as six thousand so-called Northern Indians were making the annual migration to Victoria, southern British Columbia, and Puget Sound. White inhabitants in the favored destinations, Victoria and the Puget Sound area, responded differently to these migrations. The British authorities in Victoria, intent on creating a white settler society and leaving the mixed-race fur trade customs behind, tried to keep the races apart, especially after the smallpox epidemics of the early 1860s. Native men and women were banned from the city of Victoria, with the interesting exception of Native women living with white men, who could apply for a permit to remain. The British also encouraged massive missionary interference into Native cultures because they believed that prohibition of the potlatch and other Native customs was the only way to keep "Canadian Indians" at home. In effect, they thought that erasing the racial border via forced assimilation was the only way to enforce the international one.

The scattered communities of Puget Sound, already enmeshed in commercial relationships with local Indians (who outnumbered the settlers by at least five to one into the 1860s), lacked the policing capacities of British officials and tolerated mixed-race relationships that were becoming unacceptable elsewhere in the Greater Northwest. Although all the Puget Sound tribes had agreed to move to reservations, in fact few Indians had done so, and the intermixing of races continued well into the 1870s. Many single men among the settlers continued to find wives—or at least sexual companions—among the Indian women. Although the Washington territorial legislature passed a law banning interracial marriage in 1855, and there was often local scorn for "squaw men," the practice was widespread and continuing. Just as in the fur trade, a local sexual relationship with an Indian woman was a sensible adaptation for men living in unfamiliar territory where few white women were to be found. Throughout the 1860s, Indians and whites in the Puget Sound region lived side by side without the pervasive violence that marked most mining camps. Nevertheless, interracial relations were far from placid, as is obvious from the evidence that Coll-Peter Thrush and Robert H. Keller Jr. present in their article about the trial of Xwelas, a Coastal Salish woman, for murder in 1879. She was tried and convicted of killing her third husband, a Welshman named George Phillips, a poor, alcoholic "roisterer" prone to violence. Xwelas's previous marital history sheds some light on the complex state of white-Indian relations in the region. Married in her twenties as the second wife of a prominent (polygamous) white man who deserted her to return east to fight in the Civil War, she remarried, only to be abandoned again, this time with three children to care for. The third marriage, to Phillips in 1873, was rife with argument and violence, and at her trial, Xwelas claimed self-defense. She was convicted of manslaughter, not of murder, and served two years in prison, during which she gave birth to a son, her fifth child. In the verdict, the jurors apparently considered factors such as Phillips's record of violence, the fact of her dependent children, and the need to stay on good terms with the large local Indian population. The very weight of these considerations shows, the authors say, that in the 1870s the whites in the Puget Sound region still lived in a complex, multiracial society that they did not completely control.

While the effect of the gold rushes on Native women was unquestionably catastrophic, their impact on the expectations of many white women was, to make a bad pun, unsettling. The gold rushes made nearly everyone more mobile in spite of themselves. In most mining camps, no one attempted to put down roots or to forge close connections with neighbors, for who knew who would still be there tomorrow? But many women not in the mining camps, who were seriously engaged in putting down roots, were not as settled as they had planned to be.

Melinda Applegate thought she had made a home. Settled on a Donation Land Act claim at Salt Creek (near present-day Salem, Oregon) with sisters-in-law Elizabeth and Cynthia on adjoining claims, the three Applegate women had planted gardens, raised fruit trees from seedlings, milked the forty cows they brought over the Oregon Trail, and made butter while their men raised cattle, grew wheat, and built a gristmill. But the men were restless: two brothers, Lindsay and Jesse, spent the summer of 1846 attempting to open a new and controversial trail to Oregon from California, and in 1848 Lindsay succumbed to the "gold spell," demanding that his seventeen-year-old son Elisha remain at home to bring in the harvest while he went to California. Then, in 1849, Jesse Applegate moved again, south of Eugene, to beautiful grazing country for horses at Yoncalla on the Umpqua River, and his brothers (and their wives and their children) followed a year later. These pioneers, now middle-aged, started again, but not from scratch. Charles built a large, imposing house, and could even afford to have the glass for its windows shipped around the Horn from the East Coast. There was only one odd thing about the house: it turned out to be double, with a men's side and a women's side with no interior connecting doors, for all the world like a communal dwelling for celibate female and male Shakers (which the prolific Applegates certainly were not). A descendant, Shannon Applegate, speculates that the house was built to female specifications, for she notes that Melinda, aged forty-one when she moved into the house, had no more children. (She had already given birth to sixteen.) Surprising as the Applegate move to Yoncalla may seem, the restless search for the perfect location seems to have been common, for a later study showed that, of the nearly seventy-five hundred original Donation Land Act claims, two-thirds were no longer held by the original owners or their descendants fifty years later. The three Applegate couples contributed to those numbers.

The Applegate women had been farm women back in Missouri. Sarah Yesler, of Massillon, Ohio, was the wife of a successful carpenter turned businessman who left her behind when he went to the West Coast in 1851 to scout out the best location for his sawmill. Henry Yesler decided on the new little settlement of Seattle (population approximately fifty) on Puget Sound, and in early 1853 began operation on the waterfront. The trees he needed were logged on the hills behind him and sent down to him on the skid road behind him that became a famous Seattle landmark. At first the mill was a roaring success, working around the clock to meet demand from California for rough lumber, but soon competing sawmills and fears of Indian attacks brought Henry's sawmill to a "standstill" and made him talk of selling out.

Sarah was still waiting to join him. She had sold their house in anticipation of a move and was forced to rent rooms from the new owners as she waited for Henry to send for her, which he finally did, with some uncertainty, in 1857. Perhaps he feared that she would not react well to the news that he had a mixed-race daughter by a Duwamish woman named Susan with whom he had a continuing relationship. Henry also realized that Sarah would not like to live in the cookhouse-cum-bunkhouse that

The double-sided Applegate house, Yoncalla OR (Library of Congress, Prints and Photographs Division, HABS ORE, 10-YONC,V,1—1)

he called his "castle" and that he shared with whomever needed a place to meet or to lodge. When Sarah arrived by ship in July of 1858, she discovered that he had built her a six-room house.

Sarah's first actions duplicated those of the Applegate women: she arranged for the planting of a large garden and orchard with seeds and seedlings she had brought with her. She did what was expected of the wife of Seattle's leading citizen by offering hospitality to visitors and by holiday entertaining, and she kept up a busy correspondence with relatives back home and with new acquaintances she had met in San Francisco on her way north to Seattle. Soon she had built a network of female friends that stretched from Puget Sound to Olympia to San Francisco. In fact, her new friends were so important to her, and she spent so much time visiting them, that rumors flew in Seattle that she and Henry were separated. They were not, but they clearly inhabited separate emotional worlds.

The story of another Seattle pioneer mentioned earlier, Catherine Blaine, adds still more to the picture. She refused to employ Indian women to help with domestic work, scorning them as "even more stupid" than the Irishwomen her East Coast relatives employed. She also disapproved of the sexual relations, without benefit of clergy, that were common between

white men and Indian women. Most of these relationships were less permanent and usually more abusive than the fur trade's marriage "according to
the custom of the country." They were no longer driven by the fur trader's
necessity to be on good terms with the local Natives; now, men might share
the common disdain toward Natives, but sleep with an Indian woman all
the same. Catherine Blaine and her husband David did not approve. When
Chief Seeathl's granddaughter committed suicide after a fight with her
drunken white husband, Reverend Blaine refused to officiate at her inter-
ment, claiming that to do so would indicate approval of their cross-racial
sexual union. Catherine Blaine concurred, although she was a temperance
advocate and might have been expected to have sympathy for the victim.
Intolerant she may have been, but Catherine Blaine was educated, and in
response to repeated requests she soon opened a subscription school, the
first in Seattle; by doing so, she became Seattle's first professional woman.

To the south, on the family claim along the Columbia River, Abigail
Malick, who had lost one son to the California gold rush in 1850, found
her younger children slipping from her control. Son Shin refused to do
farmwork, preferring the company of soldiers at nearby Fort Vancouver.
Later he left home and hunted for gold in Idaho. The daughters proved
equally difficult. Daughter Jane was three months pregnant when she married at age sixteen to another soldier. Daughter Susan was even younger
when she eloped to marry an actor and join his theater troupe. A year later
she was divorced. Abigail wrote to her older children, properly settled back
in Illinois, "The children. . . . Are Not Like children Raised in the States. . .
. They Will Not Mind Me." More accurately, the firm hand of patriarchal
control that settlers had planned to maintain on this agricultural frontier
faltered in the face of the new attractions and options.

Still another woman's life played out in unexpected ways in the interior
of British Columbia, where a British woman, Susan Moir, married miner,
prospector, and rancher John Allison in 1868 and went to live with him
in the Similkameen Valley. Over the years she gave birth to ten children
and partnered her husband in their ranching enterprise while around them
mineral strikes and mini-rushes undermined Native life. An observer who
came upon her leading a pack train (riding sidesaddle, of course) wondered at the "courage and endurance of a refined and educated woman
like her" living so far from "the comforts and conveniences" of civilization.
Her memoirs do not reveal her inner life, although they do clearly show
her genuine care for the Similkameen people among whom she lived and

her determination to write down their stories and customs. She gives a glimpse of some of her initial culture shock, however, when she describes her unexpectedly early first childbirth assisted by a Native midwife known only as Suzanne, whose first action on arrival was to give her patient a shot of whiskey to dull the pain. Allison goes on to say, "[she] was good to me in her way—though I thought her rather unfeeling at the time. She thought I ought to be as strong as an Indian woman but I was not."

Settler women who did not expect to move (the Applegates), a wife who isn't by her husband's side (Sarah Yesler), a woman who juggles housework and her profession (Catherine Blaine), a mother deserted by her children (Abigail Malick), and a genteel lady enjoying her rough circumstances (Susan Allison)—although none of these disruptions can compare to the devastation experienced by Native women, none of these fit the usual stereotype of the settled pioneer woman. The gold rushes that so unsettled the entire Greater Northwest disrupted the lives of Native and settler women alike. A few women in mining camps and towns found new opportunities and avenues for action, but even those most opposed to change often found themselves rebuilding familiar kin and community networks in new circumstances and in new places. In the years to come, community-building was repeated time and again across the Greater Northwest. And, although in many places whites barely noticed, as white women worked to build communities, Native women fought persistently to prevent theirs from being destroyed.

SOURCES FOR THIS CHAPTER

Both sides—Indian and white—of early settlement and accommodation in the Puget Sound area have been illuminated by Alexandra Harmon, *Indians in the Making: Ethnic Relations and Indian Identities around Puget Sound* (Berkeley: University of California Press, 1998); and Coll-Peter Thrush, *Native Seattle: Histories from the Crossing-Over Place* (Seattle: University of Washington Press, 2007). See also David M. Buerge, "Women on the Frontier," *Seattle Weekly* January 29–February 4, 1986; and Phoebe Judson, *A Pioneer's Search for an Ideal Home*, reprint of original 1925 edition (Lincoln: University of Nebraska Press, 1984).

    In the early days of western women's history, white women settlers were often depicted as kinder, gentler companions of their violent male counterparts. See, for example, Glenda Riley, *Women and Indians on the Frontier* (Albuquerque: University of New Mexico Press, 1984); and my own "Women's Literature and the American Frontier: A New Perspective on the Frontier Myth," in L. L. Lee and Merrill Lewis, eds., *Women, Women Writers and the West* (New York: Whitson Publishing Co., 1979). That perspective crumbled under the weight of evidence and the influence of feminist critics of imperialism such as Anne Stoler and Antoinette Burton, mentioned in chapters 2 and 3. A key book on US women was Brigitte Georgi-Findlay, *The Frontiers of Women's Writing: Women's Narratives and the Rhetoric of Westward Expansion* (Tucson: University of Arizona Press, 1996), which detailed the ways in which the civilizing and domesticating activities of white women, while less apparently violent, were as destructive of Native culture as those of their men. Most recently, the topic of what is now called settler colonialism underpins Margaret Jacobs's Bancroft Prize–winning *White Mother to a Dark Race: Settler Colonialism, Maternalism, and the Removal of Indigenous Children in the American West and Australia, 1880–1940* (Lincoln: University of Nebraska Press, 2009). For a wider perspective, see James Belich, *Replenishing the Earth: The Settler Revolution and the Rise of the Anglo-World, 1783–1939* (Oxford: Oxford University Press, 2009).

The varied effects of the various gold rushes on women and families are covered in Lillian Schlissel, "The Malick Family in Oregon Territory, 1848–1867," in Lillian Schlissel, Byrd Gibbens, and Elizabeth Hampsten, eds., *Far From Home: Families of the Westward Journey* (New York: Schocken Books, 1989), pp. 3–105; Sylvia Van Kirk, "A Vital Presence: Women in the Cariboo Gold Rush 1862–1875," in Gillian Creese and Veronica Strong-Boag, *British Columbia Reconsidered* (Vancouver, BC: Press Gang Publishers, 1992), and extended manuscript copy in author's possession; Edgar Fawcett, *Some Reminiscences of Old Victoria* (Toronto: William Briggs, 1912); Claire Rudolf Murphy and Jane G. Haigh, *Gold Rush Women* (Anchorage: Alaska Northwest Books, 1997); Charlene Porsild, *Gamblers and Dreamers: Women, Men, and Community in the Klondike* (Vancouver: University of British Columbia Press, 1998); and Phyllis Demuth Movious, *A Place of Belonging: Five Founding Women of Fairbanks, Alaska* (Fairbanks: University of Alaska Press, 2009). For realistic views of prostitution, see Mary Murphy, "The Private Lives of Public Women: Prostitution in Butte, Montana, 1878–1917," in Susan Armitage and Elizabeth Jameson, eds., *The Women's West* (Norman:

University of Oklahoma Press, 1987); Ann Butler, *Daughters of Joy, Sisters of Misery: Prostitutes in the American West, 1865–90* (Urbana: University of Illinois Press, 1985); Miriam Goldman, *Gold Diggers and Silver Miners: Prostitution and Social Life on the Comstock Lode* (Ann Arbor: University of Michigan Press, 1981); and Paula Petrick, *No Step Backward: Women and Family on the Rocky Mountain Mining Frontier, Helena, Montana, 1865–1900* (Helena: Montana Historical Society, 1987).

Chinese women are discussed briefly in Liping Zhu, *A Chinaman's Chance: The Chinese on the Rocky Mountain Mining Frontier* (Boulder: University Press of Colorado, 1997), but the in-depth study is Judy Yung, *Unbound Feet: A Social History of Chinese Women in San Francisco* (Berkeley: University of California Press, 1995); see Ruthanne Lum McCunn, *Thousand Pieces of Gold* (Boston: Beacon Press, 2004), for Polly Bemis. See also Priscilla Wegars, *Polly Bemis, Chinese American Pioneer* (Cambridge, ID: Backeddy Books, 2003).

The impact of gold rushers on Native people is discussed in John M. Findlay and Ken S. Coates, *Parallel Destinies: Canadian-American Relations West of the Rockies* (Seattle: University of Washington Press, 2002); Coll-Peter Thrush and Robert H. Keller Jr., "I See What I Have Done: The Life and Murder Trial of Xwelas, a S'Klallam Woman," *Western Historical Quarterly* 26:2 (Summer 1995); and Jean Barman, "Aboriginal Women on the Streets of Victoria: Rethinking Transgressive Sexuality during the Colonial Encounter," in Katie Pickles and Myra Rutherdale, *Contact Zones: Aboriginal and Settler Women in Canada's Colonia Past* (Vancouver: University of British Columbia Press, 2005), pp. 205–227.

For unsettled white women, see Applegate, *Skookum;* Linda Peavy and Ursula Smith, *Women in Waiting in the Westward Movement: Life on the Home Frontier* (Norman: University of Oklahoma Press, 1994); Margaret Ormsby, ed., *A Pioneer Gentlewoman in British Columbia: The Recollections of Susan Allison* (Vancouver: University of British Columbia Press, 1976); and her encounter with a Native midwife in Kristen Burnett, "Obscured Obstetrics: Indigenous Midwives in Western Canada," in Sarah Carter and Patricia McCormack, eds., *Recollecting: Lives of Aboriginal Women of the Canadian Northwest and Borderlands* (Edmonton: Athabasca University Press, 2011); also Schlissel, "The Malick Family."

Chapter 5
Civilizers 1860s–1870s

By the 1860s, the older residents of the Willamette Valley were ready to turn their pioneering past into history. The Oregon Pioneer Association, founded in 1873, held yearly meetings at which pioneers shared their reminiscences (some true, some embellished, and mostly by men) of the Oregon Trail. Several prominent pioneers, among them Judge Matthew Deady, wrote reminiscences and gathered historical documents. But it was a woman, Frances Fuller Victor, who wrote the history of the pioneers. An enterprising journalist who moved with her husband from San Francisco to Portland in 1864, Victor took advantage of the retrospective mood. She used her position as a paid correspondent of the *San Francisco Evening Bulletin* as an entree as she traveled around the region and solicited the reminiscences (and, where available, papers) of leading men.

She interviewed Matthew Deady and traveled south to interview Jesse Applegate, widely known as "The Sage of Yoncalla." But she was positively entranced by another old-timer, the former fur trapper Joe Meek, a colorful character full of tales of epic journeys, relations with Indians (he had had several Indian wives), and deep involvement in early Oregon politics. In 1870, separated from her husband and in need of money to support herself, Victor published *The River of the West*, a history of early Oregon starring Joe Meek. Two years later, Victor published an account of her travels, *All Over Oregon and Washington*, hoping to reach a national audience that knew very little about the remote Pacific Northwest.

But her most cherished project, for which she continued to gather material, was an authoritative, deeply researched history of pioneer Oregon. She wrote it, and histories of Washington, Idaho and Montana, Nevada, Wyoming, and Colorado as well, but she was not recognized as their author. The credit went instead to Hubert Howe Bancroft, the California bookseller and historical entrepreneur who employed a workshop full of historians, Victor among them, and produced, under his name, nearly forty volumes on the history of the West and of Central America. Victor worked for Bancroft from 1878 until 1889, when she resigned in an argument over recognition for her work. By then she was sixty-three. She lived for another twelve years, sometimes in poor financial circumstances, for in addition to claiming the credit, Bancroft had not paid well either. Victor never received the recognition she deserved for her skills as a historical researcher and writer, as well as for her determination to survive in what she called "this man's world." The Bancroft volumes, as they are known, are still consulted today for the early history of Oregon, a lasting monument to the work of Frances Fuller Victor, the Pacific Northwest's first historian.

Victor's historical writings focus on the activities of men to such an extent that one wonders whether women were there at all. Yet Victor herself was a feminist who contributed regularly to Abigail Scott Duniway's women's rights journal the *New Northwest*. She must have believed, as her contemporaries did, that "history" was a chronicle of a limited number of public activities such as legislation, economics, and wars, from which women were excluded (except, of course, as victims). Victor's acceptance of this prevalent but mistaken notion has deprived us of many female insights into the early history of the region.

Although women had no place in official history, there was general agreement that they were absolutely essential if European settlement was to succeed. First, biological necessity tinged with racism indicated that without white children, no settlement had a future, and white women had to give birth to those children. Second, women were civilizers or, to use the term later popularized by author Dee Brown, "gentle tamers." Nineteenth-century society believed that respectable women embodied the moral values essential to civilized life. It sometimes seemed that their very presence was enough to bring change, as this report from the early days of the Idaho City gold rush implies: "Society is rapidly improving here, owing, doubtless to the influence of women, a large number of whom are here."

This faith in the power and fecundity of good (white) women seemed to offer a quick solution to a region-wide preponderance of men and a shortage of white women of marriageable age. In Washington Territory, an enterprising young man named Asa Mercer tried to solve the problem by importing two boatloads of unmarried women from the East Coast in 1864 and 1866, numbering perhaps a hundred in all (he had hoped for seven hundred). Most of the "Mercer Girls," as they were nicknamed, married as expected, but a surprising number of them first forged careers as single women. For example, Lizzie Ordway, recruited from the cotton textile mills of Lowell, Massachusetts, became the first public school teacher in Seattle in 1870. Equally intense efforts to recruit women were made in British Columbia, where attracting settlers from Britain was a continuing worry in a territory where Native inhabitants still far outnumbered whites and where authorities clearly feared that a mixed-race rather than a properly white British colonial society would emerge. The

Anglican Church took the lead in importing white women from England to remedy both the gender imbalance in England, where women were a majority, and in British Columbia, where white men vastly outnumbered white women. Four times between 1859 and 1870, "assisted immigration" of white British women occurred; in all about a hundred women arrived in British Columbia via "brideships," as they were called. As with the similar female immigration scheme in Washington Territory, the motives and character of these immigrating women were the subject of much media attention and titillation, although, as Lizzie Ordway's example showed, many women had their own reasons for accepting free passage, reasons that did not necessarily include marriage. In the larger scheme of things, their scanty numbers made little difference. But symbolically their presence made a huge difference in British Columbia where, in Anne McClintock's evocative phrase, these women became the "boundary markers of empire" between the minority white and majority Native populations.

The discrepancy between public images and the personal expectations of these imported women points to a larger problem with the notion of women as civilizers. In the ideal version, the moral presence of civilizing women was enough to influence men's actions. In real life, women didn't just sit around waiting to influence men: they acted to create and stabilize the communities in which they and their families lived. They moved beyond influencing men into action themselves, but in informal ways that did not challenge male authority in the public realm. At the same time, a few missionary women were actively using their moral authority to reshape the lives of the Indian women who were dependent on them. Thus this chapter explores the two-sided aspect of the concept of white women as civilizers, first as informal builders of their own communities, and second as destroyers and rearrangers of Indian communities.

Community-building was a basic activity repeated time and again as the Greater Northwest filled—at first very slowly—with settlers. Two decades of gold rushes had left a pattern of spotty development, of nodes lacking connections except by water. Portland quickly became Oregon's major city, but in Washington Territory several towns, among them Olympia, Tacoma, Seattle, and Port Angeles, competed for primacy. For a while Walla Walla, far to the east on the Snake River, grew the fastest because of its proximity to the Oregon Trail and because of its role as a supply center to mining camps in Idaho. In southern Idaho, Boise, which began as a supply center for overland travelers, grew once it became supplier to Idaho's southern mines. In western Montana, Missoula, a remote trading post established in the 1860s, began to grow only when the US Army completed the Mullen Road that connected Fort Benton, in central Montana, to Walla Walla in the west. In British Columbia, most of the European population clustered around Victoria on Vancouver Island. The much-sparser settlement on the mainland was strung out along the Fraser River. Between the population nodes of cities and towns were agricultural areas at many different stages of development. Until the 1880s, permanent settlement was both slow and spotty, with lots of empty spaces between towns. The 1880 census recorded miniscule numbers: the white population of Oregon was 175,000; of Washington, only 75,000; and Idaho only 33,000. British Columbia, officially part of the British Dominion of Canada since 1871, counted a white population of 17,000 in 1881.

The vast majority of settlers were farmers. Outside the Willamette Valley, land was either purchased or, more commonly, "taken up" under the Homestead Act, passed in 1862, allowing a claimant (single and married men, single and widowed women, but not married women) 160 free acres for a small filing fee and the commitment to "prove up" (plant some crops, build a house) within five years. British Columbia had a similar land law, with the important exception that single women could not claim land of their own. The basic homesteading hope that hard work could make up for lack of capital, allowing poor families the land ownership they craved, lasted well into the twentieth century.

There are no accounts of novel forms of community in the early days: people wanted to be *settled* in the same familiar ways they had experienced at home, in small, homogeneous communities. In David Buerge's evocative phrase, settlers were determined to "reweave the social fabric in customary ways." Thus, community-building was deliberately not innovative but rather a cooperative effort by men and women to recreate familiar patterns left behind. Historians have understood and recorded the political and economic activities of men that helped build local communities, for their institution-building was reported in local newspapers, in "booster" literature that usually consisted of inflated claims about the economic possibilities of certain places, and in biographies of their upstanding (male) citizens. Rarely, however, have historians recognized the contribution that women's more informal and less-recorded activities made to community-building, leaving a blank, just as in Victor's histories, that needs to be filled in. In reality, in many new communities, women were often the first to press for religious services and to raise the money to bring a minister (at first, perhaps, a circuit rider who came once or twice a month) and to build churches. Similarly, they rallied support for schools (and teacher funding) for more than the minimum of three months, and for libraries. These informal efforts laid the groundwork for community institutions. Women were used to this kind of background work, and many believed that claiming credit was too "forward" and not properly deferential to their husbands. As a result, women's part in community-building became invisible and extremely hard for later historians to document. In fact, women's part in community-building was even more basic than their informal actions, for communities begin with families, and maintaining families is a part of women's work.

Farmers knew how to build communities, for no farm family was completely self-sufficient and all depended on "neighboring" in any number of ways, including supplementing their own homegrown food supply, providing enough hands for harvesting and barn raising, and helping in times of childbirth and illness. By the time of the settlement of the Greater Northwest, American farm families had perfected the art of neighboring. Men had accustomed routines of work-sharing for the farmwork that was too heavy or too time-consuming to do alone, and women had accepted methods of mutual aid. Farm people were used to working together, especially with extended family members. The Applegate sisters-in-law spent their lives working with each other and each other's numerous children. As we have seen, clan networks were especially strong in the Willamette Valley and cooperation was taken for granted, but elsewhere, as in Phoebe Judson's case, one simply imagined "family" to include non-related neighbors. As she wrote, she considered all the white settlers within an eight-mile radius on the Grand Mound prairie near Olympia to be family. The phrase had more than sentimental meaning: family were those you turned to in necessity and those you were obligated to help in return.

The patterns of social activity in rural areas throughout the region clearly show that the most comfortable and customary social networks were with one's immediate family. Few places, however, were as heavily family- and clan-settled as the Willamette Valley. In later farming communities, single men married into existing family networks, and unconnected families had to wait until their children intermarried with children of other settlers and then function within the new family networks that developed. And in these families, the "kinwork" necessary to keep the networks strong—writing letters to relatives, remembering birthdays and anniver-saries, "staying in touch"—was an acknowledged part of women's work.

Another framework with strong similarities to family networks was provided by several religious communities in the Greater Northwest, among them German Catholics in Washington, Hutterites in Montana, and Mennonites and Doukhobors from Russia in British Columbia. The best-known coreligionists, however, were members of the Church of Latter Day Saints (Mormons), who quickly spread out from their base in Salt Lake City, Utah (established in 1847), to neighboring territories, including southern Idaho, which they began to settle in the 1860s. Bound tightly together by patriarchal bonds of communal and religious obligation, Mormons in effect belonged to ready-made communities. Additionally (and shocking to outsiders), nineteenth-century Mormons practiced polyg-amy. The close ties that often formed between multiple wives were both a fascination and a mystery to outsiders, who, while accustomed to close ties between women in family networks, looked askance at these.

The rapid growth of Mormons in Idaho (thirty-one settlements by 1877, one-quarter of the state's population by 1890) prompted a politi-cal backlash. Until the early 1890s, when the president of the church dis-avowed polygamy, observant Mormon men in Idaho were not allowed to vote. When, in 1896, Idaho unexpectedly became the fourth state in the nation to enact woman suffrage, the strong vote of Mormon men in its favor may have been in reaction to their own earlier disenfranchise-ment, as well as being a practical calculation that women's votes could bolster Mormon causes. The claim at the time was that the men voted yes in grateful recognition of the work of stalwart Mormon women pio-neers. Indeed, all Mormon women were expected to be stalwart. As Susan Swetnam points out in her study of Idaho Mormon diaries, the tradition of life-writing encouraged by the LDS church produced reams of formulaic celebratory writing. While we may question whether all "pioneer mothers" were as uniformly strong and uncomplaining as their diaries claim, few expressions of discontent over physical circumstances or multiple wives are evident in these life-writings.

The hostility experienced by the Mormons in Idaho points to another aspect of communities: as clusters of like-minded people form, community norms (usually enforced by women) serve to exclude as well as include. Such, in fact, was the experience of Annie Pike Greenwood, who with her husband homesteaded a 160-acre tract on the Twin Falls North Side

Irrigation Project on the Snake River Plain of southern Idaho in 1913, as she recorded in her memoir, *We Sagebrush Folks*. Although neither Annie nor Charles Greenwood came from farm families, they threw themselves into community work. Annie started a Sunday school and a literary society and taught school for a year as well. The Greenwoods worked together to help organize the local Grange, and they organized the yearly Fourth of July celebrations. Charlie Greenwood was so popular that he was elected to the state legislature, but Annie claims that she was too much of a "maverick" to win the approval of the local women. Among her other sins, she loved to dance. Annie's observations on the gendered nature of community-building were acute, and poignant:

> Men love farming, and one of the reasons is that the normal human being is gregarious. Almost every operation on the farm that is considered men's work requires at some stage a number of men to prosecute it. There is fun in working together, joshing and laughing, but it is a pleasure that the sagebrush women knew very little about.

Because, she goes on to explain, farm women's work happened in their own kitchens, there were comparatively few times—cooking for harvest, canning—when they needed additional help aside from what they expected from their own growing daughters. On those occasions, Annie found, her neighbors turned to nearby family members or close friends for help. They had no need of Annie, for she had failed the entry test for community membership by refusing to conform to customary norms.

The Greenwoods failed as farmers, in part because they did not move to southern Idaho as part of an existing community to which they could turn for support. In the fifteen years that the Greenwoods stayed on their homestead, they noticed three distinct populations make a try at success: first the Mormons, who did well and moved on; then a large clannish group of Arkansas farmers—"one whole mountain community migrated together," Annie noted; and finally, German-Russian families who moved in as hired laborers on large farms. A fourth wave escaped Annie's notice: in the 1920s, as sugar-beet companies expanded in southern Idaho, they actively recruited farm laborers and their families from Mexico.

The Greenwoods' experience serves to underline an underappreciated factor in western community-building: the prevalence of preexisting ties between migrants. Worldwide studies of international migration have repeatedly shown that solitary migrants are rare; most people follow paths already blazed by family or neighbors, and they deliberately choose to settle near those of their own kind, thus following a pattern of chain migration. This was true of migrants to the Greater Northwest, the myths of individual adventurers (based, perhaps, on miners rushing for gold) notwithstanding. As an example, the following individual pioneer story turns out to be, upon inspection, one of linked family connections.

Daniel Wright Boone homesteaded in Washington's Palouse Country in 1877 in company with his sister Jane and his brother-in-law. In 1888, after eleven years of living as a bachelor, he went home to Illinois to visit his parents and courted a bride, Amelia Williams, the sister of his sister-in-law, and returned with her to Washington, where they lived the rest of their lives. Married in January 1889, they arrived in Pullman by immigrant train in early March, along with a brother, George Boone, and his new wife Georgia, as well as a neighbor, Ed Hough, who lived with the Boones until 1900.

Daniel Boone was a jack-of-all-trades: farmer, orchardist, blacksmith, and, in particular, a lover of trees, which he planted in profusion on his four hundred acres. Described as "a good provider of food and wood," he made frequent trips to nearby Moscow Mountain, where he spent several days at a time cutting wood. And what was Amelia doing all this time, in addition to birthing nine children? She did the other half of the work: the job of feeding and clothing the family, friends, relatives, and boarders and maintaining a well-known standard of hospitality and generosity. In addition, Amelia was the "business head" of the family: she kept the books, arranged the sale of the yearly wheat crop, and even arranged land purchases, although since the farm was held in Daniel's name, he had to sign the legal documents. At the time, everyone in their local community knew perfectly well what Amelia did. A division of labor of this kind was not at all unusual, and Amelia was surely widely admired. But when the family story was written down for the history books, all Amelia's essential work disappeared. When an article about the family was published in the local historical magazine in the 1970s, Amelia is mentioned in marriage and in death, but otherwise Boone stands alone as a heroic individual pioneer, an obvious fiction, since the account makes clear that he homesteaded in company with relatives, and that throughout his life he was surrounded by relatives and close friends. A record of Amelia's activities survived only because of the unwritten stories passed from mother to daughter to grand-daughter in the Boone family, which, owing to the nine children, became a clan of its own within a generation of settlement.

There are similar community stories. William Willingham, in *Starting Over*, discovered that in Long Valley, an eastern Oregon ranching and farming community first settled in the 1870s, one-third of the migrants came from Arkansas and the majority from the adjoining states of Tennessee and Missouri. They thus shared not kinship but a similar southern border culture that, like that of the early Willamette Valley settlers, placed heavy value on the patriarchal family and family loyalties, ties that allocated to women the role of helpmate, household manager, and maintainer of social norms. Unlike the Willamette Valley, however, geography created a circumstance that affected Long Valley and many other eastern Oregon and Washington farming communities: limited transportation meant that they remained isolated. To use Robert Weibe's evocative term, Long Valley was an "island community," where the small and largely homogeneous population reinforced the original social norms through constant interaction and multigenerational family networks. For women in these communities, there were few acceptable occupations: teaching, domestic service, and sewing were all local and did not pay enough for a single woman to consider living independently. Until transportation improved and horizons widened, there really was no alternative to living at home until one married a "local boy" and built another link in the family network. It is unlikely that many women even considered another future.

Another example of "clustering" settlement occurred in British Columbia. In *Sojourning Sisters,* Jean Barman used a set of family letters to document the kind of connection created by two sisters from Nova Scotia who migrated to British Columbia in the 1880s. Jessie and Annie McQueen came to teach school for three years to earn some money for their parents in Nova Scotia and, doubtless, to have a "western adventure." But their taste for new experience was limited: they very deliberately sought out other Nova Scotians and coreligionists to recreate the society they had known at home. As Jessie wrote home after nine months in British Columbia, "I have no use for any of 'the natives' as intimate friends"; she was really comfortable only with Nova Scotians.

One unusual community example is provided by the story of a large number of African Americans (estimates vary from three hundred to eight hundred) from San Francisco who sought refuge in Canada in 1858. Like their counterparts throughout the United States, these free black people were fleeing the danger of capture posed by the Fugitive Slave Act of 1852 that was a potential threat to them all. Facing persecution, segregation, and, in at least one case, actual arrest and reenslavement, San Francisco's black community decided to move en masse to Victoria for safety. These refugee African Americans made a deliberate choice for integration by deciding to join existing churches rather than founding their own. But in spite of their efforts, although outright segregation did not occur in Canada, black people were informally barred or restricted in many public facilities like barber shops, saloons, theaters, and hotels.*

All of the African American women in the original migration, with one possible exception, were married, but as was true of free black communities throughout North America, most of the women were in the labor force. They, in common with poor women everywhere, did laundry, domestic work, cooking, and sewing for wages. One woman, Sarah Jane Moses, ran a well-regarded boardinghouse with her husband. Two other women, Julia and Mary Hernandez, set up as cooks during the Fraser River gold rush, making enough to later buy property in Victoria. As the century progressed and the American Civil War made their freedom certain, many members of the community returned to the United States, but perhaps as many as three hundred remained. In the face of unofficial hostility, Victoria's black community took defensive measures by deliberately strengthening racial ties by frowning on marriage outside the group, by living in close proximity, and, for the women, by actively working for race betterment through charitable activities and presenting a "respectable" face to the outside world.

Settlement and community-building efforts in the Greater Northwest always had another face: "civilizing" meant something drastically different when applied to the region's Native population. Both Catholic and Protestant missions had been present since the 1830s, devoted to converting Native people to Christianity. Part of the conversion effort involved civilizing them—that is, teaching them white ways. In spite of the setback caused by the killings at the Whitman mission in 1847, the missionary effort never ceased. By the 1860s, civilizing had become a key part of governmental policy both north and south of the international boundary. For

---

* A note on terminology: I use "black" and "African American" interchangeably in this and following chapters.

Native peoples, civilizing did not mean continuity with the accustomed ways of their past, but drastic change.

In 1871, when British Columbia joined the Canada Confederation, federal agents administered policies that forced many Native people to settle onto small reserves and take up white-approved occupations such as farming, abandon Native social practices such as the potlatch, and educate young people in mission schools. These drastic measures seemed justified, in the eyes of many whites, by the visible disintegration of Native societies devastated by alcohol and white men's diseases like tuberculosis and smallpox (the epidemic of 1862–1863 killed twenty thousand people, or one-third of British Columbia's remaining Native population).

Historian Adele Perry points out that missionaries in British Columbia viewed Native women as the key to civilizing efforts. Missionaries failed to see the ways in which the traditional work of Native women was valued by their tribes, instead agreeing with Narcissa Whitman that Native women were "veritable slaves of their husbands." The heavy female labor to which Europeans objected was associated with the mobility of the seasonal round, the basic way Native people in the Greater Northwest had always lived off the land. Determined to change what they regarded as exploitation and lack of autonomy, missionaries insisted that Native women settle in one place in European-style houses, wear European clothes, and learn the personal and familial skills of settled domesticity, especially cleanliness. Additionally, Native women had to be rescued from the sexual dangers of cohabitation, polygamy, and divorce that was the sum of Native marriage in white eyes. Missionaries believed that monogamous Christian marriage was the only way to give Native women the opportunity to become as moral and civilized as white women. They understood, as had the authors of the Donation Land Claim Act in Oregon, discussed in a previous chapter, that the terms of marriage represented particular kinds of gender relations, and they were determined that those terms would now be European rather than Native. Finally, missionaries believed that Native women had to learn to work in appropriate occupations, so they trained them to become domestic servants. Thus they would learn to become docile colonial subjects or, as the missionaries saw it, civilized.

These measures, imposed initially by male missionaries, were taken up later in the nineteenth century by women, who were slowly allowed into the British Columbia mission field, first in the 1860s as the wives of male missionaries and then in the 1880s as single women on their own. For most of these British missionary women, the price of overcoming male disapproval was to be just as rigid and judgmental in their attitudes to Natives as the men. Thus most missionary women entered the field convinced of their own cultural superiority over "the women with painted faces . . . [who] looked so wild and terrible," as Florence Appleyard, a British nurse, wrote home. She went on to write, "I can realize now more than ever before how full of love one must be in order to teach these poor creatures whose faces betray that they know not the Lord Jesus."

Missionary women were convinced that they had a vital role to play as domestic and maternal examples to Native women. The belief that Native mothers were too indulgent of their children justified the discipline and regimentation that white women imposed on the children they taught in mission schools, as well as their strict training in domestic skills. In this version, true Christianity and good housewifery went hand in hand. As had been apparent since the experience of Narcissa Whitman and Eliza Spalding in the 1830s, the mission field offered opportunity to white women that they rarely found elsewhere. Because they were instructing Native women, whom they considered their cultural inferiors, missionary women had a rare chance to exercise moral *authority*, not just influence. For the female missionaries in British Columbia, the possibility of an adventurous life in the wilderness, coupled with unparalleled and uncontested scope for their maternal feelings, was very alluring.

The United States government also adopted the policy of turning Indian peoples over to the civilizing influence of missionaries. Following the Civil War, the administration of President Ulysses S. Grant adopted a new policy, ironically called the Peace Policy, to gather Indians on reservations and to assimilate them according to Christian principles. Accordingly, reservations were parceled out to different religious denominations, by a process that apparently mystified both the Indians and the churches themselves. The newly assigned missionaries were not intended to replace government-appointed Indian agents (already widely accused of corruption and incompetence) but to supplement them. Thus on the Nez Perce Reservation in northern Idaho, two Presbyterian sisters, Sue and Kate McBeth, opened a mission school in Kamiah in 1874, while the government office remained in Lapwai. The effect was to split the tribe, with Christianized Nez Perce clustering around the McBeths while traditionalists remained at Lapwai. The mingled horror and fascination the McBeths experienced when confronted with Nez Perce culture is vividly captured in Kate's description of the last traditional ceremonial dance before government banning:

> We saw all the devilish glamour and savage gorgeousness that covered every kind of wickedness that human mind can invent. Always the solemn beat of the tom-tom and the hi-yi, ki-yi, of the Indian dancers in their teepees or around the camp-fires. There was gambling going on incessantly; warriors dressed in sweeping eagle feathers, riding on horses with silver mounted trappings; women in gay blankets and highly colored handkerchiefs around their heads and daintily embroidered moccasins on their feet forever on the go or busy about their teepees; children and dogs everywhere.

The effects of missionary strictures on Native women are a matter of some dispute. Because Native women in British Columbia quickly became part of the paid labor force in the canneries, it has been suggested that they more successfully adapted to the enforced changes than did Native men. In the late nineteenth century, between one-third and one-half of the cannery workforce in British Columbia was Native women. Working just down the line from the Chinese men who gutted the salmon, Native women sliced fillets and packed them into tins. Some canneries were so eager to employ Native women that they allowed them to bring infants to work, or encouraged elderly Native women to provide day care for the working mothers. As historian Chris Friday points out, Native women in British Columbia, already accustomed to far-ranging seasonal migration, found it easy to combine these short-term cannery jobs with their traditional familial fishing activities. Further, John Lutz suggests, canneries employed entire families, the men as fishers, women as canners, and children to do light work such as labeling and stacking cans. All this may be true, but it seems to make a virtue out of what was often urgent necessity. When coupled with the continuing high death rates from smallpox and tuberculosis and the devastation wrought to tribal social structures, what is astounding is how successfully Native women worked to salvage parts of their traditional cultures.

The life of Florence Edenshaw Davidson, a notable Haida woman whose life spanned the changes (born 1896, died 1992), illustrates the tension between enforced change and cultural persistence. By the time she was born, Florence's parents had converted to Christianity, and her father, Charles Edenshaw, a famous artist, was able to earn money from whites for his work. They lived at Massett, a traditional Haida village in the Queen Charlotte Islands that was much depleted by recurrent smallpox epidemics. Although Charles had inherited a traditional Haida longhouse built to shelter an extended family, he built a small Victorian house in which only he and his wife and children lived. In the fall and winter, when the family lived in Massett, Florence recalled what she called "doings" of a mixed nature: church gatherings, family events such as weddings and mortuary potlatches, and occasional masked dances, survivals of the traditional winter ceremonies. The rest of the year the Edenshaw family traveled to a mixture of old and new events: wagework in canneries; berry, seaweed, and spruce root gathering; fishing for salmon; planting and harvesting potatoes.

Nevertheless, because they were a high-status family, Florence experienced the traditional puberty seclusion and, against her will, had an arranged marriage at age fourteen to an older but equally high-status man. Florence's husband, Robert Davidson, earned his living as a commercial fisherman and also occasionally worked as a logger. Florence helped supplement the family income by working in canneries, selling baked goods and running a small restaurant, gathering and putting up food for winter use, and going with her husband to fish camp for salmon—again a mixture of old and new. The Davidsons had thirteen children (eleven of whom lived), many more than Florence would have birthed or been able to support in precontact Haida society. After her husband's death at age eighty in 1969, Florence earned some money by taking in boarders.

When her grandson, another Robert Davidson, became an internationally recognized artist, Florence herself gained fame for her button blankets, a ceremonial art form that demonstrates the adaptability of Haida culture. When missionaries forbade the making of totem poles in the 1850s, the inventive Haida transferred the creation of ceremonial crests from ax and wood to needle, thread, buttons, and woolen blankets. Men made the designs, but women like Florence Edenshaw Davidson transformed them into art. Today, button blankets are not only valuable items for sale but also symbolize the vitality and flexibility of Haida culture. The subject of an admiring and respectful life history by anthropologist Margaret Blackman, Florence Edenshaw Davidson made an apparently successful transition from traditional to modern society. Better off financially, more widely known, and apparently free from Native scourges of alcohol, drugs, and disease, her life depicts a model transition. She spoke freely to Blackman of the satisfactions in her life, but was more reticent about the losses.

Much less is known about the individual lives of American Indian women on reservations in the Pacific Northwest during this period of wrenching change. A collection of historical photographs of Nez Perce women for the period between 1877 and 1900, used in conjunction with government and missionary records, confirms some similarities and some differences from Florence Davidson's experience in British Columbia. Like Florence Davidson, Nez Perce women moved from communal to single-family housing. They began to wear European clothes when Native clothing was banned by missionaries. They were required to adopt the European form of marriage, and they came very close to losing their language. The most significant difference, however, was that the Nez Perce were expected to take up agriculture and were pressured to give up their migratory seasonal gathering rounds because some of their accustomed routes now "trespassed" on the farmland of settlers. Women had to learn an entirely new range of agricultural skills, while trying to figure out how to maintain the traditional activities that mattered to them. Just as in the Davidson life history, the interior details of how those choices were made were not available to outside interviewers.

Two forced Indian relocations in the 1870s stand as examples of Indian resistance east of the Cascades. Both occurred in the immediate aftermath of the national scare caused by Custer's defeat on the Little Bighorn battlefield in 1876. The first relocation, the misnamed Chief Joseph's War, attracted nationwide media attention in 1877. Chief Joseph was the leader of the Nez Perce band that lived in the beautiful Wallowa Valley of eastern Oregon. White settlers began pushing into the valley in the early 1870s, and it was not long before frictions developed. According to missionary Sue McBeth, a delegation of whites in Wallowa complained to the military in 1874, "that the Indians, . . . had assembled in large numbers . . . ostensibly for the purpose of digging roots, hunting, and fishing, and that they were talking very saucily to the settlers, and had committed various trespasses upon the farmers of the country." In other words, they were on their customary seasonal round, but some of the younger members of the party could not resist a taunt or two. White complaints continued, and in

1877, sadly bowing to the inevitable, Chief Joseph ordered his people to gather their belongings and move to the main Nez Perce Reservation at Lapwai. This was not a popular decision, and some young warriors, as a parting gesture, killed several settlers who had harassed them.

General Oliver Howard, nervously in command of US troops at Lapwai, was convinced an Indian revolt was under way, as were the settlers throughout eastern Washington, who deserted their farms and fled in panic to stockades. In fact this was not a war band, but an entire tribal migration consisting of an estimated 750 men, women, and children of all ages, including the sick and the elderly, and hundreds of horses. After the Indian men protecting the migration easily won several small skirmishes ("battles"), they decided to retreat across the Bitterroot Mountains and seek refuge with the Crow Indians in eastern Montana. There ensued a four-month retreat, which covered seventeen hundred miles, avidly followed by the national press, that finally ended in the snow at Bearpaw Meadow in eastern Montana.

The Wallowa Nez Perce mistakenly believed that, once they crossed into Montana, they could travel to the Crow Indian Reservation in eastern Montana in safety. A predawn attack by Howard's troops on August 9 on a sleeping camp at Big Hole disabused them of that notion. From then until October, the warriors were constantly occupied devising evasive strategies and, when necessary, fighting to protect the retreating women and children, while lurid rumors circulated among settlers about Indian depredations. When the end came and Joseph surrendered, he and his entire band (except the 250 or so who escaped to join Sitting Bull in Canada) were sent, not to the Wallowas as Joseph had understood, but to Indian Territory (Oklahoma). Only in 1885 were the survivors allowed to return, not to the Wallowas or even to Lapwai, but to the Colville Reservation in northern Washington, where until then no Nez Perce had lived.

Joseph was a charismatic figure, and his speech, "I will fight no more forever"—or whatever the translators claimed he said, as he spoke no English—allowed whites to pity and admire the nobility of his defeat. But this was not a war with military heroes. What has been lost in the telling was the strength of the women, children, and nonwarrior men engaged in a desperate retreat. Some Nez Perce women did demonstrate military courage, for example in the fight at Big Hole, when the young warrior Wahlitits was killed, his wife, although herself wounded, grabbed his rifle and shot a soldier before being killed herself. At Bearpaw Meadow, as the remaining

Nez Perce dug deep shelter pits to protect the noncombatants from the expected attack, one anonymous woman recalled:

> We digged the trenches with camas hooks and butcher knives. With pans we threw out the dirt. We could not do much cooking. Dried meat and some other grub would be handed around. If not enough for all, it would be given the children first. I was three days without food. Children cried with hunger and cold. Old people suffered in silence. Misery everywhere.

Years later, as the war passed into tribal memory, one Nez Perce woman told an interviewer:

> People tend to think that the men were the heroes of the war, but to me the women had to gather up the deceased people, they had to take care of the orphan children. To me, these were strong women; they had to be. They had no choice. That was their job, to be strong for them. . . . They had to do this; they had to hold things together.

True to his promise to "fight no more forever," Chief Joseph went quietly with his people to Oklahoma and the Colville Reservation, but the leader of the second retreat, Northern Paiute Sarah Winnemucca, chose to speak out, publicly and frequently. Winnemucca's band of Northern Paiutes was caught up in the aftermath of the Bannock War of 1877, which was a protest against the terrible conditions at the Shoshone-Bannock Reservation at Fort Hall in Idaho. To clear the region of future threats, the US military insisted that the Northern Paiutes move away from their Nevada homeland to the Yakama Reservation in central Washington. Sarah Winnemucca, a multilingual Northern Paiute leader, had long served as a spokesperson for her people as she worked for the army as a translator and scout. When she was told that it was her task to tell her people of their fate, she exclaimed, "Oh, Major, my people will never believe me again," for she had earlier been assured by the military that they would not be moved. A week later they set out on a forced march of 350 miles over the high plateau and mountains of eastern Oregon. Because many lacked warm clothing, people froze, and mothers and newborn babies died as they traveled under armed guard. The misery continued when they finally arrived at the Yakama Reservation, for the Indian agent claimed that he had not been warned of their coming and had no extra food or shelter available. Winnemucca continued her protestations to army officials, to no avail.

So she sought a wider public audience, embarking on a national lecture tour that made her famous. Appearing in a "native costume" of her own design, she explained the misery and suffering of her people and its cause: the cruelty and corruption of Indian agents. Befriended by influential Boston reformers Elizabeth Palmer Peabody and her sister Mary Peabody Mann (widow of famous educator Horace Mann), she published her autobiography, *Life Among the Paiutes: Their Wrongs and Claims,* in 1883. In a little over a year, she delivered three hundred dramatic, emotional, and accusatory lectures to large and fascinated audiences, but her pleas to restore the Northern Paiutes to their homeland fell on deaf ears in Washington. Slowly audiences began to suffer from "complaint fatigue," and Winnemucca's credibility was damaged by hostile Indian agents who set out to blacken her reputation by accusing her of gambling, drinking, multiple marriages, and even the fact that her stage costume indecently left her arms bare. She died in 1891, with a bespattered reputation among whites and distrusted by many of her own people, because she too, like Chief Joseph, had promised to remedy the misfortunes of her people, only to find, as her biographer Sally Zanjani wrote, that "she had too often served as the messenger for white men's broken promises."

For Indian peoples throughout the United States, the culminating "civilizing" blow occurred in 1887, when the Dawes Act broke their communal reservation lands into parcels and allotted them to individual Indian nuclear families. Reformers believed that granting families their own land would turn formerly nomadic people into settled and industrious farmers. Some reservations were sunk in destitution and despair, as reformers claimed, but others were doing very well, among them the Umatilla Reservation in northeast Oregon, which was the largest livestock-producing reservation in the United States. Nevertheless, the Dawes Act applied to all reservations, regardless of the circumstances. In taking this action, reformers saw themselves as protectors of Indian rights, for in many places surrounding ranchers used the excuse of no apparent cultivation to freely graze their cattle on "unoccupied" reservation lands. Still, even from its inception, it was obvious that the Dawes Act would allow white ranchers and farmers to acquire lands not allotted to individuals. On some reservations, government officials even offered the "extra" land to homesteaders. In short, it was a landgrab cloaked in benevolent intentions.

Today the maps of most reservations in the United States resemble a checkerboard. As a result of the Dawes Act and of subsequent sales of land, few Pacific Northwest tribes control much of the land within their reservation borders or are able to assert any collective control over it. Only recently have some tribes, enriched by profits from their own casinos, begun to buy back tribal lands and to assert tribal police power over all the lands within their boundaries.

Equally devastating was the impact of the Dawes Act on personal relationships, for the system of allotment of individual plots of land to families imposed white ideas of monogamous marriage and gender roles on resistant people. Anthropologist Alice Fletcher took four years (1889 to 1892) to complete the allotment process for twelve hundred Natives on the Nez Perce Reservation in northern Idaho. She was proud that the time and care she took in her interviews with Nez Perce men and women allowed her to accurately trace complex family relationships. But the very premise upon which she worked—that she could chart stable, male-headed nuclear families—was false, and its effect on Native women devastating. Only the Christianized Nez Perce (about half the tribe) had been married by a minister; the rest equated cohabitation with marriage and were comfortable both with polygamy and with divorces accomplished by the simple act of moving out. So if a Nez Perce woman had lived with three men, which was her husband? And if the Nez Perce system of bilateral kinship was to be replaced by a patrilineal one, how were children to be assigned? Although Fletcher told the Nez Perce men that she had "come to bring them manhood, that they may stand up beside the white man in equality before the law," she could offer no such assurance to Nez Perce women, who were in fact losing their traditional autonomy. Under the double blows of Christianity and allotment, Indian women could marry only once, lost the freedom of divorce, and were expected to take up domestic work while their husbands, former hunters and fishermen, became farmers. In the end, the Nez Perce were allotted 179,000 acres, with 34,000 acres reserved for their children. In return, they were forced to cede more than twice as much land (half a million acres, or 542,276) that promptly went up for sale to whites.

The Dawes Act abrogated the rights of the Pacific Northwest tribes whose treaties specifically promised them the right to hunt and gather in "the usual and accustomed places," most of which had been within the original reservation boundaries. By selling the "extra" land, allotment ended the seasonal round, thereby robbing Indian women of their most basic role as providers. It took from everyone the seasonal structure of their lives and damaged the kinship networks that had ruled their lives. It was the single most devastating blow to Indian life that could have been imagined, and, at least in the eyes of reformers, it was for their own good.

Alice Fletcher would have been shocked if anyone had called her anti-Indian. In fact, as an active participant in the Women's National Indian Association, she saw herself as a helpful "mother" to Indian peoples, trying to save them from hostile treatment by whites. So too did the female missionaries and the female teachers at Indian boarding schools see themselves. Each of them, with deep sympathy toward Indian women and children, believed that the only way to "save" them was to make them over in their own image.

Viewed through the lens of Native defeat and devastation, the civilizing vision of the 1870s in the Greater Northwest takes on an unfamiliar aspect. We honor and celebrate the efforts of the pioneer women and men who worked so hard to build communities in the Greater Northwest, but their efforts must be set alongside the contemporaneous suffering of the people they so rapidly displaced. Perhaps it is time to adjust our vision.

Similarly, it is time to reject the "Wild West" versions of history that ignore what women actually did to settle the Greater Northwest. The image of women as civilizers, gently influencing men to do the right thing, is a fiction. The reality lies with hardworking women whose basic instinct was to build stable relationships in their own families and to reach outward to build communities with like-minded kin and family members. But, as was so frequently the case in the Greater Northwest, their quietly persistent community-building efforts were about to be overwhelmed by a new deluge of change.

SOURCES FOR THIS CHAPTER

The key text for understanding the notion of woman as civilizer in the West is Peggy Pascoe's *Relations of Rescue: The Search for Female Moral Authority in the American West, 1874–1939* (New York: Oxford University Press, 1990), in which she looks at women's search for moral authority and finds it first in their benevolent control over women of color and later in benevolent help for poor immigrant women. For women's activities in family maintenance and the notion of kinwork, see Micaela de Leonardo, "The Female World of Cards and Holidays: Women, Families, and the Work of Kinship," *Signs* 12:3 (Spring 1987), pp. 440–453.

Frances Fuller Victor deserves closer study; for now the biography by Jim Martin, *A Bit of a Blue: The Life and Work of Frances Fuller Victor* (Salem, OR: Deep Well Publishing Company, 1992), is adequate. Importation of white women is in Lenna A. Deutsch, ed., *Mercer's Belles: The Journal of A Reporter* (Pullman: Washington State University Press, 1992); and in Adele Perry, *On the Edge of Empire: Gender, Race, and the Making of British Columbia, 1849–1871*; and their significance in Anne McClintock, *Imperial Leather: Race, Gender and Sexuality in the Colonial Conquest* (London: Routledge, 1996).

Although historians have looked closely at the pioneering settlement of the Willamette Valley, details of community settlement elsewhere have not been much studied. The writing that has most shaped my thinking about community settlement in the West is a largely overlooked essay by Kathleen Conzen, "A Saga of Families," in *Oxford History of the American West*, edited by Clyde A. Milner II, Carol A. O'Conner, and Martha A. Sandweiss (New York: Oxford University Press, 1994), pp. 315–357.

The books I found helpful include Susan Swetnam, *Lives of the Saints in Southeast Idaho: An Introduction to Mormon Pioneer Life Story Writing* (Moscow: University of Idaho Press, 1991); Annie Pike Greenwood, *We Sagebrush Folks* (New York: D. Appleton-Century Company, 1934; reprint Moscow: University of Idaho Press, 1988); Jean Barman, *Sojourning Sisters: The Life and Letters of Jessie and Annie McQueen* (Toronto: University of Toronto Press, 2004); William F. Willingham, *Starting Over: Community Building on the Eastern Oregon Frontier* (Portland: Oregon Historical Society Press, 2005); and Daniel Boone in "Daniel Wright Boone—Settler," *Bunchgrass Historian* 7:4 (Winter 1979) (Colfax, WA: Whitman County Historical Society), coupled with the memories of family females told to me by Katharine Meyer, a Boone descendant (in author's possession). For the African American community in British Columbia, see Sherry Edmunds-Flett, "'Abundant Faith': Nineteenth-Century African-Canadian Women on Vancouver Island," in Catherine A. Cavanaugh and Randi R. Warne, *Telling Tales: Essays in Western Women's History* (Vancouver: University of British Columbia Press, 2000).

For missionary ideas about Native women, see Adele Perry, "Metropolitan Knowledge, Colonial Practice, and Indigenous Womanhood: Missions in Nineteenth-Century British Columbia," in Katie Pickles and Myra Rutherdale, eds., *Contact Zones: Aboriginal and Settler Women in Canada's Colonial Past* (Vancouver: University of British Columbia Press, 2005); Sarah Carter, *The Importance of Being Monogamous: Marriage and Nation Building in Western Canada to 1915 (*Edmonton: University of Alberta Press, 2008); Myra Rutherdale, *Women and the White Man's God: Gender and Race in the Canadian Mission Field* (Vancouver: University of British Columbia Press, 2002); and Allen Conrad Morrill and Eleanor Dunlap Morrill, *Out of the Blanket: The Story of Sue and Kate McBeth, Missionaries to the Nez Perces* (Moscow: University Press of Idaho, 1978).

Studies of Native women in transition are scanty. Chris Friday has looked at the work of Native women in BC canneries in "Orchestrating Race, Gender, and the Meaning of Work in Pacific Northwest Salmon Canneries," unpublished paper, 2001, copy in author's possession; and John Lutz pays attention to women workers in *Makúk: A New History of Aboriginal-White Relations* (Vancouver: University of British Columbia Press, 2008). Also see Margaret B. Blackman, *During My Time: Florence Edenshaw Davidson, A Haida Woman* (Seattle: University of Washington Press, revised and enlarged edition 1992); and Caroline James, *Nez Perce Women in Transition 1877–1990* (Moscow: University of Idaho Press, 1996).

About Chief Joseph's War, see Alvin Josephy, *The Nez Perce Indians and the Opening of the Northwest* (Boston: Houghton Mifflin, 1997), supplemented by Caroline James, *Nez Perce Women,* for women. For Sarah Winnemucca, see Sarah Winnemucca, *Life among the Piutes: Their Wrongs and Claims*, Mrs. Horace Mann, ed. (New York: G. P. Putnam's Sons, 1883); Sally Zanjani, *Sarah Winnemucca* (Lincoln: University of Nebraska Press, 2001); and Rosemarie Stremlau, "Rape Narratives on the Northern Paiute Frontier: Sarah Winnemucca, Sexual Sovereignty, and Economic Autonomy, 1844–1891," in Dee Garceau-Hagen, ed., *Portraits of Women in the American West* (New York: Routledge, 2005).

About the Dawes Act, see Frederick E. Hoxie, *A Final Promise: The Campaign to Assimilate The Indians, 1880–1920* (Lincoln: University of Nebraska Press, 1984); Joan Mark, *A Stranger in Her Native Land: Alice Fletcher and the American Indians* (Lincoln: University of Nebraska Press, 1988); E. Jane Gay, *With the Nez Perces: Alice Fletcher in the Field,*

1889–92 (Lincoln: University of Nebraska Press, 1991); and Dolores Janiewski, "Learning to Live 'Just Like White Folks': Gender, Ethnicity and the State in the Inland Northwest," in Dorothy O. Helly and Susan M. Reverby, eds., *Gendered Domains: Rethinking Public and Private in Women's History* (Ithaca: Cornell University Press, 1992). More recently, Nicole Tonkovich, in *The Allotment Plot: Alice C. Fletcher, E. Jane Gay, and Nez Perce Survivance* (Lincoln: University of Nebraska Press, 2012), argues that the Nez Perce used the allotment process to preserve family stories and cultural properties in ways that evaded Fletcher's understanding.

Finally, for a moving, fictionalized look at white settlement/Native displacement, see the poems of Jana Harris, *Oh How Can I Keep on Singing? Voices of Pioneer Women* (Princeton, NJ: Ontario Review Press, 1993), and the beautiful video/DVD of the same name (Seattle: Moving Images Video Project, 2001, 2008).

Chapter 6
Women Together, Women Apart 1880s–1890s

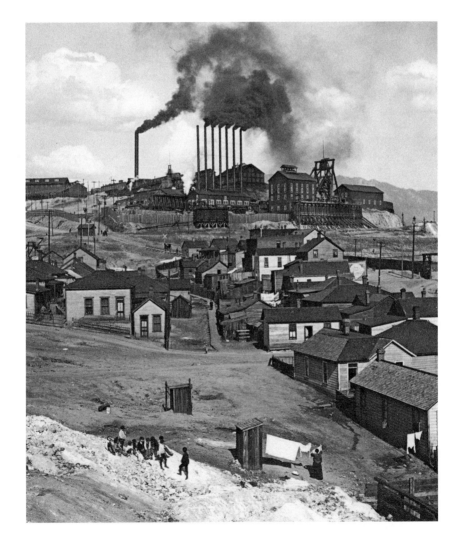

In June 1890, a group of working women in Butte, Montana, announced they had formed the Butte Women's Protective Union, one of the first labor unions in Butte and the only all-woman union in Montana. This dramatic assertion of women's solidarity as wageworkers would have been unheard of in the Greater Northwest just ten years before. What had happened?

The railroad had arrived, bringing with it fundamental changes. Although the transcontinental railroad connected the eastern parts of the country to San Francisco in 1869, the Northern Pacific Railroad did not reach Portland until 1883 and Tacoma in 1887. The Canadian Pacific reached Vancouver in 1885, and in 1893 the Great Northern Railroad linked Seattle to St. Paul, Minnesota. Almost overnight, an isolated, sparsely populated, and underdeveloped region was transformed, as its resources fueled large-scale industrialization throughout the nation. National corporations transformed the landscape as they built extractive industries to exploit the Greater Northwest's abundant natural resources. Sucking in labor from all over the world, railroads brought thousands of strong young men to work in the rough, temporary, and physically demanding conditions of agriculture, logging, mining, and fishing. Ships brought a stream of immigrants from unaccustomed places in Europe and Asia to what seemed to everyone to be a land of inexhaustible natural resources. As a result of this industrial transformation, the Greater Northwest developed a distinctively masculine spirit of toughness and bravado that suited the physically demanding new industries and the violent confrontations between labor and capital that ensued. In response, women of all kinds— rich, poor, Native, immigrant—changed in ways that bonded some of them together and drove others apart. Divided by class and race, women nevertheless cooperated with women like themselves to adapt their communities to these changes. Strength in numbers, many women discovered, fostered their own confidence and conviction.

The mining industry provides the most dramatic example of the transition to industrialism. Throughout the West, as gold rush–era mining camps faded away, they were replaced by a few great mining towns located on particularly rich deep lodes of copper and silver, owned by giant corporations that often controlled the state's politicians as well as the wageworkers in the mines. By 1890, Butte and Anaconda in Montana and Wallace and Kellogg in the Coeur d'Alene mountains of northern Idaho had become famous strongholds of powerful unions of miners who challenged—sometimes peacefully, sometimes not—their capitalist employers. The dangerous life of the hard-rock miners who worked the deep mines bred a rugged masculine bravado that was reflected in the raucous, wide-open public spirit of their mining towns, where at least half the population was single men. Yet although these mining towns were much more visibly male-dominated than agricultural communities, women were vital to the solidarity that knit these communities together. Women never worked in the mines, and few worked outside their homes. But they supported their husbands' union activities by figuring out how to feed their families during strikes, by keeping families together when men left to seek work elsewhere, and by helping other women in similar circumstances. In effect, as the men worked to keep the union together, they counted on their wives to keep family and community together. Men took for granted a gendered division of labor in which women devoted themselves to home and family, but miners' wives did much more than that.

As women did elsewhere, mining town women created community by supporting the churches and encouraging the schools. And as elsewhere, they supported their men by joining the female auxiliaries of the fraternal organizations like the Masons or similar groups to which the men belonged. In most towns, female auxiliaries were primarily polite social groups, but in mining towns they were directly linked to the unions that shaped the men's lives. The Irishwomen who lived in Anaconda, for example, formed a women's auxiliary to the Ancient Order of Hibernians (AOH), the organization that combined cultural, political, and economic concerns by providing sick and funeral benefits to members and their families. While the male AOH members were most concerned about the politics of the Anaconda Smelter Workers Union and the freedom struggles in Ireland itself, the women were stalwart supporters of the Catholic Church and other local concerns. As was customary, women provided food for social functions, but their most intense effort was devoted to St. Patrick's Day festivities—an early morning mass, a parade, evening entertainment followed by a dance—that raised the money for the funeral and widows' benefits that provided a bit of security for workers' families, while at the same time fostering ethnic pride and solidarity. The women's auxiliary in Anaconda fully supported the men when they went out on strike. In fact, as historian John Hinde found in his study of Ladysmith, a coal-mining town on Vancouver Island, women were especially crucial to community solidarity during strikes. Calling on neighborhood ties, women stretched their resources to aid their own and others' family economies while at the same time organizing special events such as dances to bolster community morale while the strike lasted.

In all of the region's great union strongholds, these traditional female support roles bred a new and more activist role for women. In good times, miners earned good wages, but how long until the next strike? Or the next mining accident? As miners depended on each other underground, so their families depended on women aboveground. The neighborhood ties that women built sustained families through the bad times and bred a respect among women for work that crossed ethnic and gender lines. Neighbors understood and respected the women whose economic circumstances compelled them to earn income by taking in boarders and laundry and by working as cooks, waitresses, and domestic servants, all jobs that were scorned by the middle-class women of the region's cities. In addition to respect for domestic work, mining town inhabitants were quick to recognize the right and need of women wageworkers to foster solidarity by forming their own unions.

Thus when thirty-three women came together in 1890 to form the Butte Women's Protective Union, the *Butte Daily Miner* welcomed them warmly, if a bit condescendingly: "The ladies of Butte—God bless them!—are not going to be behind their brothers in demanding their rights." The women who formed the union represented the limited range of women's work opportunities in towns with male-dominated industries. While the men labored in the mines, Butte's women worked in the service industries that provided the food and comfort for single miners, just as wives supplied them for their husbands and families. Women ran boardinghouses, worked in laundries and as waitresses and hotel maids, as the "bucket girls" who daily filled miners' lunch buckets, and as nursemaids and domestic servants to the families of mine managers—and of course as prostitutes, although they were not invited to join the union. Recognizing that they all shared the low wages and poor working conditions characteristic of "women's work," the Butte Women's Protective Union (BWPU) opened membership to all working women and vowed to band together to improve not only their individual circumstances but also the social condition of all women. Within five years of its founding, the BWPU was providing lodging, health care, child care and legal advocacy, a library, and classes in topics from job skills to citizenship.

In contrast to Butte, the emerging class system in the region's major cities made life very difficult for poor women. Labor in most major industries was seasonal: loggers could not work in the winter, harvest was limited to late summer, canneries and fisheries functioned only when the salmon were running. This "surplus army of labor" suited companies very well, but it degraded the conditions in the region's cities—Vancouver, Seattle, Portland, Spokane, Missoula, and Boise—all of which had huge temporary male populations that drifted in during slack times and left again when work was available. Seattle's Skid Row (originally Henry Yesler's skid road), one of the earliest haunts of loggers, gave its name to the districts of other cities where the transients congregated, areas where they could find cheap boardinghouses and restaurants, saloons, and brothels. Frequently these districts also housed racial/ethnic groups such as the Chinese and Japanese men who built most of the region's railroads. Interethnic violence was exacerbated by the Skid Row tolerance for drinking and brawling as well as the uncertain employment situation. Anti-Chinese riots in Seattle and Tacoma in 1886 were notorious results, but on a daily basis, disorder and violence were common in the cities.

Lacking the neighborhood and union solidarity of the mining towns, poor women in these cities were really on their own. Only women married to skilled workers had any hope of stability and security for their families. Those who were married to unskilled workers faced a future of transiency and long periods of spousal absence or outright desertion. Because of the predominance throughout the Greater Northwest of male-dominated extractive industries, there were few job possibilities for working-class women except poorly paid domestic jobs working for middle-class families: cooking, laundry, or domestic service, and none of these tolerated children. Middle-class city women never considered hiring Indian or other nonwhite women as servants. Prostitution flourished in these circumstances and was easily found in the red-light districts of cities, along with saloons, cheap restaurants, and cheap lodging in "flop houses."

On the East Coast at this time, young immigrant women flocked to unskilled factory jobs in the garment trades, but few of those factories existed in the Greater Northwest. The only industrial jobs were in the salmon canneries, which employed Native women and Asian men because they were the cheapest workers available and the easiest to let go, or local white women who regarded temporary cannery jobs as a way to supplement family wages and spend some time with other women. Until well into the twentieth century, the major occupation available to women in Northwest cities was live-in domestic service. (In Portland in 1880, for example, 55 percent of working women were in domestic service, another 20 percent in the needle trades, and none in factory work.) Although middle-class women believed that domestic service offered young women a safe and protected environment, native-born working women sought other options, because in reality it was restrictive, exploitative, and poorly paid. As a result, in Seattle in 1900, domestic servants were predominantly young Scandinavian women who, in contrast to most other ethnic groups, had migrated alone, without family members. They could not afford to live on their own, so they chose domestic service, with all of its drawbacks, because it gave them a place to live and because they knew that if they left one position they could easily find another.

At this time, every middle-class family expected to have servants, at least a live-in maid-of-all-work who did general housework and cooking. For the maid, a twelve-hour day was the rule, not the exception, because there was so much to do. Daily she lit fires in stoves and fireplaces, prepared and served meals and cleaned up afterward, made beds, dusted, answered the doorbell, and ran errands. To this was added the weekly cycle of washing, ironing, and mending, followed by the polishing of silver and glass, sweeping and window cleaning, and a day devoted to cleaning the kitchen. More affluent families also employed a cook and a nursemaid, and many families "sent out" their laundry or hired a laundress to come in one day a week. Still, the work routine was not only exhausting but lonely. Added irritants were the need to wear a uniform and being at the beck and call of one's "family" at all times. These circumstances explain why domestic service quickly became the niche for immigrant women (with adequate English) who had no better options.

Emily Berg, one of Seattle's Scandinavian "old-timers" interviewed by Janet Rasmussen in the 1980s, recalled the ways she and other young women had found to assert their independence. Berg moved from position to position, working as a maid for a female schoolteacher, then for a doctor who paid better wages, and later for a rich family in Portland where she was just one of many servants. Then she and her sister quit to visit the 1915 World's Fair in San Francisco. "When I came back to Seattle, I had just a lousy fifty cents in my pocket," so at four o'clock in the morning she called the bakery where her sister worked and asked for a job. She kept working even after she married, variously running a restaurant, working as a waitress, and working in a laundry. She never did return to domestic service.

We know very little about the poor women who were part of the huge transient workforce of the 1880s and 1890s, but we can infer some things about their circumstances from the range of benevolent organizations that middle-class women created to meet their most urgent needs. For the railroads brought not only a large new working class but also a sizable increase in the number of middle-class women ready to assume a benevolent role toward their poorer sisters. Nationwide, female responsibility for benevolence had begun early in the nineteenth century as charity work by church women, and by the time of the Civil War had grown into very large undertakings such as the Sanitary Commission that raised millions of dollars for soldiers aid and their widows and orphans. Benevolence was a well-established, accepted female activity.

The middle-class women and their husbands—lawyers, doctors, merchants, businessmen, journalists, ministers—who moved to the Greater Northwest intended to live as their counterparts lived in the East. They were not pioneers. They expected to settle in a style to which they were accustomed. But the cities they encountered were not what they expected. At a time when state and federal governments provided no assistance to the poor and unfortunate—no welfare, no unemployment insurance, no Medicaid—middle-class women assumed benevolent responsibility as a way to counteract the casual and transient atmosphere of Skid Rows by providing charity to poor women and children. In their activities was an urgency that went beyond customary benevolent charity. Reacting to the disorder and danger posed by the region's rootless young male workforce, benevolent women wielded their acknowledged roles as protectors of poorer women to improve society in general. The women's clubs of the Greater Northwest intended to alleviate the ill effects of industrialization, not to challenge it. Unions fought battles to achieve decent wages for workingmen, but neither they nor women's clubs raised the issue of the poor wages and conditions faced by working women. In fact, most middleclass women and men of all social classes believed that women should not be in the workforce at all. Woman's place was in the home; the workplace belonged to men. Therefore it followed that the women who *were* in the workforce were either disreputable or pitiable. In either case, they were in need of rescue.

In the 1890s, the number of women's clubs throughout the Greater Northwest multiplied in a wave of women's joining. Already there were many well-known and accepted forms of female association, from church-related charitable and fund-raising groups such as the earliest recorded women's club in Idaho, the 1864 Ladies Mite Association in Idaho City, to the women's auxiliaries of the vast number of men's fraternal organizations, ranging from the Masons to the Knights of Columbus to (as we saw in Anaconda) the Ancient Order of Hibernians.

What was new in the late nineteenth century were study clubs, a new kind of women's club in which women met together to enrich their own lives and form social bonds through literary, social, or cultural activities. A woman's club of this new kind, Sorosis, with a focus on female self-improvement, was formed in New York City in 1868, and the women of the remote Northwest did not lag much behind. The first handwritten constitution of the Woman's Club of Olympia in the early 1880s baldly stated: "The object of this club is the mutual aid and improvement of its members in their daily life whether it be for their domestic, social, intellectual or political advancement." This was new: women were stating their own needs, no longer claiming that all their efforts were on behalf of others. From these small beginnings, women's organizations were to blossom into full-scale civic reform in the decades to come. And as historian Sandra Haarsager argued in *Organized Womanhood*, the activity of the clubs demonstrated that "women had their own imagined West, quite different from the West of the dime novels or the gold-seekers . . . [one that had] spaces for women, homes, and community values expressed through social policies and cultural institutions."

Women's clubs provided a quick way of belonging for newcomers to the community, and they were also a form of social ordering. For example, when a local chapter of the well-known literary club, the Fortnightly Club, was formed in the 1890s in Pullman by Harriet Williams Bryan, wife of the president of the new Washington State College, membership was limited to faculty wives of whom she approved. Working-class women did not belong to groups like the Fortnightly. Some women's groups, like the Columbian Club in Boise, attracted wealthy, socially prominent women while others, like the Culture Club of Rupert, Idaho, was made up of farm women. In the small African American communities of Portland and Seattle, black women came together in groups like the Dorcas Charity Club in Seattle for sociability but also to help "uplift" poor members of their community, for these respectable clubwomen knew very well that whites judged blacks by the worst, not the best, of the race. The vast proliferation of women's clubs meant that individual women could find the activity and the companionship they desired, at the same time that their exclusivity confirmed boundaries between women as well.

Many of the clubs formed by eastern "transplants" had cultural purposes. The Seattle Ladies Musical Club formed in 1891 "to develop the musical talent of its members and to stimulate musical culture in Seattle." The group's first musical director, Marguerite Blanke Churchill, a former student of Franz Liszt, fostered both talent and high performance standards for its members by, among other things, limiting full membership to those who could pass an audition and participate in monthly concerts. Associate membership was offered to those who wished to attend concerts and/or sing in the club's chorus. By 1900 the club had already reached beyond its own talent to establish a successful concert series that brought many of the world's most famous musicians to Seattle to perform. In the days before radio or sound recordings, the opportunity to hear music performed by highly talented artists brought indescribable pleasure to the listeners.

Some of the clubwork of transplanted eastern women was nationalizing in intent, in the sense that establishing eastern values was the primary aim. A striking example of this sort of activity was shown by the Spokane chapter of the Daughters of the American Republic, founded in 1900. One of the members was Elizabeth Tannatt, wife of a former Civil War general prominent in eastern Washington. Elizabeth initiated and carried through the erection of a monument in Rosalia, near Spokane, commemorating the deaths of two US soldiers in the first serious conflict between US troops and eastern Washington Indians in 1858. Never mind that the Indians—a confederation of Nez Perce, Spokane, and Coeur d'Alene tribes at least six hundred strong—routed the troops led by Colonel Edward J. Steptoe. What was important was the commemoration of the efforts of loyal American soldiers. In this way, through the efforts of well-meaning, deeply patriotic women, the centuries-old history of the indigenous inhabitants of the region was overlaid by a new history marked by events meant to unify the nation, not to acknowledge different versions of local history.

The social exclusivity of some women's clubs makes all the more extraordinary the rapidity with which women's clubs in urban areas moved from study into action on behalf of poorer members of their communities. For example, in Seattle in 1884 a group of women, including Sarah Yesler, Babette Gatzert, Caroline Sanderson, and Mary Leary, founded a Ladies Relief Society to help the poor regardless of their race, religion, or nationality. Their agenda, and the size of their membership, grew to meet the need. The Seattle group went on to found an orphan's home, a day-care center, and a refuge for widows staffed entirely by volunteers and dependent for support on the society's fund-raising efforts with Seattle's business leaders and wealthy that later grew into the Seattle Children's Home.

In each of the region's major cities—Seattle, Portland, Tacoma, Boise, Spokane, Vancouver, and Victoria—women's clubs founded and maintained key civic institutions such as libraries and hospitals with the agenda of making them available to all. In Boise, the women's Columbian Club, composed of the wives and daughters of wealthy Boise men, expanded the existing public library in Boise into what eventually became a statewide circulating library. First, the Columbian Club donated the land for a large public library and obtained a grant from Andrew Carnegie for the building itself. As in his other library grants throughout the country, the canny Scotsman donated the money for the building only after the city government had pledged to pay the ongoing operating costs. But, mindful of the large rural population of Idaho, the Columbian Club lobbied the state legislature to establish a State Traveling Library. At first ten cases of books circulated among Idaho communities that had no libraries, consigned at each stop to a local women's club. Eventually more than two hundred cases of books circulated throughout the state free of charge, transported by the railroads that had been persuaded to generosity by the clubwomen.

Hospitals were another urgent urban need, and here the Sisters of Providence, headed by the tireless Mother Joseph, founded more than two dozen throughout the Northwest, beginning with the first hospital in Vancouver, Washington, in 1858. The nuns were assisted by a group of twenty Vancouver women of all faiths, calling themselves Ladies of Charity, who raised donations for the hospital. Seattle's Providence Hospital was first built in 1877 in the same way. The Children's Orthopedic Hospital in Seattle was begun by a group of wealthy women in 1907 when they realized that hospital care was not available or affordable to crippled and handicapped poor children who needed long-term care. In a move unusual for the time, the clubwomen worked together with the women of the African American Dorcas Club to help fund the hospital care of young black children. Orthopedic Guilds throughout the city began creative fund-raising that included everything from fancy social events to "pound parties" where each guest brought a pound of food for the hospital. Beginning with the first Fresh Air Cottage in 1908, Children's Orthopedic Hospital quickly expanded into a major institution that served young patients from all over the region.

In Spokane, the eastern Washington boomtown created by the railroad and the wealth of the Coeur d'Alene mines, the Ladies Benevolent Society formed in 1887, intending, as women's groups did elsewhere, to provide a hospital and orphanage to help the poor women and children who were flooding into the city. But they encountered competition from an unexpected source. The Sisters of Providence, led by the redoubtable Mother Joseph, had beaten them to the punch and had begun building the city's first hospital (designed by Mother Joseph) in 1886. To raise the funds for the building, the nuns held bazaars in Spokane and also engaged in Mother Joseph's famous "begging tours" of mining districts, where, it is said, they donned miners' gear over their habits and ventured underground to solicit funds from miners at work.

Back in Spokane, the Protestant benevolent women viewed the nuns askance, first because they spoke French, but mostly because they were Catholic. Although Catholic priests and nuns had been active in the Greater Northwest since the 1830s, they had ministered mainly to Indians and had little contact with settlers, who were predominantly Protestant and, like most Americans at the time, anti-Catholic. Nevertheless, the Sisters of Providence successfully concluded contracts in 1887 with Spokane County administrators and the Spokane City Council for the care of the indigent sick, thus providing a stable source of funding for the hospital. This was too much for the benevolent ladies, who promptly decided to erect a "Home for the Friendless" of their own.

Delayed by the need to raise funds and by the fire that devastated downtown Spokane in 1889, it was not until 1890 that they were able to dedicate the home, built in part by funds they had been granted from the city's formal Fire Relief Committee. The benevolent women intended the home to be simultaneously a hospital, a nursery, and a rest home, and on that basis they underbid the Sisters of Providence in 1891 to provide invalid medical care. But they were trying to run a multipurpose home with hired employees (supervised by benevolent volunteers) in contrast to the nuns, who did the work themselves. Facing this reality, the Ladies Benevolent

Society withdrew from the contract three weeks after it had been signed, and redesignated their home as an orphanage, not a hospital. In effect, they ceded medical tasks to the nuns, while reaffirming their commitment to poor children. As Nancy Engle, who discovered this interesting conflict while researching the history of women in early Spokane noted, "At the heart of the dispute [between the two groups of women] lay the question of who should have the power to define the experiences of Spokane's needy children." The dispute was papered over, the turf divided peaceably, and the two groups of women thenceforth provided help to Spokane's poor and sick. The arrangement was certainly an improvement over the previous policy of Spokane city and county officials, who had earlier met the need by providing poor people with one-way train tickets out of Spokane.

Temperance was the first region-wide female reform. There were few other regions of the country where the conflict was more clearly drawn between the nineteenth-century ideal of women's moral authority and the boisterous masculine ethos that characterized lumbering, mining, and the other major regional industries. Saloons and Skid Rows were antithetical to the hopes of middle-class women to define the values of the new communities of the West. Temperance was an issue that divided the sexes: while most men shrugged their shoulders, women saw alcohol as a serious threat to community life. In spite of the fulsome praise politicians and businessmen heaped on the community-building efforts of "the gentler sex," when these sentiments came in conflict with the economic reality of the profits to be made from the thirst of the masses of laboring men, the women lost.

Temperance had been an important national reform issue before the Civil War and became identified as a women's cause in the Midwest in 1873 and 1874 when bands of praying and singing women entered saloons and refused to leave until they shut down. Inspired by their success, a group of women in Portland adopted the same tactics, targeting the Webfoot Saloon, owned by a former member of the Portland City Council. But in Portland the tactics that worked in the Midwest were a failure. In response to their persistence and their prayers, several groups of respectable women were arrested for disturbing the peace (and on one occasion, for nearly provoking a riot). Their arrest and trial were "extremely sensational," the journalist Frances Fuller Victor reported after she had spent three days in police court. Although not a marcher herself, Victor was sympathetic to the women's cause and impressed by the strong feelings temperance evoked on both sides. She documented the women's unsuccessful battle against alcohol in a pamphlet, *Women's War with Whiskey or, Crusading in Portland*.

What made temperance a women's issue? Public drinking in taverns, bars, and saloons was an essential aspect of male sociability that deliberately excluded women. "Good" women did not drink alcohol at all, or at least not in public. The only women in saloons were prostitutes, or assumed to be such. Temperance women believed that saloons and bars distracted men from family life. Further, there was ample evidence that male drinking often cost families desperately needed money and that it was the major cause of domestic violence. No wonder, then, that when the national Woman's Christian Temperance Union (WCTU) was formed in 1874, it adopted "Home Protection" as its slogan.

In the Greater Northwest, following the Webfoot Saloon debacle, when WCTU chapters formed in the 1880s, members chose methods that were not so confrontational. WCTU members were largely educated women of the middle class, many of them recent arrivals to the region. As they grouped together under the irreproachable slogan of "home protection," they undertook a wide variety of activities to provide alternatives to the saloon and to help poor women and children whose lives had been damaged by alcohol-abusing men. In Portland and in some other towns, WCTU women raised money to erect public drinking fountains to provide the thirsty with another beverage. In many towns they established and staffed reading rooms and "coffee houses" as alternatives to the saloon. In Boise, Caldwell, and Lewiston, Idaho, among others, these reading rooms were the nucleus from which public libraries grew, nourished by continuing fund-raising by WCTU members. One woman in Caldwell raised seventy-five dollars by giving a series of ice cream socials. In Portland and Seattle, WCTU members founded orphanages and children's homes. In both Portland and Tacoma, WCTU members founded homes for unwed mothers and successfully lobbied their state legislatures for financial support.

The first WCTU chapter in British Columbia was formed in Victoria in 1882, following a visit by Frances Willard, director of the American organization. Although many BC women shared the American faith in temperance, their efforts were less successful than in the United States because of demographic differences. In British Columbia, rootless young men made up the majority of the population (outnumbering women two to one), and it was simply impossible to close down the taverns that were their acknowledged meeting places in far-flung mining and logging towns.

Furthermore, the largely British elite in the province favored moderation, not the sweeping measures of prohibition sought by impetuous Americans.

Always, a primary concern was to keep the issue of temperance before the general public by such methods as writing articles for newspapers, passing out pamphlets and pledge cards, and organizing groups of child members of the Loyal Temperance Legion to march in parades. Equally important was constant lobbying of state officials. The women who devoted considerable time to the WCTU received first-class political training. It may be that the WCTU's greatest influence was on its own members. Historian Sandra Haarsager points out that the WCTU played an important role in creating "a distinctly female consciousness and cohesion, a sisterhood that supported collective action on what we would label feminist causes, such as equity in women's legal, political, and educational status." In fact, as time went on it was clear that a generation of women who had learned their political skills in the WCTU were moving on to other women's groups, hoping to expand women's authority in still other directions. These topics are the major subject of the next chapter.

As Greater Northwest women were beginning to mobilize to accomplish their civilizing mission, other social changes were under way. A new aspect of the population surge that began in the 1880s was the foreign migration elicited by the needs of corporate extractive industries. The largest new group was Scandinavians, who had originally settled the upper Midwest and who, once that region was logged over, were vigorously recruited by Greater Northwest lumber companies. North and south of the international border, railroad companies recruited settlers from all parts of Europe to fill up the rural parts of the Greater Northwest. From as far away as Russia came Volga Germans to farm the Palouse wheat country that was so much like their lands at home, while religious freedom was one of the factors drawing Mennonites and Doukhobors to British Columbia. Portland added Italian and Jewish communities to the Chinese who were already there, while Boise became a center for the Basque men who herded sheep while Basque women ran the boardinghouses that welcomed them when they came in from their lonely work in remote places.

It would be many years before women among the new immigrants— Chinese, Basque, Italian, Scandinavian, and others—had the opportunity to speak publicly for themselves, because the newly established immigrant communities, all of which faced some degree of hostility from whites, quickly produced male leaders as spokesmen. Within these racial/ethnic communities, women's supportive roles, as always, found practical and private expression in neighborhood and organization activities but remained largely invisible to the general public and (with the exception of Butte) are not yet well documented by historians.

There are, however, a few extraordinary migration stories. In 1896, the Canadian federal government mounted a campaign to attract settlers to the western provinces. Although the major focus of the campaign was to fill up the agricultural provinces of Alberta and Saskatchewan, British Columbia attracted a substantial number of new immigrants, 60 percent of whom (175,000) were British. The odd result was that although its total population was quite diverse, British Columbia became more British than at any other time in its history. Indeed, the province became so adamantly a part of the Empire that the British practice of driving on the left side of the road remained in force until 1919.

Among the new British migrants were a group of women who were known as "distressed gentlewomen." By the late nineteenth century, the gender imbalance in Great Britain was large, with a million more women than men. As early as the 1880s, various "assisted emigration" schemes for British gentlewomen were implemented. Official thinking was that working-class women could fend for themselves, but that middle-class gentlewomen, raised only for a proper marriage, needed help. The assumption was that the female migrants would promptly find husbands in their new locations and indeed most did. But in the meantime, the migrating women had to be equipped with some employable skills. And so, apparently without a hint of irony, training programs were set up to teach middle-class women the domestic skills—cooking, cleaning, laundry, and dairy work, as well as gardening—that they did not know because they had expected to always have servants. In 1910 alone, nearly one thousand assisted gentlewomen went to Canada, most to the newly opened prairie provinces but some to British Columbia as well, where their numbers added to the British dominance of the population.

Hardening racial attitudes were bad news for the Chinese men north and south of the border, most of whom had been hired as temporary contract laborers to build the region's railroads. Although their actual percentage of the population was small, the Chinatowns that they built as defenses against white prejudice became themselves targets of hostility. British Columbia had the lion's share of Canada's Asian population (twenty thousand out of twenty-two thousand in 1901) and, owing to the anti-Chinese riots in Seattle and Tacoma in 1886, Portland attracted most of the Asian immigrants to the Pacific Northwest once the mining rushes faded and railroad-building was completed in the 1890s. These Asian communities clustered around a handful of rich merchants and a number of smaller services, with a considerable transient population working in coastal canneries or other seasonal activities.

The United States passed the Chinese Exclusion Act in 1882, banning all but merchants, students, and their families. The Canadian government disenfranchised Chinese men in 1885 and imposed a fifty-dollar-per-head tax on new immigrants that rose by 1904 to five hundred dollars per head. As a result, the growth of Chinese communities in North America was stunted, for most wives remained in China because of the exclusion laws, the expense, or because of understandable fears of violence against them. A recent study of Chinese women in British Columbia during the period of 1871 to 1902 found that less than 1 percent of them were merchants' wives. Often, concubines or second wives accompanied their husbands to British Columbia while the primary wife remained in China to manage family affairs. Concubines were one group within a larger class of Chinese women in bondage, which also included household servants and prosti-tutes, the latter of whom were actually quite few in number. In 1902 in Victoria, Chinese prostitutes were outnumbered by white prostitutes 150 to four. But in white eyes, all female Chinese immigrants were prostitutes, and lurid stories about them were frequent items in West Coast newspapers. In Victoria, the Women's Missionary Society, like its American counterpart in San Francisco, operated a rescue home for Chinese women and girls, hoping they would flee prostitution and be retrained as domestic servants for white families or be helped to find a suitable marriage partner, usually a Chinese man who had converted to Christianity. As it turned out, many of the presumed prostitutes had been sold by their parents as servants, not as prostitutes, to wealthy families in accordance with common practice in China at the time. At least in some cases, the missionary women found that "many of these girls are quite as well cared for, if not better treated, than many domestics in European homes." The Chinese-Canadian journalist Sui Sun Far (aka Edith Eaton), born in Montreal of British and Chinese par-ents, was one of the few who challenged the negative stereotype of Chinese women, sympathetically presenting their alienation and bewilderment in sentimental stories published in popular journals and collected under the title *Mrs. Spring Fragrance.*

In part because of the special animosity directed at Asian immigrants, African Americans encountered somewhat less prejudice in the Pacific Northwest (with the exception of Oregon) than in other parts of the country. Avoiding Oregon because of the clause in its 1857 constitution excluding black people from entering the state, African American migrants focused on Seattle, where a handful of blacks in 1870 grew to a community of over four hundred by 1900. Seattle's black population faced the paradox of remarkably few restrictions on their civil liberties—they could vote, go to school, serve on juries, frequent restaurants and theaters, live in a different part of the city than the Skid Row section to which the Chinese and Japanese were confined—but they faced severe job restrictions, limited to low-paying service occupations such as domestic servants or nurses or, for men, janitors, porters, and bootblacks.

There were really two black communities in Seattle, one composed of transient, often jobless, and sometimes criminal men and women who frequented Skid Row, and another of middle-class black families living in another neighborhood. Families of professionals, businessmen, and skilled artisans formed the core of the black middle class. As elsewhere, women helped to found community institutions. The first black church in Seattle—the First AME Church, incorporated in 1891—grew out of services initially held in Mrs. Elizabeth Thorne's restaurant. The first African American chapter of the Woman's Christian Temperance Union, the Frances Harper Union, was organized among AME churchwomen in 1891, led by former slave Emma Ray, who had migrated with her husband to Seattle in 1889. The chapter folded, however, when the pastor disapproved of the amount of effort the women were spending on poor African Americans on Skid Row or in jail, rather than on more respectable and deserving poor. A more successful later effort, the Dorcas Charity Club, was founded in 1906 by Susie Revels Cayton, simultaneously devoted to the pursuit of culture and self-improvement for its members while also organizing charity and "uplift" for poorer blacks. Cayton, the daughter of a Reconstruction-era black senator from Mississippi (the only black senator until modern times), was the associate editor of the *Seattle Republican*, a black newspaper founded by her husband, Horace R. Cayton.

This is not the whole story of this decade of growth and ferment in the Greater Northwest. At the same time that middle-class women were building community institutions, the women who taught in the Indian boarding schools of the Greater Northwest were taking a step beyond the Dawes Act by targeting Native children. In an effort to remove them from "bad" traditional influences, several generations of young Indian children were forced to attend boarding schools like Chemawa in Oregon (est. 1880), Puyallup/Cushman and Fort Spokane in Washington, and a host of smaller schools. In British Columbia, fourteen boarding schools and twenty-eight day schools enrolled some 40 percent of Native children by 1900. Brought to the schools often against their own and their parents' wishes, children were given English names, forbidden to speak their own languages, and dressed in European clothing. For the children, the experience was terrifying. Okanagan Indian Christine Quintasket vividly remembered her first day at a Jesuit-run boarding school on the Colville Reservation in northern Washington:

> Father was holding my hand when we went through the big white gates into the clean yard of the school. A high whitewashed fence enclosed all the huge buildings, which looked so uninviting. . . . Since I could not understand English, I could not comprehend the conversation between Father and the kind woman in black [the nun who was the superior of the school] . . . . When my father was ready to leave, I screamed, kicked, and clung to him [but] he gently handed me to the sister . . . [who] tried to calm me [but] I screamed all the louder and kicked her. She picked me up off the floor and marched me into a dark closet under the long stairway to scream as loud as I could. She left me to sob myself to sleep.

Indian parents gave up their children reluctantly, often only after extreme pressure from priests or Indian agents. They believed that in exchange their children would be taught the skills—domestic work for girls, mechanical skills for boys—that would allow them to find work in the white world. The Indian children provided the daily labor that allowed consistently underfunded schools to keep operating, but the promise of genuine domestic or mechanical training usually remained unfulfilled. Nevertheless, boarding schools often served as a last resort for Native parents in poverty; they knew their children would be fed and clothed, and they hoped to retrieve them in better times. The truth was that for many Indian children, boarding schools were deathtraps: gathering children together helped spread the deadly white diseases of smallpox, measles, and tuberculosis.

How did the white women who taught in the schools and worked on Indian reservations justify their harsh treatment of young children? Most genuinely believed that the only course for Native peoples was assimilation or extinction. The rigid control was necessary, they believed, to exterminate the old ways and enforce the new. In the incredible words of Captain Richard Pratt, superintendent of the best-known boarding school, Carlisle in Pennsylvania, it was necessary to "kill the Indian, save the man." Inevitably, such an inflexible system provided ample opportunity for sadism and sexual abuse, and for resistance. Their harsh and frightening experiences often fostered solidarity among Native children and reinforced their determination to hold on to their cultural identity. At Chemawa, children ran away when they could and frequently collaborated on other kinds of resistance. One choice made by some young women was to become pregnant, which automatically resulted in dismissal (i.e., a chance to return home). Yet in this grim picture there were lighter moments, such as encouraging students to play sports, especially the newly invented game of basketball. Some young women responded enthusiastically to the opportunity, none more so than the girls basketball team from the Fort Shaw Indian boarding school that won the Montana state championships and went on to play before an international audience at the St. Louis World's Fair in 1904. A reporter for the *St. Louis Republic*, amazed by the skill and speed of the "eleven aboriginal maidens" suggested, in explanation, that "the natural agility of the Indian maiden" had been enhanced by their training. In any case, their game was "the fastest thing of the sort ever seen in this city."

Enforced assimilation showed still another female face in 1890, when the US government created the field matron program aimed at girls returning to reservations. The program was created at the insistence of the Women's National Indian Association, the group in which Alice Fletcher was so active, to encourage—or perhaps enforce—the new domestic roles that young women had learned in boarding schools. Field matrons taught domestic skills with the deliberate purpose of providing a white maternal model to Indian girls in contrast to their own mothers. As Merial Dorchester, special agent for the Indian School Service, explained, "Often all that an Indian girl needs to keep her pure and true is to know that near her is a kind-hearted [white] woman ready with sympathy, advice, and help." The confusing mixture of religiosity and capitalism embodied in the program is captured in this description by field matron Lida W. Quimby on Washington's Puyallup Reservation:

> The Government did wisely when it inaugurated field matrons' work. Theirs to supplement all school and missionary work: to visit the sick and aged; theirs to advise, direct, encourage and teach all who desire to learn; to visit from house to house, trying to induce wage earning and quicken the indolent pulse of self-indulgence to activity for higher things; to awaken the soul and create a desire for better living.

Understandably, some Native people chose to avoid the heavy hand of government and missionary benevolence by living off their designated reservations on their own. For most British Columbia Natives, there was no choice. In contrast to the United States, British Columbia had no formal federal treaties and no government subsidies, however meager. All along the coast, Native peoples struggled to retain and exercise the fishing and hunting rights that were guaranteed in British Columbia custom but were encroached on by commercial operations such as salmon canneries and white fishermen and hunters. In combination with traditional activities like fishing and clamming, the custom of seasonal wagework continued. Native women had long been a major source of workers at canneries; another seasonal occupation was hop-picking in the Puget Sound, Fraser Valley, and

Indian women selling handicrafts (Courtesy of the Burke Museum of Natural History and Culture, catalog number 2617/6)

Yakima Valley. Families followed the harvest, crossing the international border without a thought, as they always had. Native families worked as a group picking hops during the day and then visited and gambled at night, much to the dismay of nearby whites, who disapproved of the gambling.

In the Puget Sound area, as in British Columbia, the major Native activity was fishing, not farming. Tribal treaties guaranteed Native people their customary fishing and hunting rights, and they were determined to exercise them. In 1887, one observer estimated that no more than three-fifths of the Indians on Puget Sound reservations were actually there: the rest were elsewhere, some men working at white occupations such as logging, some fishing and following other traditional pursuits. Indian women remained limited to work as domestic servants or to marriage or cohabitation with white men. As the Puget Sound area boomed in the 1880s and 1890s and population increased, so did pressure on Indians to retreat to reservations and take up allotments, but tangled tribal and racial bloodlines interfered with tidy land allocation.

Customary as Native efforts on both sides of the border to continue seasonal activities may have been, it is important not to romanticize them. Most Native peoples lived in poverty and faced constant prejudice, discrimination, and encroachment on their treaty rights, as well as interference in their personal and parental lives. They turned to their own kin, not to reservation agents, for support. And, it is very clear, they were determined to resist assimilation and find their own path between their own traditions and the white world.

Many Natives exemplified a middle way in their own persons, for the number of full-bloods continued to drop and the number with at least one white parent rose. The Puget Sound area was well-known for its mixed-race population as well as for the substantial degree of intermarriage between different tribes. The same intermixing occurred in other coastal areas, especially where logging camps were located near reservations. Sometimes the mixed-blood children were the result of rape or prostitution, for there is no question that white men preyed on Indian women, especially in male-dominated settings like lumbering towns. More commonly there were marriages, although not always long-lasting ones. Annie Miner Peterson, a Coos Indian woman of coastal Oregon, was warned by her aunt, "Do not stay at the village of the white people, because they are no good." Nevertheless, Peterson worked as a domestic servant for an Irish family and later worked in the cranberry harvest until she married (successively) a mixed-race logger, another mixed race sawmill worker, and finally, after she moved to Portland, a Swedish fisherman. In logging country, where mixed-race marriages and liaisons were common, Annie's granddaughter Iola pointed out, "If you could pass for white, you did." Iola was admitted to Chemawa Indian School in 1925, even though her father was Norwegian. At the school she found others who didn't look Indian, including "Swedes with brown eyes, and a girl from Alaska [with] black hair and blue eyes." Annie made her way in life by working at a variety of waged occupations for whites (primarily domestic service, laundrywork, and cranberry harvesting) and Native crafts. She was a skilled basket weaver. She hunted and fished, and when times were tough she lived with relatives. Late in life she was discovered by anthropologists, who came to her because she spoke both Hanis and Miluk Coos, which were dying languages that the anthropologists were eager to preserve. Almost incidentally, they also documented the many ways in which Annie survived—just barely—in the white world. It is ironic to consider that Annie's story survived only because what anthropologists treasured was the traditional language and ways that whites had destroyed.

The abrupt transition of the 1880s transformed the Greater Northwest from a remote, primarily agricultural hinterland into a natural-resource bonanza. The workers in these enterprises brought a new energy to the region and launched a three-decade struggle between labor and capital over the terms and conditions of work itself. The organized women's groups of the Greater Northwest, like groups in other parts of the country, mobilized their well-known female methods of benevolence to help the women and children who were casualties of the labor struggles. But the Greater Northwest women did more, working to shape a society that would curb the worst excesses of the harsh new natural-resource economy. Union wives, poor single women and middle-class women's groups, immigrant and Indian women, each in their own sometimes conflicting ways, worked to extend or preserve their own visions of community, efforts that were to bear fruit early in the twentieth century.

SOURCES FOR THIS CHAPTER

For women in Butte, see Janet L. Finn and Ellen Crain, eds., *Motherlode: Legacies of Women's Lives and Labors in Butte, Montana* (Livingston, MT: Clark City Press, 2005); and Janet L. Finn, *Tracing the Veins: Of*

Copper, Culture and Community from Butte to Chuquicamata (Berkeley: University of California Press, 1998). Laurie Mercier has pioneered the study of the role of women's auxiliaries to miners' unions in *Anaconda* (Urbana: University of Illinois Press, 2001), and in "'We Are Women Irish': Gender, Class, Religious, and Ethnic Identity in Anaconda, Montana," in Elizabeth Jameson and Susan Armitage, eds., *Writing the Range: Race, Class and Culture in the Women's West* (Norman: University of Oklahoma Press, 1997), and with Jaclyn Gier, in *Mining Women: Gender in the Development of a Global Industry* (New York: Palgrave Macmillan, 2006). See also John Hinde, *When Coal Was King: Ladysmith and the Coal-Mining Industry on Vancouver Island* (Vancouver: University of British Columbia Press, 2003). For urban working women, see Carlos Arnaldo Schwantes, *Hard Traveling: A Portrait of Work Life in the New Northwest* (Lincoln: University of Nebraska Press, 1994); Patricia Susan Hart, *A Home for Every Child* (Seattle: University of Washington Press, 2010); David Katzman, *Seven Days a Week* (New York: Oxford University Press, 1978); and Janet Rasmussen, *New Land, New Lives: Scandinavian Immigrants to the Pacific Northwest* (Seattle: University of Washington Press for the Norwegian-American Historical Association, 1993).

For urban women's organizations in the Pacific Northwest, the most comprehensive source is Sandra Haarsager, *Organized Womanhood: Cultural Politics in the Pacific Northwest, 1840–1920* (Norman: University of Oklahoma Press, 1997). See also Brenda K. Jackson, *Domesticating the West: The Re-Creation of the Nineteenth-Century American Middle Class* (Lincoln: University of Nebraska Press, 2005); Mildred Andrews, *Seattle Women: A Legacy of Community Development* (Seattle: YWCA of Seattle-King County, 1984); Mildred Tanner Andrews, *Washington Women as Path Breakers* (Dubuque, Iowa: Kendall/Hunt Publishing Company, 1989); and Nancy Engle, "Benefiting a City: Women, Respectability and Reform in Spokane, Washington, 1886–1910" (PhD dissertation, University of Florida, 2003).

On temperance, see Dale E. Soden, "The Women's Christian Temperance Union in the Pacific Northwest: The Battle for Cultural Control," *Pacific Northwest Quarterly* 94:4 (Fall 2003), pp. 197–207; Sandra Haarsager, *Organized Womanhood*; and Carli Crozier Schiffner, "Continuing to 'Do Everything' in Oregon: The Woman's Christian Temperance Union, 1900–1945 and Beyond" (PhD dissertation, Washington State University Department of History, 2004).

For British immigration to British Columbia, see Jean Barman, *The West beyond the West*; and Susan Jackel, ed., *A Flannel Shirt and Liberty: British Emigrant Gentlewomen in the Canadian West, 1880–1914* (Vancouver: University of British Columbia Press, 1982).

For racial/ethnic women, see Jeronima Echeverria, "A *Euskaldun Andreak:* Basque Women as Hard Workers, *Hoteleras*, and Matriarchs," in Elizabeth Jameson and Susan Armitage, eds., *Writing the Range: Race, Class, and Culture in the Women's West* (Norman: University of Oklahoma Press, 1997); Tamara Adilman, "A Preliminary Sketch of Chinese Women and Work in British Columbia, 1858–1950," in Gillian Creese and Veronica Strong-Boag, eds., *British Columbia Reconsidered: Essays on Women* (Vancouver: Press Gang Publishers, 1992); Yuen-Fong Woon, "Between South China and British Columbia: Life Trajectories of Chinese Women," *BC Studies* 156/157 (Winter 2007/Spring 2008), pp. 83–107; Denise Chong, *The Concubine's Children* (New York: Penguin Books, 1994); Annette White Parks, *Sui Sin Far/Edith Maude Eaton: A Literary Biography* (Urbana: University of Illinois Press, 1995); and Quintard Taylor, *The Forging of a Black Community: Seattle's Central District from 1870 through the Civil Rights Era* (Seattle: University of Washington Press, 1994).

For Indian boarding schools, see Cary Collins "Oregon's Carlisle: Teaching 'America' at Chemawa Indian School," *Columbia* 12:2 (Summer 1998), pp. 6–10; Carolyn J. Marr, "Assimilation Through Education: Indian Boarding Schools in the Pacific Northwest," http://content.lib.washington.edu/aipnw.marr.html; Jay Miller, ed., *Mourning Dove: A Salishan Autobiography* (Lincoln: University of Nebraska Press, 1990); Brenda J. Child, *Boarding School Seasons: American Indian Families, 1900–1940* (Lincoln: University of Nebraska Press, 1998); Cathleen D. Cahill, *Federal Fathers and Mothers: A Social History of the United States Indian Service, 1869–1933* (Chapel Hill: University of North Carolina Press, 2011); Mrs. Lida W. Quimby, "The Field Matron's Work," iweb.tntech.edu/Documents/Quimby on Field Matrons.htm.; Ursula Smith and Linda Peavy, *Full-Court Quest* (Norman: University of Oklahoma Press, 2008); Alexandra Harmon, *Indians in the Making*; and Lionel Youst, *She's Tricky Like a Coyote: Annie Miner Peterson, an Oregon Coast Indian Woman* (Norman: University of Oklahoma Press, 1997).

Chapter 7
Bold Spirits 1890s–1920

The nationwide depression of 1893 hit the Pacific Northwest hard. Natural resources prices plunged, farms failed, the Northern Pacific Railroad went bankrupt. In these circumstances, ordinary people sometimes seized on extraordinary ways to survive. One of the most dramatic examples was that of a Norwegian immigrant woman, Helga Estby, who lived near Spokane with her husband and eight children. Facing the foreclosure of their farm, Helga decided to take up a challenge publicized by New York's *World* newspaper: a prize of $10,000 to anyone who could walk across the country in seven months—more than enough money to save the farm. In May, Helga and her daughter set out to walk the thirty-five hundred miles to New York, following railroad lines so they wouldn't get lost and working in towns along the way to pay for their food and lodging. Because they arrived in New York a heartbreaking two days past the deadline, Helga never got the $10,000. But as Linda Hunt found out when she rediscovered Helga's lost story and retold it in *Bold Spirit*, Helga had risen to a challenge that few at the time believed women could meet.

Although few did so as dramatically as Helga Estby, many women in the Greater Northwest were ready to push beyond accepted boundaries and rise to new challenges. In the countryside, young farm women sought new options, while in the cities the conditions faced by workingwomen required newer and bolder solutions than a previous generation of benevolent women had considered. In sharp contrast, in this era of reform that we now call the Progressive Era, Indian women were abandoned on the reservations to which they had been consigned.

For the Greater Northwest's Indian people, the early years of the twentieth century marked a new nadir. In the United States, the hopes that had prompted the Dawes Act of 1887 had faded. The Nez Perce Reservation had been the first to be allotted in 1889; slowly over the next several decades others followed—Yakama, Colville, Umatilla, Flathead, and Warm Springs, among others—often as a result of substantial outside white pressure in spite of tribal opposition. Soon, Congress became reluctant to spend the money to support newly allotted reservations that had been promised. Reservation lands diminished as neighboring ranchers and farmers leased and bought Indian allotments, creating a checkerboard of landholdings that damaged or eliminated traditional food supplies like roots, berries, and wildlife.

In a stunning analysis of death certificates on the Yakama Reservation in *Death Stalks the Yakama*, historian Cliff Trafzer reveals the appalling price the Yakama paid for their enforced transition to "civilization." Between 1888 and 1940, tuberculosis and pneumonia, two diseases associated with poverty, malnutrition, and poor sanitation, killed the Yakama, Trafzer calculated, at a rate twenty times higher than that of the white population. Similar figures from British Columbia show that the Native population dropped from an estimated sixty thousand in 1860 to twenty thousand in 1911. Equally shocking, the Indian Health Service on the Yakama Reservation was unable to stem an infant mortality rate five times that of whites.

Tuberculosis was the scourge of poor people of all races until the 1940s, when drugs were developed to combat the disease. But before then, the figures show that even with adequate medical treatment, the death rate among Indians remained exceptionally high. Elizabeth James's study of the model Fort Lapwai sanatorium school (1909–1939) in Idaho explored the reasons this was so. Poverty among Indian peoples and persistent underfunding of Indian health services were obvious causes, but there were cultural factors as well. The Lapwai sanatorium school isolated young people from their families for health reasons, but just like the boarding schools, its agenda was to train them in white ways by cutting them off from their families. Administrators particularly blamed alcohol, intermarriage, and "superstitious beliefs" (there were many more medicine men and healers on the reservation than there were white medical staff) as dangerous practices. As well-meaning doctors insisted on erasing traditional ties, young Nez Perce died at a rate that imperiled the tribe's cultural survival. Torn between white demands and the remnants of traditional culture, Trafzer's conclusion that many died because of anomie—cultural loss leading to collective depression—seems correct. But most white people blamed the failure of Indians to become successful farmers not on the lack of the promised training and equipment, or on the breakup of reservation lands, or on disease, but on the inherent inferiority of people who could not rise to the standards of "civilization."

Meanwhile, rural women throughout the Greater Northwest, no longer as isolated as their mothers had been, became aware in the 1890s that city women had modern conveniences such as electric lights, refrigeration, streetcars, and steam laundries, while farm women still cooked on wood-burning stoves and did laundry by hand. Affluent urban women had servants and electrical appliances, while rural women had to wait until electrification in the 1930s to lighten their grueling daily load. Simply getting three meals a day on the table when everything was cooked from scratch was a nearly full-time job on top of other domestic tasks, all of which had to be done with less help from children than before, because local school boards now frowned on the practice of pulling children out of school to work at home. As a result, as one Montana farm woman put it, "You had to make every minute count."

Everyone knew that hard physical labor was the farm woman's lot, but early in the twentieth century influential critics of farming implied that farm men (who were working even harder) were selfish to deny their wives the comforts enjoyed by urban women. The real cause was economic instability: fluctuating farm prices meant that money had to be spent carefully, and always first for equipment that would increase output. Too many farmers had seen neighbors lose everything in bad years when they could not keep up payments on land and equipment they bought in good times.

Although farm women knew how important their work was to the success of the farm enterprise, they also knew that urbanites regarded their out-of-date clothing and careworn appearance with pity and condescension. Urbanites were confirmed in their impressions by the influential Country Life Movement, which focused its attention on the poor education, lack of culture, and hardscrabble lives of many of the nation's farm families. All this accentuated the fact of rural poverty. As Annie Greenwood sarcastically noted, "If you see a man, and he's got a fairly good suit and coat, why, that's a tramp; if you see a man in a ragged coat and worn-out overalls, that's a farmer!" Farm daughters, pondering this rural-urban gap, increasingly wondered how they, following their more footloose brothers, might leave the farm for the big city.

One new opportunity for young farm women emerged in the 1890s. The region's land-grant colleges offered them courses in home economics, or domestic science as it was also called. The Morrill Education Act of 1862 mandated each state to establish an inexpensive college to provide practical and agricultural knowledge to the children of rural farmers. The regional land-grant colleges—Oregon Agricultural College (1868), and Washington State College and the University of Idaho (both established in 1889)—were coeducational from their beginnings. This itself was novel.

Most male administrators and professors were uncomfortable about women students, who at the very least were a "distraction" and whose intellectual abilities they doubted. Furthermore, because parents insisted that their daughters be protected, colleges had to spend money to build female-only dormitories and hire supervisory "matrons" to enforce strict rules covering dating, hours, dress, and behavior. These rules lasted for a very long time. Indeed, to this day US senator Patty Murray, graduate of Washington State University, boasts of her successful challenge to the rule that women students could not wear pants to dinner in their own residence halls—in the 1960s!

The first women who attended land-grant colleges were segregated from men—Oregon Agricultural College (OAC) even prohibited conversation between the sexes during and between classes. As it turned out, they were also segregated by coursework, as young women themselves sought the new academic specialty of domestic science. At OAC, for example, of the sixty-six women enrolled in 1892–1893, only two were not majoring in household economy, as it was called there.

Aside from being considered the perfect vocation for farm women, what *was* domestic science and why were women attracted to it? Housekeeping in its broadest sense—cooking, sewing, home design and management—had been proclaimed as women's special vocation by female educators such as Catharine Beecher in the 1840s. But in the 1880s, the founder of the discipline, Ellen Swallow Richards, a chemist, insisted that domestic science was indeed a science on a par with the other sciences. Home economics was, in her eyes, the way to rationalize, dignify, and elevate the vital household functions women performed every day. "Who is to have the knowledge and wisdom and time to carry out the ideals [of society] and keep the family? Who, indeed, but the woman, the mistress of the home, the one who chooses the household as her profession . . . because she believes in the home as the means of educating and perfecting the ideal human being."

The region's land-grant colleges quickly established courses and then departments in home economics, and young women flocked to them. At the University of Idaho, courses in home economics were compulsory for all freshman and sophomore women, but compulsion was unnecessary: the first year forty-five young women enrolled, and more in subsequent years. Historian Michelle Tabit, who studied the program's development, describes modest beginnings. Women students took courses in cookery, theoretical and practical; household economy; hygiene; and homemaking. Courses in sewing and home design and decoration came later as the curriculum developed. The aim throughout, as the university catalog announced, was to combine the findings of scientific research with the practical needs of the home.

Idaho was an agricultural state, and home economics was felt to be the perfect field of study for young women, who were expected to return home and become farm women themselves. It was hoped that home economics would stem the flow of young women to the city and improve the quality of rural life for men and women alike. These were no small claims, but in Idaho they were largely successful, especially when state and federal funding became available for farmers' institutes and rural extension programs that continue at land-grant colleges to this day. A similar Canadian program, Farmer's and Women's Institutes, reached British Columbia in 1909. The provincial Ministry of Agriculture funded lecturers to visit rural areas to discuss a range of topics from "home economics, child welfare, prevention of disease, [and] local neighborhood needs," to "industrial and social conditions." In some locations, Women's Institute (WI) lecturers served as catalysts for permanent groups devoted to community improvement as, for example, in Nelson, British Columbia, where the local WI supported a variety of measures including libraries, parks, and health facilities. In the United States, the University of Idaho Department of Home Economics began outreach to rural women in 1912, via home demonstration agents who traveled throughout the state holding meetings on topics as varied as fly extermination and child care, although, in contrast to British Columbia, not on wider social and economic issues. Rural women flocked to demonstrations, and later to extension Homemakers Clubs, to learn skills to improve their homes and families. And in the process of meeting a need, a career in domestic science opened for women graduates of the University of Idaho. They could teach home economics in high schools, work as extension agents, as dieticians, or with agencies like the Red Cross and the Public Health Service. Thus home economics became a female profession. But as it became a viable vocation, the wider social mission of the field's founders, the notion that homemakers had the power and moral authority to reform society, faded, and with it the idea of the home as the locus of holistic learning. But in the meantime, the home economics departments of the region's land-grant colleges flourished.

The perception of University of Idaho administrators that young women were seeking new options was correct. Just as elsewhere in the country, the booming cities of the Greater Northwest exerted a strong pull over rural

young women. Nationally, the long demographic transition from rural
to urban majority was already under way, although it did not become
a reality in the Greater Northwest until after World War II. For young
women, the lure of urban life raised new issues; young men were supposed
to be independent, but the thought of young women living on their own,
separate from their families, alarmed many parents. Young women who
wanted to leave their rural families needed to find a secure job, if only
because their parents were unwilling to loosen the "family claim" without
the assurance that their daughters would be safe.

The occupation that best satisfied the aspirations of young women
and the worries of their parents was teaching. Public schools began in the
region in the 1870s, but at first they were an uneven patchwork of one-
room schools for grades one to eight that typically offered short sessions
(four months was common) conducted by poorly paid local young women
who often had just a little more education than their pupils. From the first,
urban schools were better, with longer terms and better-qualified teachers.
In the 1880s, the new middle-class migrants from the East spurred a move
to catch up to the rest of the country and establish high schools. That
required trained teachers and led to the establishment in Washington of
two normal schools for teacher training, the first in Cheney (1890) and
the second in Ellensburg (1891). In 1899, a third normal school opened
in Bellingham. Historian Karen Blair has looked at the experience of these
young normal-school students in some detail.

At first, the basic requirement for entrance, an eighth-grade diploma
or passing an equivalency test, was a hard standard for many applicants
from poor rural schools to meet. Some students who showed promise were
admitted to the preparatory division, where they were pushed hard to
catch up. Tuition and books were free to applicants who signed a pledge
to teach for two years. Most of the students were white Protestant young
women (there were only a few male students) from rural families. There
were no nonwhite applicants.

The two-year curriculum of the early normal schools was rigorous.
Students learned the subjects they would teach: math, science, Latin, history, geography, and civics, with a scattering of courses on pedagogy, school
management, and practice teaching. For many students, this course of study
was hard going, but most persevered. One of the things that helped was the
close friendships they formed with other young women in college literary
societies. In contrast to the structured coursework, members of these literary

clubs developed their own topics for study, discussion, and public perfor-
mances. Literary works (Dickens and Twain, for example), current events
(the Spanish-American War), and social issues such as woman suffrage were
popular topics. Thus, historian Blair asserts, attendance at a normal school
was a stimulating, demanding, and sociable experience for young women.

In contrast, the real world of teaching was a shock. Poorly equipped
rural schools, poor pay, and censorious community standards were common. All female teachers knew they would lose their jobs if they married
(although male teachers did not), but young women on their own were such
a disturbing novelty to many communities that they suffered constant sur-
veillance, gossip, and speculation. As a result, most teachers married after
they had fulfilled their two-year teaching commitment. Probably they had
always intended or hoped for marriage—almost all women *did* marry—
and the two years at hard labor were balanced by the rare opportunity for
education and lifelong friendship that the normal schools provided.

For the teachers who didn't marry, the goal became the opportunity to teach in a better-paid, better-equipped, and larger urban school.
Increasingly, urban schools attracted groups of older single women teachers who were sustained by their friendships with other women teachers.
Probably some of these close female friendships were physical as well as
emotional, but only in large cities did lesbian living become quietly possible. In the Greater Northwest, female households did not attract much
public attention. In part, this was because female sexuality among "respectable" women was a not a matter for open discussion. Newspapers, did,
however, pay close attention to reports of cross-dressing women. Accounts
of unquestioned males discovered on their deathbeds to have been biologically female made for great newspaper copy that was both sensational and
titillating. The most popular explanation was that a few women wanted
the opportunity to work at male trades, but as historian Peter Boag has
shown in *Redressing America's Frontier Past*, cross-dressing was a much
more complex activity than that. Viewed through the eyes of the women
themselves, cross-dressing was more widespread and more indicative of
lesbian desire than the general public realized at the time.

Montana author Mary Clearman Blew looked carefully at the choices
available to her schoolteacher aunt in *Writing Her Own Life: Imogene
Welch, Western Rural Schoolteacher*. Although a generation younger than
the first normal-school students, Imogene's life perfectly exemplified the
conflicts and opportunities faced by the first single women teachers. She

was eighteen when she obtained the two-year degree from Montana's only normal school in Dillon, in 1928. She taught in rural schools for twelve years, sometimes boarding with families, sometimes living in isolated and potentially dangerous "teacherages." The threat of rape, assault, and harassment from roving bands of boastful young men was very real. Imogene carried a gun.

Imogene expected to get married, as had all her female relatives, but a local romance didn't work out for her. Instead, following a disabling haying accident that ruined her chance of finding a local job, she suddenly took a teaching position in western Washington, at a school near Bremerton. This was breaking free with a vengeance. Blew writes that all of the family was baffled by her independence:

"I wonder what Imogene thinks she's doing out there?"

"She's bought a *Buick*?"

"Her own house? What does a single woman want with her own house?"

Although Imogene returned home every summer to spend time with her family (and especially her young niece, Mary), she did not move back to Montana. Blew draws a sensitive portrait of a woman who loved her family but refused their efforts to absorb her and who gradually came to depend on other single female schoolteachers for emotional support.

The 1900 census reveals that these new teachers and home economists helped swell the ranks of professional women from 7 percent of the female workforce in 1880 to 18 percent in 1900. However, careers in home economics and teaching were beyond the means of most rural women, some of whom nevertheless migrated to the cities hoping for the best. The range of jobs available to white American-born young women was limited. Forty percent of Oregon's workingwomen remained in domestic service, while those in retail trade made up another 13 percent. Women's work, at all levels, had two major characteristics: gender segregation and low pay. The two reinforced each other; as women were limited to a small number of occupations, men shunned those jobs and refused to allow women into better-paid trades, thereby contributing to even lower wages in the overcrowded women's sector. Another aspect of female service work, as most women's jobs were classified, was that they required what sociologist Arlie Hochschild has termed "emotional labor," in which women, whether as domestic servants, telephone operators, or retail clerks, were expected to

be neatly dressed, politely spoken, and attentive to the wishes of the customer. This marked a little-noticed gender distinction in the workforce at
the time: to be neatly dressed and well-spoken was never a job requirement
for miners, loggers, or fishermen.

As the census figures show, the easiest job to get remained that of
domestic servant, but young American women migrating to the city overwhelmingly preferred independence. Historian Mary Lee Spence found
that although waitressing, like domestic service, was "strenuous work,
notorious for long hours, low pay, and . . . bone-tiring labor," it "brought
a sense of freedom and camaraderie not experienced in the dreary isolation of [domestic] service." This was a new occupation for women; until
1920, the majority of waiters, especially in high-end restaurants, were men.
Women began at the low end of the trade, and at first their morality was
questioned because they mixed with strange men and took tips. But from
the woman's point of view, the trade was easy to learn, and the possibility
of good tips outweighed the almost certain prospect of male harassment.
Soon more and more restaurants employed "pretty waiter girls."

Another new possibility was to become a telephone operator. At the
time, every telephone call, whether from one side of town to the other or
across the country, went through an operator. The work was not physically
strenuous, but it was mentally stressful. To be a successful operator, recalls
one, you had to be "nervous, dedicated, and quick" and able to keep track
of a dozen or so calls at a time on a switchboard full of holes and blinking
lights. You also had to speak standard American English, with no racial
or ethnic accent. In the big cities, massed rows of young white women,
very closely supervised by an older woman, were a common photographic
opportunity. In cities, the job offered sociability and the anonymity of a
large group. In contrast, in rural areas, the opportunity to be a telephone
operator was highly prized, well paid, and alarmingly visible. The famous
western writer Dorothy Johnson remembered that her switchboard in
Whitefish, Montana, was a great place to observe the life of the community,
because, she recalled, "the telephoning public had a dark suspicion that we
spent our spare time listening in, and very often the public was right." The
rural telephone operator knew everyone in town, and they knew her. Even
though Johnson recalled that all operators at times wanted to pull out all
the plugs and yell "To hell with you," in fact, she says, "we felt an awful
responsibility toward our little corner of the world. We really helped keep
it running, one girl at a time all by herself at the board."

Some young women in the cities found work as retail clerks (classified as trade by the census). Even the best positions, in large department stores, were marked by long hours, strenuous work (in particular long hours of standing), and low pay. Most large stores hired only young white women who were well-dressed, well-spoken, "mannerly," and quick. Again, like waitressing, the occupation was at first considered dangerous because a clerk had to deal with a "promiscuous" (that is, men as well as women) crowd of customers. In contrast to most women's occupations, clerking in large stores held some possibility of advancement, but this was not true in smaller shops, where the likelihood of sexual harassment was, like waitressing, something women had to expect.

Throughout the Greater Northwest, there were no factory jobs to speak of. Some light manufacturing concerns (men's overalls, candy, cigar-making) employed women in low-paying positions. And they were invariably white; there were no jobs, aside from domestic service, open to African American or other racial/ethnic women. Some small traditional occupations, such as dressmaking and millinery, continued to employ young women, but in reality the range of possible occupations was narrow. Clerical work, at the top end, required special training in typewriting and stenography, and thus was too expensive for most women at the turn of the twentieth century, although as high schools became more common, more and more young women prepared themselves at public expense by taking typing and business classes. Laundrywork was at the bottom end of the list: it was notoriously very hard, wet, physical work and was done by only the poorest white women and racial/ethnic men (African American men were often hired for their strength).

In 1903, the Oregon legislature, imbued by the progressive spirit of the time, passed a bill that limited women's work in factories and laundries to ten hours a day. The challenge to it by Curt Muller, the owner of a Portland laundry, took the issue all the way to the US Supreme Court, where a landmark 1908 decision, *Muller v. Oregon,* confirmed the Oregon law. The court's decision, specifically based on the argument that limitation was necessary to protect the reproductive health of women, was the basis for subsequent protective labor laws throughout the nation. They were among the first laws to regulate private enterprise on behalf of the general welfare.

From the very beginning, women's protective legislation was controversial. Many workingwomen believed that unionization was a better way to address the issue of wages and working conditions, but women in many occupations were very hard to organize, at least in part because they could not afford union dues out of their very low wages. Protective legislation seemed the best available option, even though it played into persistent stereotypes of women as dependent, domestic, and of value mainly for their childbearing potential. Following the *Muller v. Oregon* victory, protective legislation spread throughout much of the nation and remained in force until the 1960s, by which time there was overwhelming evidence that the law was being used to prevent women from entering better-paid male-dominated occupations.

According to Alice Kessler-Harris, the foremost historian of workingwomen in the United States, *Muller v. Oregon* "changed the face of industry for women" because, by putting the spotlight on women workers, it galvanized "a generation of reform-minded men and women [to] . . . agitate for regulation and proscription." To a much greater extent than has been appreciated, the states of Washington and Oregon were national leaders in the movement for women's labor reform.

In the forefront was the Portland-based Oregon Consumers' League (OCL) and similar groups in Seattle and Vancouver. The OCL lobbied successfully for regulation of food preparation and, in a stiff battle with the Oregon Dairymen's Association, won a city ordinance inspecting and regulating dairies and requiring tuberculin testing of cows. The OCL was always carefully prepared with statistics, reporting in 1909, for example, that "six hundred and eighteen babies less than a year old died in Portland last year, and tuberculosis or dirty milk was the cause of every death." In 1913, the league achieved the passage of a compulsory statewide minimum-wage law for women and child workers (the first in the nation) and, in 1917, fought an exemption sought by canneries by securing an amendment requiring the payment of overtime after ten hours. The bill set up the Oregon Industrial Welfare Commission to regulate and enforce the wage law, a step followed by the states of California and Washington and the province of British Columbia. The commissions followed the practice of the OCL by conducting detailed investigations, all of which confirmed the initial findings of low wages and poor working conditions for female and child workers. In these efforts the Oregon commission worked closely with the state's labor unions, and frequently had the support of members of the Portland Woman's Club, formed in 1895, which early showed a concern for working women and children, as they and other groups lobbied for stricter child labor laws and better working conditions for women. Still, the moving force in Oregon for reform for workingwomen was Caroline Gleason (later Sister Miriam Theresa), executive secretary of the commission, which points to the important role that members of the Catholic Church played in labor reform.

Most of the women's groups in the Greater Northwest were more conservative than the OCL. As we saw in the previous chapter, women in the region's cities formed ladies' relief societies and charitable associations in the 1880s and 1890s to help poor women in customary ways: hospitals, orphan's homes, day-care centers, refuges for widows, and similar institutions, staffed entirely by volunteers and dependent for support on private fund-raising. But by the turn of the twentieth century, it was obvious that these volunteer efforts were not enough. Poor women who could not earn a living, children left in orphanages because their parents couldn't feed them, unwed mothers shunned by society, and desperate and starving Indian women—all these, and others, were the special concerns of benevolent charity, and it wasn't enough. Women were ready for the next bold step, convincing state and local governments to establish and fund basic social services.

In the 1890s some women's clubs in Washington, Oregon, and Idaho began to join a national movement toward super-organization and affiliated with the General Federation of Women's Clubs. At the state level, federations of clubs reinforced each other to lobby their legislatures on behalf of social welfare laws and funding. Child labor laws and public health issues, in particular efforts to control and treat tuberculosis (but not, it should be noted, on Indian reservations), and conservation and beautification measures were issues that concerned the women's clubs of the Greater Northwest. The common denominator of lobbying efforts was their success at forcing legislatures to take on financial responsibilities for public welfare measures that had heretofore been considered matters for private charity.

The equivalent Canadian umbrella group, the National Council of Women of Canada (NCWC) was equally successful in the "North-West" (the name for the provinces that composed the former Hudson's Bay Company fur trade territory). The NCWC's greatest success was the founding of the Victorian Order of Nurses in 1898 to assist western rural women—typically referred to as pioneer mothers—in childbirth by providing trained district nurses and establishing cottage hospitals, that is, childbirth centers. In British Columbia, the provincial Women's Council banded together with other women's groups in Vancouver to successfully lobby for minimum-wage laws for women, raising the age of marriage to sixteen, compulsory school attendance, the establishment of a Children's Aid Society, widows' pensions, and woman suffrage. However, with a few exceptions (such as the minimum wage), the extensive array of women's groups in Vancouver focused primarily on women's charitable and social causes such as temperance, while it was unions that were concerned with working conditions.

Although the same division of social concerns was true in the United States, in the 1890s some national women's groups began to devote themselves to urban reform causes that became popularly known as "municipal housekeeping." The ideology that justified these efforts was simply domesticity writ large; as reformer Rheta Childe Dorr explained, "Women's place is Home, but Home is not contained within the four walls of an individual home. Home is the community." The woman who was widely seen as the exemplar of the movement, Jane Addams, founded Hull House in Chicago, a settlement house devoted to serving the needs of the new urban immigrant poor, in 1889. Addams found that the customary female benevolent activities of educational, health, and cultural programs were not enough help. She became a vigorous advocate for the poor over issues of urban services, such as garbage collection, sewers, and clean water supplies, that were available in middle-class neighborhoods but not in the slums. Settlement houses in Portland and Seattle followed Addams's example. The Seattle settlement house was established in 1906 by Babette Gatzert, wife of a Seattle mayor, and the Council of Jewish Women began with cultural programs—courses in English, Americanization, sewing, and religion—for new Jewish, Italian, and Slavic immigrants and later added free baths and medical care. The settlement-house model of active reform attracted young college-educated middle-class women to work in them, and from this beginning the new profession of social work, female-dominated from its beginnings, emerged.

"Municipal housekeeping" was an umbrella term that covered many different reform activities by women. A closer look at the reforms in three cities, Portland, Spokane, and Seattle, and three women, Lola Greene Baldwin, May Arkwright Hutton, and Alice Lord, illustrates its diversity.

The moralistic strand in women's reform concerns was exemplified in the career of Portland's Lola Greene Baldwin. In company with most of Portland's women's groups, she had a special concern for the safety and reputation of "women adrift," as young women arriving in the city without family were known, fearing that, without protection, they might be lured into prostitution. The Portland Woman's Union, formed in 1887, opened a "homelike" boardinghouse for young women workers while, in 1889, the Woman's Christian Temperance Union opened a refuge home for "fallen women" (unwed mothers), staffed by volunteers from their organization. In 1900, a Young Women's Christian Association (YWCA) opened, providing low-cost rooms, meals, and employment advice.

In 1904, expecting many visitors to Portland for the upcoming Lewis and Clark Exposition, the YWCA established its Travelers' Aid program, staffed by a matron who met trains to provide information for single female newcomers. In this, they were reflecting a nationwide concern that world's fairs and large expositions posed a special risk for young women who might succumb to "evil agents who would deceive the innocent," as the YWCA program in Chicago put it. A group of Portland women offered Lola Baldwin, an experienced social worker and newcomer to Portland, a special female-protective position for the exposition. Baldwin quickly arranged for "morally safe" housing and respectable temporary employment, an advice bureau, transportation assistance, and even meal vouchers and medical care for emergency cases. Satisfied with the arrangements, Baldwin told the press, "We do not expect to eradicate the social evil in Portland [i.e., unmarried sex or prostitution], but we do expect to improve it."

In 1908, Baldwin, with the support of most women's groups, was hired by the Portland Police Department to officially continue her female-protective work. She thus became the first full-time city-funded policewoman in the country, a "municipal mother," as an admiring article put it, officially mandated to protect the morals of Portland's "women adrift." In Baldwin's eyes, "office girls" and retail clerks were the most at risk: rich girls were protected by their families and poor ones knew how to take care of themselves.

On behalf of these at-risk women, Baldwin inspected boardinghouses, examined job offers, monitored restaurants and public amusements, and even managed to drive shady fortune-tellers out of town. She also responded to complaints of sexual harassment (then called "indecent liberties"), but it is clear that most cases went unreported because women feared losing their jobs. She regulated public entertainment, once even attempting to arrest the "Red Hot Mama" Sophie Tucker on indecency charges. Of course she did everything she could to suppress prostitution and its accompanying scourge, venereal disease, for which there was then no cure. In Baldwin's eyes, prostitution was a public health menace.

Of particular concern to Baldwin were the popular dance halls of the time, which attracted "unruly" and unsupervised young women and men—a "promiscuous crowd," Baldwin said—of mixed social classes. Baldwin objected to the music (ragtime and jazz), the "suggestive" dance moves, and the presence or proximity of alcohol. After extended local controversy, Baldwin finally emerged from the fray in 1913 with an ordinance that closed the dance halls on Sundays, required a uniform entry charge (no more free entry to young women), set a curfew of 9:00 p.m. for unaccompanied young women, and, last but not least, banned all dances but the waltz. Ridiculous as these regulations may seem today, at the time they represented the moral position of most female reformers as they attempted to maintain cultural standards and set limits on public behavior. Social control, whether it was control by parents over children, by the wealthier over the poor, by native-born over immigrant foreigners, or by a political elite over the masses, was a strong thread in the progressive reform impulse nationwide. In that impulse, the protection and regulation of young women was seen as vital to their own safety and to social order. Just as, a generation earlier, white women had been regarded as "the boundary markers of empire" in British Columbia, now single young white women, women "adrift," became the boundary markers of public order. In reality, young women experiencing the freedom of their escape from parental control, and without any sense of their own historical significance, were considerably less interested in reform than were the benevolent women who tried so hard to protect them.

In Spokane, the issue of a police matron mobilized women's groups— but in a more radical context—and the leader who emerged, May Arkwright Hutton, was a much more controversial figure than Lola Baldwin. Hutton had been a hardworking boardinghouse keeper in the Idaho mining town of Wallace until her husband Al, a blacklisted former union member, struck it rich, and the Hercules Mine made the Huttons millionaires. May and Al bought a mansion in Spokane and lived lavishly. They founded an orphanage and supported day-care centers to help poor workingwomen, a typical charity for benevolent women but, in May's case, probably based on her own firsthand experience and observation. She was a forthright woman, committed to the welfare of the working class, all her life. And she expressed a common opinion among Pacific Northwest workers when she said, "One of these days this country is going to wake up and find that more than half the people are socialists." She allowed as how she was a socialist, "or nearly one."

Many middle-class Spokane women had a genuine concern for poor women and children, but reaching out to radicals was a much less common response. It occurred, however, in Spokane in 1909, where radical politics and women's reform impulses briefly coincided.

Spokane was a major hiring center for the region's army of transient workers seeking harvesting and lumbering jobs. With the support of the Industrial Workers of the World (IWW), an explicitly socialist union, whose members were commonly called "Wobblies," workers held demonstrations to protest the corrupt employment agencies that preyed on the job-seekers. When in 1909 the Spokane city government, prompted by the employment agencies, prohibited public street speaking except by religious organizations, the Spokane Free Speech Fight was on.

IWW speakers deliberately violated the ordinance, and when one person was arrested another promptly stepped up to take his place. Hundreds were arrested, but hundreds more arrived in the city to join the fight, including one of the IWW's best-known organizers, Elizabeth Gurley Flynn. The nineteen-year-old Irishwoman—the "Rebel Girl," she was called—was a dynamic and unusual speaker who was remarkably effective at reaching her largely male audiences. As Flynn took her turn on the free-speech soapbox, she too was arrested, and soon found herself housed with prostitutes and other women in the city jail. Far from being silenced, Flynn spoke up from her prison cell on behalf of her cellmates, claiming that the male jailers had sexually assaulted one of them. This lurid claim, added to the fact that Flynn also said that jailers refused to make any allowances for her own pregnancy, brought the Woman's Club of Spokane into the battle.

Clubwomen in Spokane had been lobbying for a police matron since the 1880s. Although there were only a few women prisoners, and most of them prostitutes, the clubwomen nevertheless believed they deserved protection from abuse by male jailers. Claiming that they could not afford the costs, successive Spokane city councils denied the requests until 1901, when they approved the creation of a position for matron, but only on an as-needed basis, offering Salvation Army captain Bertha Smith the position at fifteen dollars a month. So matters stood until Flynn's arrest and accusations in 1909. Four days after Flynn's release on a $5,000 bond,

May Arkwright Hutton introduced a resolution to the Woman's Club for a resident (not occasional) police matron, stressing the need to prevent "indignities" by male jailers that harmed the city's reputation. The resolution was approved unanimously, but the police temporized, claiming both lack of money and lack of office space for a female employee at the city jail. In February 1910, some clubwomen, tired of waiting and perhaps inspired by the IWW street tactics, decided to visit the jail en masse and then "storm" the city council meeting. "Astonishing Spectacle at Council Meeting," headlined the *Inland Herald* the next day. Faced with a delegation of thirty-five indignant women claiming that the conditions at the city jail for women were "indecent and a blot upon the fair name of the City," the city council unanimously passed a bill to employ three matrons (each for an eight-hour shift) for seventy-five dollars a month. By June, two of the three matrons were hired, although (unlike Portland, where Lola Baldwin was backed by the Portland Woman's Club) not the women that the Woman's Club of Spokane had recommended.

In fact, the police matron controversy left the Woman's Club deeply divided, with a significant portion of the membership extremely uncomfortable about any perceived association with the IWW and with Flynn herself, who proudly proclaimed, "Yes, I am a Socialist. And let me tell you, socialism is no dream." Even members of the Woman's Club who were sympathetic to socialism, such as Hutton herself, were unwilling to endorse the radical syndicalism of the IWW. But the actions of the Woman's Club of Spokane in the midst of the Free Speech Fight eased the way for collaboration with unions and working-class groups later in 1910, when they worked together successfully for woman suffrage in Washington.

In Seattle, experiencing a heady boom caused by the Klondike gold rush, reform took still another shape. Seattle was a union town where, like Butte before it, the power of the men's unions provided the impetus for women to organize too.

At the height of the Klondike gold rush, ten thousand men (and a few women) a year were surging through Seattle, where they stopped briefly to outfit themselves and to wait for ships to carry them north. In the boom that followed, Seattle service workers in hotels, bars, and restaurants worked long hours. In just one example, waitresses were rushed off their feet, working ten to fifteen hours a day, seven days a week, for wages of three to six dollars a week. In response to these conditions, a dynamic leader, Alice Lord, organized the waitresses. The Seattle Waitresses' Union, with sixty-five founding members, was one of the first women's unions in the country, and one of the first to be chartered by the American Federation of Labor. It grew to represent more than two hundred waitresses by 1902, for whom the union had obtained a sizable increase in wages and, equally important, a ten-hour working day. That was just the first thing on the waitresses' agenda. Alice Lord, by now a member of the Seattle Central Labor Council and the Washington State Federation of Labor, led the fight for the eight-hour day (estimated to affect 90 percent of workingwomen), passed by the state legislature in 1911, and a minimum-wage law for women, enacted in 1913. Both laws put Washington, along with Oregon, in the vanguard of states with progressive labor legislation for women.

Just who were the Seattle workingwomen that Lord worked so hard to help? Like the rest of Seattle's workers, the female workforce changed rapidly in the Klondike boom years. By 1910, the former predominance of domestic service was on the wane, and sales and clerical jobs were sharply rising. Of the nearly twenty thousand women employed in 1910, 37 percent were in domestic service, as opposed to 33 percent in sales and clerical, a proportion that was destined to continue to skew in favor of the latter. The minimum-wage and hour laws were aimed squarely at them, and women in a number of trades—typographers, tailors, cigar-makers, retail clerks—joined mixed-sex unions. The proportion of unionized women must have been one of the highest in the country at the time. The high point probably came in 1916, when the Waitresses' Union founded the Federation of Union Women, which organized hotel and domestic maids, candy and cracker makers, telephone operators, "lady barbers," and elevator operators.

Lord's legislative and unionizing efforts were successful, in part, because of the support of Seattle's male unionists, who were almost entirely white skilled workers in unions affiliated with the American Federation of Labor. In fact, in common with their counterparts in skilled unions throughout the country, male unionists had grave doubts about union women. Many men doubted that women could successfully organize at all. As the local labor paper, the *Seattle Union Record*, confessed in 1901, "When the Waitresses Union was organized in this city, there were small-minded people who looked upon it as something of a joke [but the waitresses] have shown that women can maintain a union as successfully as men." Many more union men doubted that women should be in the workforce at all. After all, it was the boast of skilled workers that they earned enough to support their wives and daughters at home. What would happen if many women entered the workforce, or even considered entering male trades? Surely the effect would be to undercut the wages that skilled workers so highly prized.

Another source of support for Seattle's union women was middle-class reforming women engaged in the benevolent and protective activities already described. There was some tension between the two groups, as many benevolent women were at first disinclined to take up wage and hour issues, continuing to believe that domestic service was the best choice of occupation for single women. Union women retorted that many middle-class women demanded much more than eight hours a day from their own domestic servants and paid them a pitiful wage as well. But as soon as benevolent women realized how necessary union support was to a successful suffrage campaign, the rapprochement began. By 1909, when the woman suffrage campaign began in earnest in Washington, union women were onboard.

There had been suffrage organizations in the Greater Northwest since 1871, the year of Susan B. Anthony's first western lecture tour, when Anthony was shepherded around the region by her young (as she was then) follower, Abigail Scott Duniway. It was on that tour that Anthony told an appreciative crowd in Victoria that "the present condition of women is similar to that of slavery before the [Civil] War." The same opinion did not go over as well south of the US-Canada border, where the reaction, judging from newspaper reports, was hostile, at least among men, who characterized her as a "disappointed and sarcastic woman," bent on revolution, not reform.

Nevertheless, suffrage was a popular cause among the region's women. WCTU members on both sides of the international border always supported suffrage, and over the years growing numbers of clubwomen, deeply involved in lobbying, came to feel their lack of the vote keenly. In fact, it was the women most deeply committed to social reform who began to see suffrage as the ultimate reform: once women had the vote, they could change the world (or at least their own communities and states). This was a mistaken hope, for all women did not vote identically any more than did all men, but the lack of female unanimity, which became apparent in the 1920s, was still a future shock for the generation of hopeful suffragists.

The commanding figure of Abigail Scott Duniway is most closely associated with woman suffrage in the Greater Northwest, a cause she championed for more than forty years, but she also worked for almost all the progressive reforms of her time, except for temperance. Duniway's family traveled the Oregon Trail in 1852, thus making her a member of the pioneer generation. Most of the women of that generation were much more interested in continuity than in change. They worked hard to recreate the social order they had left behind, and did not want to see it disturbed. Duniway, on the other hand, was a questioner and a fighter from the first.

For fifteen years (from 1871 to 1886) she independently published the *New Northwest*, a newspaper in which she regularly reported her extensive regional travels on behalf of woman suffrage. In 1886, for example, she reported traveling three thousand miles in Washington and Oregon and giving 181 public lectures on suffrage. No other region of the country had such a tireless advocate for women's rights. The Pacific Northwest's most persistent and eloquent advocate for suffrage—"the best lady talker on this coast," a man once called her—had a strong influence on the suffrage campaigns mounted throughout the region. But in spite of all her efforts, votes for women were not easily won in Oregon. Five referenda on the subject were held—in 1884, 1900, 1906, 1908, and 1910—before the sixth successful vote in 1912. Abigail Duniway, by then an old woman, was photographed casting the first woman's vote, a worthy prize for her persistence.

British Columbia also had a stalwart supporter of woman suffrage in British-born Helena Gutteridge, who first came to Vancouver in 1911 as one of the suffragists sent out by the embattled British movement, embroiled in dramatic arrests and hunger strikes at home, hoping to gain support from women in "the colonies." Gutteridge's main concern was the needs of workingwomen, which she fostered by becoming secretary of the Vancouver Trades and Labour Council, advocating for a minimum-wage law and founding the BC Woman's Suffrage League to garner their support. The wider woman suffrage movement in British Columbia, closely allied to the Woman's Christian Temperance Union, welcomed Gutteridge's efforts but, because of class differences, was sometimes taken aback by her assertiveness and lack of deference to her "betters."

In the 1870s and 1880s, however, these events were still in the future. First, suffragists had to figure out how to make the best of a difficult situation: unable to act directly themselves, they had to use their influence and persuasive skills to convince men to favor extending the vote to women. It is not surprising that it took years of effort, for all the weight of established custom and privilege favored the status quo. While in other regions of the country and in British Columbia suffrage advocates depended on the organized womanpower of the WCTU, Duniway always insisted on a clear separation between suffrage and temperance activity. Early history in Washington seemed to bear her out. There the territorial legislature had enfranchised women in 1883, but when women used the vote to turn their towns "dry" in local option campaigns, the liquor interests supported a challenge to suffrage that was upheld by the territory's supreme court in 1887, thereby depriving women of their briefly held right to vote.

Serious lobbying by women's groups in Washington, Montana, and Idaho to write woman suffrage into their state constitutions all failed in 1889, the year the first two became states, as did Idaho a year later. That defeat appears to have discouraged women in Washington and Montana during the 1890s, but the story was different in Idaho. There, both the Republican and Populist parties supported woman suffrage, and the issue was scheduled to be on the 1896 ballot. Duniway argued for what she called a "still hunt" campaign, avoiding large rallies and quietly persuading important men to influence other men to vote favorably. As Duniway blandly said, it was important "to impress upon all men the fact that we are not intending to interfere, in any way, with their rights; and all we ask is to be allowed to decide, for ourselves, also as to what our rights should be." In her eyes, temperance campaigns did threaten to interfere with the rights of the drinking man. But she did not draw attention to the fact that the second clause, allowing women, not their fathers or husbands, to decide their own rights was even more offensive to many men.

Duniway thought that "outsiders" like the eastern officials of the National American Woman Suffrage Association (NAWSA) should stay out of the 1896 campaign. Fortunately for Idaho, NAWSA ignored her and sent veteran organizer Emma Smith DeVoe to work in tandem with local suffrage workers. Idaho carried woman suffrage in 1896 by a margin of two to one, making it the fourth state (after Wyoming, Colorado, and Utah) to enfranchise women. A special factor in Idaho was the overwhelming support for suffrage among Mormon men, who themselves had been denied the vote until the LDS church renounced polygamy in 1890. Now Mormon women in Idaho, like their sisters in Utah, could vote.

The decorous, low-key "still hunt" publicity-shunning method seemed to be further vindicated in the Washington campaign of 1910, again organized by Emma Smith DeVoe. Its success was marred only by an open argument between DeVoe and May Arkwright Hutton. Their disagreement was not about the still hunt, which they both favored, but about style. DeVoe had built her career on her charming, deferential, "womanly" style of persuasion, and she was embarrassed by Hutton's hail-fellow-well-met manner as well as by her assumption that her wealth gave her the right to disagree with some of DeVoe's decisions. In effect, the two ended up dividing the state along customary east-west lines, with DeVoe in charge of the Seattle campaign and Hutton directing efforts east of the Cascades. In spite of their disagreement, suffrage passed overwhelmingly in Washington in 1910, by a two-to-one margin in every county of the state. The scale of the Washington victory is credited with reviving the suffrage movement nationally, and it was important for the careers of the two leaders. Hutton became the first woman ever elected as a delegate to the Democratic National Convention in 1912, and DeVoe organized and became the head of the National Council of Women Voters, representing the enfranchised women voters from western states. Under DeVoe's leadership, the council played an important role in the national campaign for woman suffrage and was a precursor of the League of Women Voters, the major post-suffrage nonpartisan women's political organization.

Suffrage victories in Washington in 1910 and California in 1911 gave a strong boost to the campaign in Oregon in 1912. The repeated failures in Oregon had been an embarrassment to Abigail Scott Duniway. The failure of the 1906 campaign especially annoyed her, for it was what she called a "hurrah" campaign, featuring large rallies addressed by the president of NAWSA, Dr. Anna Howard Shaw, who was widely known for her brilliant, sarcastic speeches. This intervention by "outsiders" into Oregon politics earned, for Shaw, Duniway's undying enmity, and she was not reticent in saying so. But, much closer to home, a key factor in the defeat was the opposition of the state's most influential newspaper, the *Oregonian*, whose editor was Harvey Scott, Abigail's brother.

In 1912, the highly organized women's groups of Oregon tried again, this time with a new sort of campaign. First, in common with the Washington suffrage effort, organizers reached beyond the comfortable middle class to actively involve working-class women and men. One example of this inclusive approach was the formation of Everybody's Equal Suffrage League, open to anyone for a membership fee of twenty-five cents. A second innovation, which imitated the successful California suffrage campaign of 1911, was the careful use of the new techniques of mass advertising. Posters, banners, and buttons were freely available, and a truck festooned with bunting made an appearance every day at noon during Rose Festival Week in June. This "suffrage lunch wagon" was a popular and mobile advertisement in an age when motorized vehicles were still a novelty. Duniway, herself old and ill, functioned more as a symbol than as an active campaigner. A huge banquet held in her honor in October, just before voting day, provided a sentimental culmination to the campaign, and this time Oregon voters narrowly approved suffrage.

Montana was the last of the Northwest states to gain suffrage in 1914. There the final success owed a special debt to Missoula's Jeannette Rankin, who provided the energy and organizational ability to reach into the far corners of the state. Montana's campaign effort was marked by large gestures, such as a mile-long suffrage parade at the Montana State Fair in Helena in 1914, headed by a marching band from Anaconda followed by Rankin and Dr. Anna Howard Shaw, automobiles, horseback riders, floats, union marchers, and a group of men representing the Montana State Men's League for Woman Suffrage. Suffrage carried at the polls by a margin of 3,714 out of 78,890 votes, and two years later Jeannette Rankin of Missoula took her seat as the first woman ever elected to Congress.

In British Columbia, women's efforts to obtain the vote were tied directly to party politics. When the British Columbia Liberal Party adopted suffrage in 1912, after concerted lobbying by women's groups, the women knew that their goal was in sight. In 1916, the Liberal Party won the provincial election and, when they took power, pledged to support both prohibition and suffrage, the two causes that Duniway had tried so hard to keep apart. World War I decided the issue: in 1917 the Canadian government granted the vote to war nurses and immediate relatives of military men and extended it to all women in 1918. Similarly, the American president, Woodrow Wilson, used the war as a reason to support suffrage, and the Nineteenth Amendment, the so-called Susan B. Anthony amendment, became law in 1920.

Suffrage was achieved as a result of the immense efforts that women of the Greater Northwest put into every campaign, slowly shifting the hostile public mood that had greeted Susan B. Anthony in 1871. The larger political tides of populism and progressivism played their part in changing attitudes, but surely as important was the positive recognition of all the community work of the region's women's clubs. This community work, as women themselves knew, was deeply political. Women created and maintained privately funded social services on behalf of women and children and then, over time, came to realize that private charity was not enough. Social welfare, they insisted, was a community responsibility. In effect, women defined the society taking shape in the Greater Northwest by insisting that social welfare was a basic function of government. Now that they had achieved the vote, women's groups looked forward to enacting their vision.

SOURCES FOR THIS CHAPTER

Linda Hunt's discovery of Helga Estby's lost walk is a story in itself, beginning with a high school History Day paper, "My Grandmother Walked Across America," that historian Jim Hunt thought might interest his wife Linda, an English teacher. She slowly reconstructed Estby's saga and told it in a compelling way in *Bold Spirit: Helga Estby's Forgotten Walk across Victorian America* (Moscow: University of Idaho Press, 2003; New York: Random House, 2006).

On Indian health, see Clifford Trafzer, *Death Stalks the Yakama: Epidemiological Transitions and Mortality on the Yakama Indian Reservation, 1888–1964* (East Lansing: Michigan State University Press, 1997); and Elizabeth James, "'Hardly a Family is Free from Disease': Tuberculosis, Health Care and Assimilation Policy on the Nez Perce Reservation, 1908–1942," *Oregon Historical Quarterly* 112:2 (Summer 2011), pp. 142–169.

For rural women, see Laurie K. Mercier, "'You had to make every minute count': Women's Role in Montana Agriculture," *Montana: The Magazine of Western History* (Autumn 1988), pp. 50–61; and Annie Pike Greenwood, *We Sagebrush Folks*.

For land-grant colleges and the beginnings of home economics, Andrea G. Radke-Moss, *Bright Epoch: Women and Coeducation in the American West* (Lincoln: University of Nebraska Press, 2008), was a mine of information. For the history of the development of the profession, I relied on Michelle M. Tabit, "Remaining Relevant: Home Economics at the University of Idaho, 1902–1980" (PhD dissertation, Washington State University Department of History, 2004); and on information generously provided to me by Alberta Hill, former Dean of the WSU College of Home Economics, about the University of Idaho School of Home Economics and the Washington State University College of Home Economics. General information about Women's Institutes in British Columbia is in Barman, *The West*; the vignette about the Nelson Women's Institute is in Brenda Hornby, "Life in the Town of Nelson, British Columbia," in Sharon A. Cook, Lorna R. McLean, and Kathryn O'Rourke, eds., *Framing Our Past: Canadian Women's History in the Twentieth Century* (Toronto: McGill-Queen's University Press, 2001).

For teachers and their education, see Karen Blair's fine article, "Normal Schools of the Pacific Northwest: The Lifelong Impact of Extracurricular Club Activities on Women Students at Teacher-Training Institutions, 1890–1917," *Pacific Northwest Quarterly* 101 (Winter 2009/2010), pp. 3–16; and Mary Clearman Blew, *Writing Her Own Life: Imogene Welch, Western Rural Schoolteacher* (Norman: University of Oklahoma Press, 2004).

Regarding women's wagework, see Joanne J. Meyerowitz, *Women Adrift: Independent Wage Earners in Chicago, 1880–1930* (Chicago: University of Chicago Press, 1988). Arlie Hothschild's insight about "emotional labor," in *The Managed Heart: Commercialization of Human Feeling* (Berkeley: University of California Press, 1983), is quoted in Joan Sangster's thoughtful *Transforming Labour: Women and Work in PostWar Canada* (Toronto: University of Toronto Press, 2010). Also see Mary Lee Spence, "Waitresses in the Trans-Mississippi West: 'Pretty Waiter Girls,' Harvey Girls and Union Maids," in Susan Armitage and Elizabeth Jameson, eds., *The Women's West* (Norman: University of Oklahoma Press, 1987); and Dorothy Johnson, *When You and I Were Young, Whitefish* (Missoula, MT: Mountain Press Publishing Company, 1982).

For women's reforms, see Mildred Andrews, *Seattle Women: A Legacy of Community Development*, and her *Washington Women as Path Breakers*; Margaret Hillyard Little, "Claiming a Unique Place: The Introduction of Mother's Pensions in British Columbia," in Veronica Strong-Boag and Anita Clair Fellman, eds., *Rethinking Canada: The Promise of Women's History* (Toronto: Oxford University Press, 3rd ed., 1997), pp. 285–303; and Beverly Boutillier, "Nursing Nation Builders: The Council Idea: Western Women, and the Founding of the Victorian Order of Nurses for Canada, 1896–1900," in Catherine Cavanaugh and Randi Warne, eds., *Telling Tales: Essays in Western Women's History* (Vancouver: University of British Columbia Press, 2000), pp. 174–199.

For Portland, Spokane, and Seattle reforms, see Janice Dilg, "'For Working Women in Oregon': Caroline Gleason/Sister Miriam Theresa and Oregon's Minimum Wage Law," *Oregon Historical Quarterly* 110:1 (2009); Nancy Woloch, *Muller v. Oregon: A Brief History with Documents* (Boston: Bedford Books of St. Martin's Press, 1996); and Alice Kessler-Harris, *In Pursuit of Equity: Women, Men and the Quest for Economic Citizenship* (New York: Oxford University Press, 2003). Elaine Zhand Johnson, "Protective Legislation and Women's Work: Oregon's Ten-Hour Law and the *Muller v Oregon* Case, 1900–1913" (PhD dissertation, University of Oregon, 1982), provided an important corrective to my assumption that women's groups had proposed the law. It was in fact proposed by the Oregon State Federation of Labor.

For reforming women, see Gloria E. Meyers, *A Municipal Mother: Portland's Lola Greene Baldwin, America's First Policewoman* (Corvallis: Oregon State University Press, 1995); Patricia Voeller Horner, "May Arkwright Hutton: Suffragist and Politician," in Karen Blair, ed., *Women in Pacific Northwest History: An Anthology* (Seattle: University of Washington Press, 1988); "Flynn, Elizabeth Gurley (1890–1964)," HistoryLink.org, essay 7309, www.historylink.org; Nancy Engle, "Benefiting a City," and her article, "A Blot upon the Fair Name of the City," *Columbia* (Summer 2013), pp. 10–15; John C. Putnam, *Class and Gender Politics in Progressive-Era Seattle* (Reno: University of Nevada Press, 2008); and Mildred Tanner Andrews, "Lord, Alice (1877–1940)," www.historylink.org.

For suffrage, see Ruth Moynihan, *Rebel For Rights: Abigail Scott Duniway* (New Haven: Yale University Press, 1983); G. Thomas Edwards, *Sowing Good Seeds* (Portland: Oregon Historical Society, 1990); Beverly Beeton, "The Suffrage Idea in Idaho," in Beverly Beeton, *Women Vote in the West: The Woman Suffrage Movement, 1869–1896* (New York: Garland Publishing, 1896), pp. 116–135; Rebecca J. Mead, *How the Vote Was Won: Woman Suffrage in the Western United States, 1868–1914* (New York: New York University Press, 2004); Jennifer Ross-Nazzal, *Winning the Vote for Women: Emma Smith DeVoe* (Seattle: University of Washington Press, 2011); Kimberly Jensen, *Oregon's Doctor to the World: Esther Pohl Lovejoy and a Life in Activism* (Seattle: University of Washington Press, 2012); "A Radical Woman," [Helena Gutteridge] Labour Heritage Center; and Linda Kealey, "Helena Gutteridge Biography," www.jrank.org/history/pages/7338/Helena-Gutteridge.html.

Chapter 8
Crosscurrents 1916–1929

||||||||||||||||||||||||||||||||||||||||||||||||||||||||||||||||||||||||||||||||||||||||||||||||||||||||||||||||||||||||||||||||||||||||||||||||||||||||||||||||

"**I** want to stand by my country, but I cannot vote for war. I vote No," said Montana representative Jeannette Rankin, on April 2, 1917, when President Woodrow Wilson asked Congress for a declaration of war against Germany. Forty-nine other House members voted no, but they were all men. Rankin, the first woman ever elected to Congress, was assumed to speak for all women. Of course she did not, although she did believe that war and peace were women's issues.

In her commitment to pacifism, Rankin had illustrious company. Although the national suffrage organizations threw their support behind the war effort, renowned reformer Jane Addams and many other activist women worked hard for peace: Addams founded the Woman's Peace Party, lectured widely throughout the United States, and, in 1915, led a delegation to an international conference of women pacifists in the Netherlands, where they formed the Women's International League for Peace and Freedom (WILPF). Rankin never regretted her "No" vote, and after she lost her bid for election to the Senate in 1918, she acted as WILPF's congressional lobbyist throughout the 1920s and 1930s. In 1941 she had a rare chance to reconfirm her pacifist beliefs when, elected to the House again by Montana in 1940, she cast the sole "No" vote against American entry into World War II.

Rankin's career exemplified the strengths of the prewar women's reform movement and its political limits. Carried into political office on a wave of reform that culminated in the success of woman suffrage in Montana in 1914, Rankin had not risen through the ranks of the traditional party system. Now, although she had the distinction of being the first woman elected to Congress, she found that she could not act alone, except to say "No." Further reforms, especially on a matter like pacifism that was widely considered a "woman's issue," could not move forward without substantial cooperation *inside* Congress as well as outside support. Although they had won the battle for the vote, women now had to begin the slow work of making their opinions matter within political parties. And in a break with their elders, young women believed that organized women's groups had outlived their usefulness and that the best way forward in a man's world was not in groups but as individuals. However, like political women, they were to find that although they had access, there were obstacles in the path to acceptance.

First, though, the entry of the United States into the war in 1917 demanded patriotism, and most middle-class clubwomen delivered.

Suffrage organizations were particularly strong in their support: Dr. Anna Howard Shaw, a former president of the National American Woman Suffrage Association (NAWSA) chaired the woman's committee of the Council of National Defense. Acting with the committee's approval, a Portland woman, Dr. Esther Pohl Lovejoy, made a major contribution to the international health of women and children. Lovejoy had been Portland's public health officer from 1907 to 1909, the first woman in the country to hold such a position. When the United States entered the war in 1917, she went to France as a representative of the Medical Women's National Association to investigate the needs of women and children in the war zone. Deeply shocked by the extent of the rape, violence, and poverty she encountered, she spoke as openly as the propriety of the time allowed: "Warfare is much worse for women than for men. Men have the right of death and they die fighting gloriously for their ideas. But women must live and be confiscated with the goods and the chattels." During the war, Lovejoy wrote and spoke about what she had seen, raising funds for what became known as the American Women's Hospitals Service Overseas for refugee women and children. At the war's end, she kept going, devoting the next fifty years to this cause, eventually helping women in twenty-eight nations.

At home, members of Portland's WCTU chapters and many other women's groups spent their meetings rolling bandages and making "comfort bags" for soldiers, while many women volunteered to staff Red Cross chapters that saw departing soldiers off to war. These seemingly routine efforts required substantial time, money, and womanpower, as the records of the Canteen Department of the Spokane Red Cross demonstrate. Between August 1917 and July 1919, under the leadership of canteen captain Mrs. Thomas (Lenna) Baird, the forty members of the committee met every troop train traveling from Fort Lewis, an army training and mobilization point near Tacoma, to the East Coast. They served the soldiers food, coffee and soft drinks, cigarettes, candy, flowers, and good will. These were essential services, for there was often no food service on the military trains. Most soldiers had never before left home and were grateful for friendly faces on the first leg of their long journey to the front. The Canteen Committee included a first-aid nurse, who was much in demand, and mail service. Because troop movements were secret, Mrs. Baird commonly received word (by telegram) only a few hours in advance and had to scurry to organize her crew before the train arrived. She was not the only woman who had to ask her husband to drive her to the train station. On one memorable occasion, when the Ninety-First Division went through to the front, the Canteen Committee worked eighteen hours a day for ten days, sometimes counting two thousand soldiers in the station at one time. In all, the Spokane Red Cross later calculated that they had greeted nearly two hundred thousand soldiers. White-haired, motherly looking Mrs. Baird was a troop favorite, receiving letters from some for years afterward. As a contemporary article retelling this remarkable story of service said, Lenna Baird was "Mother to 200,000 Boys."

Even before the war ended, the Canteen Committee met a new emergency, the influenza epidemic of 1918. The women took over the kitchen of the Spokane YMCA and cooked special diets for influenza patients for sixty-nine days. South of Spokane, nearly nine hundred soldiers were temporarily stationed at Washington State College when the flu hit in October. Hundreds of soldiers and students were affected; a total of forty-one people died on the campus alone. At the height of the epidemic, a fraternity house, two churches, the gymnasium, the mechanic arts building, and the college hospital were all used to house the sick. The entire home economics faculty and sixty students mobilized and prepared more than nine hundred special diets daily until the need subsided. Scenes like this were common all over the United States and Canada—indeed, all over the world. The epidemic was so serious and so pervasive that an estimated quarter of the entire US population was affected, and worldwide, three times as many people died of influenza than had been killed in the war itself. It was a horrific end to a terrible war, and presaged a turbulent peace.

Only three months after the end of the war in November 1918, the growing class division between militant workers and patriotic members of the middle class exploded in the Seattle General Strike of February 1919. The wartime boom had attracted tens of thousands of workers to Seattle, swelling its population by more than a third. Women as well as men joined the migration, although, unlike the future boom in World War II, they were not employed in the shipbuilding industry. Women found "women's work" as waitresses and sales clerks, clerical and laundryworkers, and many of them eagerly joined or created female unions, usually with support from male unions. But there were limits: the "Lady Barbers" Union was formed because the male barbers union would not admit them (although they did help the women form their own union), and there were very large segments of female occupations, such as teachers and clerical workers, that male unions were uninterested in organizing.

Seattle had never been a center of heavy industry, but government control over shipbuilding made it a union stronghold that was strongly influenced by the Industrial Workers of the World. The shipbuilders unions were strengthened and radicalized by the war, as workers saw that government control brought them better wages and working conditions than had the owners. It seemed that there really *was* an alternative to capitalism, just as IWW speakers kept saying!

In this heady wartime atmosphere, militant speakers, huge rallies, and socialist papers and pamphlets became almost commonplace. Famous figures like William Z. Foster (later head of the US Communist Party), Elizabeth Gurley Flynn, and the radical Portland couple John Reed and Louise Bryant were frequent speakers.

The effects of the exciting, although often very vague, socialist ideology can be charted with some accuracy in the career of Anna Louise Strong, who moved to Seattle to live with her father, a respected Congregationalist minister, in 1915. Strong was a pacifist who had worked with Jane Addams at Hull House and with the Children's Bureau, a government agency founded by reforming women of the National Consumers League. Owing to her own background and her father's reputation, Strong was elected to the Seattle School Board in 1916, the first woman ever elected and the youngest (she was thirty). Shocked by the notorious Everett Massacre in 1916, in which sheriff's deputies killed five IWW members, Strong's sympathies moved very much to the left. Soon she was writing articles for the IWW paper, the *Daily Call*. She made such an effective public appeal for free speech at the trial of a well-known labor socialist who had resisted the draft that he was acquitted, but Strong herself was recalled from her school board post by disapproving voters. While Strong was moving left (a direction that especially alarmed many Americans after the Bolshevik Revolution in Russia in November of 1917), few members of the middle class were moving with her, as the Seattle General Strike proved. The strike was called by the shipyard workers, locked in battle with the owners who refused wage increases to match wartime inflation and who clearly hoped to break the union. Sixty-five thousand union members, most of them in skilled trades and including six thousand women (waitresses, bookbinders, laundryworkers, telephone operators, and others) went out on strike while working together to continue to provide essential services to city residents. These successful cooperative efforts were what made the Seattle General Strike extraordinary, but what most middle-class Americans heard at the time was the vaguely threatening message of Anna Louise Strong, carried away by the romance of revolution. In a *Seattle Union Record* editorial that was reproduced nationally, she described the strike as "the closing down of the capitalistically controlled industries of Seattle," but went on to admit, "We are starting on a road that leads—NO ONE KNOWS WHERE!" Most Americans, including Ole Hansen, the mayor of Seattle, knew where it would lead—straight to Bolshevism. He called in the National Guard. After four days, the strike collapsed and class lines further hardened. Labor militancy was quashed by firing the shipyard workers and by systematic repression of IWW members locally and nationwide.

It was clear to Strong that it was time for her to move on, and she did. Following the lead of John Reed and Louise Bryant, she went to Russia, where she became an enthusiastic supporter of the communist enterprise. Using Russia as her "home base," she covered the world's revolutionary spots—Mexico, Poland, Spain, China—as a journalist for the rest of her life, eventually dying in Beijing, China, in 1970 at the age of eighty-five. Increasingly discredited as Soviet ideals revealed their tarnished reality, Strong's internationalism is still worth mention, not just for her own enterprise but also because she was part of a larger group. Internationalism encompassed a diverse group of women, from Jane Addams, Jeannette Rankin, and Esther Pohl Lovejoy at the moderate end to radicals like Strong and her sister socialist Agnes Smedley (a miner's daughter from Colorado who ended up in China). Internationalism in one form or another drew some of the most talented women of their generation and forms a little-studied counterpoint to the activities of other political women in the 1920s.

For radical women who did not leave the country, the 1920s were hard. Elizabeth Gurley Flynn, the hero of the Spokane Free Speech Fight, saw friends deported in the wake of the Palmer Raids in the "Red Scare" of 1919, others jailed, and the IWW effectively broken. Beginning in 1920, she threw herself into the defense of Nicola Sacco and Bartolomeo Vanzetti, the Italian anarchists who were eventually executed in 1927. "These seven terrible years were too much for me," she wrote. Early in 1927, her health collapsed, and she took refuge with Dr. Marie Equi, the radical fighter for women's rights, in Portland. Equi had begun practicing medicine among the poor in Portland in 1903. She began as a Progressive, was active in the movement for woman suffrage, and was a member of the Portland Woman's Club. Converted to socialism by an IWW-backed cannery strike in 1913, Equi actively supported strikes by Wobbly lumbermen and was an outspoken member of the American Union Against Militarism (the same group to which Jane Addams and Anna Louise Strong belonged).

Equi was just the sort of radical that the government was determined to silence: after the US Congress passed the Sedition Act in May of 1918, she was immediately indicted and spent ten months in San Quentin prison. She was not again active in radical causes after her release, but she did shelter Flynn from 1927 to 1936, nursing her back to health and, as Flynn later claimed, entangling her in an intense emotional relationship. Because Equi herself was an up-front lesbian there was speculation, then and later, about the relationship between the two women. In 1936 Flynn left Portland and returned to politics, now as an acknowledged member of the Communist Party, which she had joined secretly (as was common) in 1925. In Flynn's case, the failure of her radical hopes propelled her in a still more radical direction, along with many others in the 1930s. Her reengagement in politics took her back to the East Coast, and she never lived in the Pacific Northwest again.

Another radical Oregon woman chose another path, one she followed for the rest of her life. Activist and journalist Julia Ruuttila, the daughter of an IWW organizer, began her career in the 1920s by organizing a ladies auxiliary to her husband's lumber mill workers' union. As she said, "Now that was in the day when not many women, wives of workers, had jobs of their own, so the auxiliary was extremely important to them because it was something they could belong to. We weren't welcomed in the PTAs and clubs that other women found activity in. We were the wives of lowly workers and lived on the other side of the tracks." Throughout the 1930s, Ruuttila continued to work on union causes both as an organizer and as a writer for the *Timber Worker*, the logging union paper; the *Dispatcher*, the paper of the International Longshore and Warehouse Union (the source of much labor protest); and the *Peoples World*, the Communist Party paper. Logging and longshoremen's unions were in the forefront of the battle that raged into the 1930s to force owners to accept the new unions of unskilled and semiskilled workers that made up the new Congress of Industrial Organizations. Journalists like Ruuttila were essential to the CIO's successful struggle in the Northwest.

But for less radical working-class women, the sudden collapse of union militancy in the 1920s created fissures in the community solidarity of strongholds like Seattle and Butte. Some of these fissures arose from the gendered myopia of union leaders. Chastened by the failure of the Seattle General Strike, the city's male unions turned to more peaceful strategies based on selective consumer boycotts. At the turn of the century, the boycott had been a powerful weapon in the hands of middle-class women's groups like the National Consumer League in support of better working conditions for retail clerks and (on the East Coast) female factory workers. But when the Seattle Building Trades Council called a boycott in 1920 of Bon Marché, one of Seattle's largest department stores, for their plans to hire nonunion construction workers, it was a failure. Male unionists had assumed that all union-associated women would support the boycott, but they had failed to consult beforehand with the female retail clerks union members who might lose their jobs. Nor, apparently, had they consulted their own wives. Historian Dana Franks believes that the union men did not realize the extent to which their own wives now managed tight postwar household budgets by careful buying of consumer goods, such as inexpensive clothing, rather than making them at home. This was the beginning of a fundamental shift in women's domestic activities. Helped along by the burgeoning advertising industry, women shifted from home producers to consumers as manufacturers discovered the market for inexpensive consumer goods for the home and targeted advertising to housewives.

Although the 1920s was a very hard decade for the region's radicals and working-class women, it at first seemed to be the world that female reformers had been working for. In 1916, one of Jeannette Rankin's congratulatory messages had come from the wife of a Butte miner, who wrote, "I am especially happy in your election because I feel that the women of Montana can depend on their woman representative to achieve legislation for their benefit, hitherto unaccomplished by men." At first that seemed to be happening. The passage of the Eighteenth and Nineteenth Amendments (Prohibition and woman suffrage) in 1919 and 1920 enacted two goals that the nation's women's clubs had long sought. Two other long-sought goals, however, were unsuccessful. A proposed constitutional amendment banning child labor passed Congress but failed to be approved by the required number of states. A second bill, the Sheppard-Towner Act to provide prenatal and childbirth care for rural women, met a mixed

reaction in the Pacific Northwest. Because the act required matching
state funds, Idaho rejected it immediately, whereas Montana eagerly welcomed federal funds. Montana had the highest maternal death rate in the
nation, mainly due to lack of nearby medical care for widely scattered
rural women. The Sheppard-Towner Act funded public health nurses who,
hosted by local chapters of the statewide network of women's clubs, visited rural towns to provide health care and information to mothers and
infants. As a result, there was a significant drop in maternal and infant
mortality. Unfortunately, the Sheppard-Towner Act was barely up and running before opposition from the American Medical Association killed it in
1929. The AMA objected because public health nurses, not doctors, staffed
the outreach to rural women.

In British Columbia, a similar although much more limited program of
public health nurses (there called the Victorian Order of Nurses) had been
established in 1897 for rural women and children in the west at the prod-
ding of the National Council of Women of Canada. In 1918, the British
Columbia Child Welfare Association was instrumental in distributing
copies of *The Canadian Mother's Book* across the province. In 1919, the
University of British Columbia established the first nursing degree program in the British Empire, only to be countered by the provincial equivalent of the AMA, which argued that two years of training were sufficient:
"The overtraining of nurses is not desirable and results largely in the losing
of their usefulness." In Seattle, the University of Washington offered its
first course, in public health nursing, in 1918. The doctors' attitudes, so
reminiscent of the medical hostility that greeted the efforts of the legendary
British reformer, Florence Nightingale, in the 1860s, hampered the profes-
sionalization of nursing in North America until university-based programs
broke their control. Before then, most nursing schools were attached to
large hospitals, which favored clinical experience rather than "book learning" and used student nurses as cheap labor.

These legislative disappointments were accompanied by political
ones. Few women enjoyed the electoral success that seven women in tiny
Umatilla, Oregon (population 198), had experienced in 1916. Fed up with
an all-male city council that paid its bills so late that the street lights were
cut off and the city sidewalks were unswept, seven women mounted a
"stealth" attack. Taking advantage of the fact that few residents bothered
to vote and that write-ins were allowed, they nominated and voted for
each other and got other women to do the same. All seven women were

elected, including Laura Starcher, who beat her own husband for mayor by a twenty-six to eight vote margin. In the next four years, the female majority on the city council improved water and light services, instituted garbage collections, budgeted for street and sidewalk projects, put up railroad-crossing signs, founded a library, and took action to combat the influenza epidemic of 1918. In 1920, however, none of the women ran for reelection, and they did not publicly explain why. Perhaps they simply concluded that they had accomplished their goals.

Elsewhere, women who ventured directly into party politics (as opposed to the collective lobbying at which women's groups were so skilled) rapidly encountered difficulties. In Washington, two women, Dr. Nena Jolidon Croake of Tacoma and Frances Axtell of Bellingham were elected to the state legislature in 1912, only to find themselves ignored or ridiculed when they spoke on the floor of the house. A later female member of the state senate, Spokane attorney and prohibitionist Reba Hurn, was condemned as too brash and "pushy." The first hard lesson women were learning about politics was that access did not automatically entail acceptance.

In British Columbia, suffrage leader Mary Ellen Smith's legislative career illustrated the wax and wane of reform sentiment. Smith was first elected to the BC legislature in 1918, running on the slogan "women and children first," which epitomized the social concerns of the BC women's movement. She started brilliantly, successfully introducing women's minimum-wage legislation and a range of other social welfare measures. In 1921, she became the first female provincial cabinet minister in the British Empire; however, chafing at cabinet discipline, she returned to the floor of the legislature. By then the reform movement had peaked, and further legislation stalled. Later in the decade, in another "first," she served briefly as acting speaker of the legislature but lost her seat in the Conservative Party victory of 1928. Important as her double "firsts" were as a model, Smith found, as Rankin had, that alone she could not translate the strength of the women's outside reform movement into legislation.

At the local level, however, politics seemed more promising. In Seattle, an all-male precedent was broken when two women were elected to the city council in 1922. Kathryn Miracle, a former boardinghouse keeper and real estate broker, ran as a businesswoman. Bertha Landes, a married middle-class woman who had the backing of Seattle's powerful women's clubs, garnered a record-breaking 82 percent of the votes. Landes, who had been active in Seattle's women's clubs since 1905, ran as a "municipal housekeeper," the term she and other clubwomen used to argue that cities, mismanaged by corrupt male politicians, could be cleaned up by women who applied their domestic skills and values to civic betterment. An important corollary was that women entered politics not out of personal ambition but on behalf of "home protection" (an old WCTU phrase). On the city council, Landes was an activist, favoring comprehensive city planning and strict regulation of hours and conditions in public entertainment and licensing of dance halls, massage parlors, and public bathhouses. Her stance brought her into conflict with the mayor, who argued that Seattle needed to continue to attract the "tourist dollars" (as he put it) of the loggers and other workers who had long sought the cheap lodging and entertainment of Skid Row. Part of remaining attractive, Mayor Brown believed, required turning a blind eye to the "rum runners" and profiteers who were making a mockery of Prohibition. Because British Columbia had quickly repealed its prohibition legislation at the end of World War I, Vancouver found itself conveniently located to profit from this illegal liquor trade.

For her part, Landes fought especially hard for regulation of all-night dance halls, many of which were, as she claimed, fronts for prostitution and the sale of bootleg alcohol. Her concern echoed the longtime desire of middle-class clubwomen, and officials such as Portland's Lola Baldwin, to protect innocent young women from corruption. Landes's city ordinance, which included chaperones, a minimum age of eighteen, and bans on some especially intimate dances, was enacted in the face of considerable opposition. When, in a brief stint as council president and acting mayor, Landes closed down a number of nightclubs and fired the police chief, the lines were clearly drawn. She was the "clean-up candidate." When she ran for mayor and won in 1926, Bertha Landes became the first female mayor of a large American city. Widely praised for her integrity, efficiency, and progressive agenda, Landes nevertheless lost her bid for reelection in 1928 to a businessman who ran against what he called "petticoat rule." In the aftermath, the *Seattle Times* blamed women themselves for her loss: "Seattle has shelved all claims of women to higher places in local government; and this shelving, it must be remembered, has been done by women themselves."

Landes's loss revealed that there was not, as both suffragists and opponents had expected, a monolithic "women's vote" that would automatically support a reform agenda. It also underlined the great balancing act required of politically active women: to be feminine was to be perceived as weak, but assertion brought charges of "petticoat rule" or, worse, suspicions of lesbianism. And in Northwest cities in the 1920s, still a third factor was at work. As ideas about acceptable social behavior changed, the desire of older female reformers like Landes to protect innocent young women by setting strict boundaries on public expressions of sexuality began to seem quaint. Young working and middle-class women who bobbed their hair, wore short dresses, and smoked and drank in public were impatient with restraints. Rebelling against the strictures of older women reformers, young women sought personal freedom through education and employment, or in freer notions of sexuality. In the process, they refused to join the organized club movement that had created the reform tradition to which Landes's generation of middle-class women had been so committed.

The 1920s was the decade in which it became acceptable to talk publicly about sex. Popular Freudianism, in particular the idea that sexuality was a natural and innate instinct that should not be repressed, was especially liberating for young women who delighted in the chance to rebel against Victorian strictures about the need for female purity and piety. Margaret Mead, whose immensely popular anthropological study, *Coming of Age in Samoa* (1928), did so much to foster freer discussion (and practice) of sex, expressed the new mood of privileged college women of the time when she remembered, "We belonged to a generation of young women who felt extraordinarily free—free from the demand to marry unless we chose to do so, free to postpone marriage while we did other things, free from the need to bargain and hedge that burdened and restricted women of earlier generations."

Less outspoken middle-class young women shared Mead's sense of new possibilities. Nationally, there was an upsurge of women entering the professions of social work, medicine, academics, and the law. In 1930, women earned one-third of all graduate degrees and made up 30 percent of college and university faculties, a figure not reached again until the 1980s. Less ambitious and less affluent white women, while still planning on marriage, dipped their toes into what was still considered the male world of business by taking jobs for two or three years in the rapidly expanding field of clerical work.

The "business girl" who wore nice clothes and worked in an office, side by side with men, was a signal of women's shifting expectations. Clerical

jobs offered women the opportunity for clean work that was more intel-
lectually stimulating than domestic service, factory work, or retail sales,
and that paid better as well. The invention of the typewriter had opened up
office work for women in the late nineteenth century, supposedly because
women had the "quick, nimble fingers" needed to operate the machine. In
actual fact, it was education and social class that mattered. Most "type-
girls," as they were first known, had high school educations and spoke and
dressed as if they were daughters of the middle class (even though some
were not). This was not a position to which nonwhite women or immigrant girls with foreign accents and odd clothes might aspire, although in
the next generation their American-born daughters might.

By 1920, clerical work accounted for 25 percent of the female workforce in the city of Portland. When combined with the figure of 16 percent
for women in the professions, it appeared that a major change in the status of women's work had occurred. But there were important limitations.
Most professional women held "women's jobs"—teaching, nursing, and
social work. Similarly, in clerical work in business offices, two clear hierar-
chies had emerged: one for women, and another for men. Men could start
as clerks or accountants and expect to move up the ladder to managerial
positions, but women could not. The majority of female clerical workers
were low-level typists, file clerks, office machine operators, and the like;
the elite few were private secretaries with better wages, more independence, and more responsibility and control. From there, however, there
was no further possibility of promotion. A woman could dream of marrying the boss, a fantasy fueled by the movies and popular literature of
the day, which used romance to divert women from the full realization
that they were stuck in dead-end jobs. The attractive, well-spoken, highly
competent private secretary was in fact her boss's servant, expected to give
him trust and deference whether he deserved them or not. She was, as the
phrase said, his "office wife." Still, compared to the alternative job possibilities, the autonomy and financial reward of such a position was one that
many young women in the 1920s thought worth striving for. Probably, if
they thought about it at all, what labor historian Joan Sangster describes
as "pressures on female workers to behave in appropriately deferential and
feminine ways" at work seemed to women workers no different from what
their fathers expected of them at home.

Nowhere have the social consequences of shifting gender expectations in the 1920s been studied more perceptively than in Butte. In *Mining Cultures*, historian Mary Murphy charted the changes that began to shift the balance away from unquestioned male dominance of work and politics. Wartime events caused irrevocable changes, from which the miners' union never fully recovered. In 1917, a combination of antiwar protests, a terrible mine disaster and subsequent strike, and IWW agitation led the federal government, in the new mood of wartime patriotism, to send in federal troops to protect the mines from possible sabotage by the miners themselves. Troops remained until 1921, when the Anaconda Company completely closed the mines in response to the postwar depression. When they reopened in January 1922, a third to a half of the city's prewar population had moved on. Butte, which had prided itself on its reputation as a hard-drinking wide-open town—as, in effect, a man's town—never fully recovered. Prohibition, which was the law of the land, made it much more difficult for Butte's famed saloons to continue to function as the key institution in miners' lives. And other national changes, including the mass production of inexpensive consumer goods such as women's clothing and the popularity of "outside" values spread by radio and films, served to undercut the former unquestioned male dominance. These changes probably had a disproportionate impact in the Greater Northwest because so much of its prewar industry and social life had been so masculine.

During the labor shortage of World War I, some Butte women had worked in sawmills, driven trucks and streetcars, and even worked on the railroad. Although they did not keep the jobs at the war's end, they were no longer willing to be excluded or limited. Women flocked to the new clerical positions, and even in such customary work as waitressing they formed a union to press—and win—their demand for higher wages.

But the real arena of change was not in the workplace but in leisure activities. Ironically, Prohibition opened up some public spaces: for example, a young woman who would never in her life have walked into an old-time Butte bar was perfectly comfortable drinking with her boyfriend at a speakeasy or a roadhouse that offered bootleg liquor. Many young women in Butte welcomed the easy new clothing styles, the bobbed hair, the new sexual freedom for women (or at least the idea of it), and the autonomy and variety of working in an office rather than as a domestic servant. And the increased personal freedom and public visibility of young women made it easier for older women like Elizabeth Kennedy and other members of the

Good Government League to play a more active role in politics, although for a long time, like League of Women Voters chapters elsewhere, their role was one of public watchdog rather than direct participant. Still, by the end of the 1920s, public places in Butte were less rigidly gendered than they had been before, and women of all ages could move about more freely.

As young women became more visible in the world of business, other older women shifted their attention from reform activities to cultural concerns. The ladies musical clubs that had been founded throughout the region in the 1890s were the first step in fostering professional-level musical talent. They were particularly important to many middle-class migrants who missed the cultural richness of the eastern cities they had left behind. But only the coastal cities—Vancouver, Seattle, and Portland—had the population and the wealth to support larger efforts. In all three cities, efforts to establish symphony orchestras had begun earlier—the Portland (now Oregon) Symphony boasts that its founding in 1896 made it the first in the West—but all three were on shaky financial ground until the 1920s, when elite women organized fund-raising that stabilized them. In Vancouver, the key figure in the founding and funding of the symphony in 1919 was Isabella Rogers, the wife of a wealthy industrialist. Earlier, in Seattle, Harriet Overton Stimson and her friends in the Seattle Ladies Musical Club inaugurated the Seattle Symphony in 1903. Her granddaughter recalled that Stimson not only picked the music to be performed but also recruited a conductor from New York. As a final touch, Stimson and her friends raided their husband's closets to provide the orchestra with the requisite coats and tails, while their owners sat in the audience in business suits. Many of the same women came together in the 1920s, this time mobilized by the legendary Nellie Cornish, to put the symphony on a firm financial basis.

Nellie Cornish herself came from a poor family led by an erratic but hopeful father who, like Dickens's Mr. Micawber, was always sure that "something would turn up." Certainly his daughter had plenty of optimism and determination. A piano and voice teacher, she founded the Cornish School in Seattle in 1914. With help from wealthy patrons, the school rapidly expanded from teaching children to training music teachers to becoming a full-fledged school of the performing arts. Within three years, with six hundred students, the Cornish School was the largest music school west of the Mississippi. By 1921 it had its own building, which the school (now the Cornish College of the Arts) still occupies. Throughout the 1920s, which Cornish described as the school's "golden age," the school, guided firmly by "Miss Aunt Nellie," sought out and fostered new talent. The friendship and financial support of Seattle's wealthiest women was a major key to the school's success, but another was Cornish's own innovation and enthusiasm. As one of her "finds," dance teacher Martha Graham, described her, Nellie Cornish was "a small, round plump little lady with the dynamism of a rocket."

At the same time as Cornish's success, another determined musical woman in eastern Oregon was creating another cultural institution. Mary V. Dodge moved to Burns, a town of fifteen hundred in far southeast Oregon, in 1910 with her husband, a civil engineer. There they lived in a tent for eight years as Mott Dodge worked on an irrigation project and Mary began giving violin lessons to children. Within two years, the lessons had blossomed into the Sagebrush Orchestra, composed of between twenty and thirty local children. A few years later the group was touring the state. Automobile travel itself was a challenge. One former student remembered that driving the orchestra members from Burns to Bend took ten or twelve hours "winding around through the sagebrush," with fourteen flat tires en route. When Dodge moved to Portland in 1918, the Sagebrush Orchestra collapsed, but she promptly began an expanded youth project from her new position as the music director of the Irvington School Orchestra. By 1924, she had built a new youth orchestra and persuaded Jacques Gershkovitch, a guest conductor for the Portland Symphony, to lead it. The musical group, now called the Portland Youth Philharmonic, is today the oldest youth orchestra in the United States.

Meanwhile, a few woman artists were beginning to gain some recognition. For sheer determination, the prize would certainly go to Emily Carr of Victoria. Carr's parents were part of the distinctive British migration to British Columbia, and she was firmly brought up in that tradition, which did *not* include being an unmarried professional artist with a completely inappropriate interest in Native art. Over the years Carr made several long and venturesome trips to Native villages, including one in 1912 to the Queen Charlotte Islands, where she painted a series of pictures of Haida totems, which were then literally decaying and falling to the ground. In the same decade, Carr also traveled to Paris, then the acknowledged center of the art world, where she was influenced by postimpressionist experiments with color and form. Carr's efforts to reconcile the two artistic styles were long and difficult, and were met at home in Victoria with such disdain and incomprehension that she virtually stopped painting and ran a boardinghouse for fifteen years. Finally, in the late 1920s, the artistic climate changed. Carr's work was appreciated in Toronto and Ottawa, and she was welcomed by the Group of Seven, a group recognized as Canada's leading painters. Carr began painting again, and she exhibited internationally. Today she is recognized as one of the first artists who, by her focus on Natives and nature, helped define the modern Canadian spirit. And she is also recognized for the determination that helped her persist in what one biographer tactfully calls "an artistically unadventurous society."

Another adventurous artist, Seattle's Imogen Cunningham, had better luck than Carr in finding a welcoming artistic community—in San Francisco, not Seattle. Cunningham opened her own photographic studio in Seattle in 1910, and she quickly gained a reputation for portraiture. That reputation turned scandalous when her photographs of her husband posed in the nude on Mount Rainier were published. They are believed to be the first photographs of a male nude ever taken by a female photographer. Soon after that the family found it convenient to move to San Francisco. There Cunningham found a comfortable teaching position at Mills College in Oakland and the artistic companionship of the famous Group f/64, photographers that included Edward Weston, Ansel Adams, and Dorothea Lange. Even as her photographs gained widespread recognition, Cunningham maintained her ties to Seattle. It will come as no surprise to learn that some of the closest ties were with the Cornish School.

While the cities of the Greater Northwest grew and prospered in the decade following World War I, the region's farmers, still the majority of the population, never recovered from the abrupt wartime boom and postwar slump. During the war, farmers had been exhorted to expand, leading to postwar overproduction and debt. Many farmers simply lost their land as banks foreclosed. Others struggled on in the face of a prolonged drought, thereby contributing to continuing overproduction and low prices. The Republican governments of the 1920s refused to consider farm relief, and only the grotesque spectacle of farmers destroying their crops for lack of customers in the 1930s finally brought New Deal aid in the form of the Agricultural Adjustment Act, which came too late to save many small farmers.

Among the worst hit by the agricultural depression were many of the homesteaders who had staked their claims in the hopeful—and wet—years early in the century. Oregon's high-desert Lake County experienced a homesteading rush that began in 1905, accelerated in 1909 with the passage of the Enlarged Homestead Act, and ended in failure after 1915. By 1920, more than half of the initial one thousand homesteaders, defeated by lack of water for their crops, had given up their claims. Some left with literally only the clothing on their backs, abandoning the shells of the homes they had worked to establish. One old-timer, recalling the departure of his closest neighbors, said, "On the morning they left, when they were about ready to go, they drank a cup of coffee there. And then they left their coffee cups and plates on the table, just as if they were going to go out for a minute and come back. And those cups stayed there for years."

In another memoir from the same era, Alice Day Pratt, a single woman homesteader, recorded her hardscrabble experience in nearby Crook County. She stuck it out for eighteen years, from 1911 to 1929, and, in *A Homesteader's Portfolio*, left a moving appreciation of the beauty of the land and her ties to it. Pratt was far from being the only single woman to claim a homestead of her own, although there may have been fewer female claims in the Pacific Northwest than in the Dakotas, where Elaine Lindgren has shown that over 15 percent of the homesteaders were women. However, Lindgren's careful study also showed that the women who succeeded in proving up usually had family or close friends nearby on whom they could rely. In contrast, Pratt was a loner. She had no neighborly ties and no one (that is, no men) to whom she could turn for help for the heavy work of plowing and harvesting. That she finally failed and had to leave her beloved homestead should be no surprise. Farm folk simply did not survive without neighboring.

One unusual group of women homesteaders were deliberately destined to fail as farmers. Early in the century, a number of single young women, as well as some men, took up timber claims in the dense white pine forests of northern Idaho. Obviously, they were not planning to be serious farmers; in fact, they had been recruited by the region's timber companies, who were intensively cutting these very forests. How better to obtain lumber cheaply than by providing the homesteaders with a modest stake, waiting the few years for them to "prove up," and then buying their claim at a reasonable price? One of the homesteaders was young Ione "Pinky" Adair, who took up a claim with a "nest" of other women homesteaders from Moscow, Idaho. She lived on her claim for several summers (the snows were too deep in the winter) until driven out by the Big

Burn of 1910, a huge forest fire that burned three million acres of timber and came perilously close to burning Wallace, the key mining town in the Coeur d'Alenes, as well.

Pinky actually ended up cooking for the crew of firefighters that arrived to evacuate her and, in the excitement, forgot to notify her parents in Moscow (to the south, out of the fire zone). They lost a good deal of sleep worrying about her, she admitted later. If fire had not driven Pinky out, the federal government would have, for the newly created US Forest Service, a product of Gifford Pinchot's conservation efforts to preserve the American wilderness, regarded forest homesteading claims as a lumber company fraud and prosecuted claims holders. Years later, doubtless influenced by childhood stories of Pinky Adair and other displaced homesteaders, Moscow author Carol Ryrie Brink published a novel, *Strangers in the Forest,* depicting the clash between federal conservation efforts and the hopes of the homesteaders. The novel contains some evocative scenes of the isolation and fascination of living on a claim in the deep forest, and culminates—how else?—in the dramatic rescue of the homesteading heroine from the Big Burn by the conservationist hero.

By 1922, 75 percent of the homesteaders had left their claims in eastern Montana where, in the earlier boom years, thirty million acres had been "taken up." As had always been the case, the survivors fattened on the failures, adding to their own acreage by buying land at bargain prices. Attrition and consolidation were normal, but what was different this time was that there was no new land on which to try again. The families who left the land in the 1920s sought wage jobs (mostly for men) in town, not new family frontiers on the land.

Equally devastating, although slower acting, was the effect of failed farms on the rural towns that had served their immediate needs for supplies and sociability. It was rather like a slow leak in a balloon, as gradually it became clear that the town would not grow, the railroad would not come, opportunity would not knock. Many small towns simply disappeared, while others shrank and lost their businesses, which consolidated in the larger towns that the remaining farm families, with their new automobiles, could now reach with ease.

For the farm families that survived in the Greater Northwest, the hard times of the 1920s and 1930s marked the beginning of a fundamental transformation. Together, the internal combustion engine and electrification changed the nature of farming. (By 1939, 64 percent of Washington's farms had electricity, 54 percent of Oregon's, 52 percent of Idaho's, and only 13 percent of Montana's.) Tractors and mechanized harvest equipment began to replace horses, and automobiles allowed greater range of movement. For farm women, electrification transformed housework for those who could afford new appliances like electric stoves, refrigerators, and washers (though many could not until after World War II). As one woman said when electricity arrived, "We thought we were in heaven." Changes that affected everyone on the farm included electric lighting, indoor flush toilets, and the marvelous new connection to the wider world, the radio. But imagine what a difference even a small appliance like an electric iron meant to a woman who had spent years heating heavy "sad" irons over her stove.

The 1920s brought little but continuing poverty and disease to the Indian peoples of the Greater Northwest. Many of the realities of reservation life for women are unpublished, but we do have, in some detail, the experiences of one exceptional woman, Christine Quintasket (Humishuma), a Southern Okanogan woman who tried to make her way in two worlds. It was a constant struggle to make ends meet. Working variously as a housekeeper, a teacher at Indian schools in the United States and British Columbia, and as a cross-border migrant farmworker, Quintasket had ambitions beyond survival: she wanted whites to understand the realities of contemporary Indian life. Her novel, *Cogewea the Half Blood: A Depiction of the Great Montana Cattle Range*, published in 1927, was the first novel ever published by an American Indian woman. Notable as was her achievement, the novel makes hard reading today. Quintasket, who used the pen name Mourning Dove, was influenced by popular dime novels and quite deliberately used melodramatic language to write a romance about Cogewea, torn between the true love of the mixed-blood Jim and the blandishments of the nefarious white man, Densmore, whose real purpose was to acquire her land. Quintasket's original manuscript suffered an unknown degree of didactic rewriting by her patron and mentor, Lucullus McWhorter, a white man and well-regarded Indian sympathizer. The resultant "mix" makes Cogewea almost unreadable today, where it is generally viewed as a cultural marker in efforts to describe an Indian world that whites preferred to ignore.

At McWhorter's urging, Quintasket went on to gather traditional Salish stories that she published under the title *Coyote Stories*. McWhorter, like the anthropologists who hounded Annie Miner Peterson, was convinced that Indian culture was disappearing and needed to be recorded and preserved. Although Quintasket agreed, at least in part, she was more aware than McWhorter of the cost of her compliance: "It has been with the greatest reluctance that I consented to ... chronicling ... the ... oral philosophy of the Okanogans. ... And now, on the threshold of publication, there is a heart-shrinking from what I realize will be regarded by older members of my ... tribe as irreverent sacrilege." Her fears were well placed. When Christine Quintasket died at the Washington state mental hospital at Medical Lake in 1936 at the age of forty-eight, the cause of death was recorded as "exhaustion from manic depressive psychosis." But on the Colville Reservation, among her own people, the belief was that she died of spirit sickness because she broke tribal taboos. As Mary Nelson explained in 1988, "Oh Humishuma, Humishuma! You know what they say! The old people say, Humishuma, she told too much, too much." Perhaps this tension between the impulse to preserve traditions through secrecy and the desire to promote understanding through disclosure was a true indicator of the stresses that Native people experienced at the time.

In another, contrasting, case, after years of neglect and enforced assimilation, some Northwest tribes found themselves invited to participate in mainstream events. In the 1920s, as the Pendleton Round-Up became a major tourist attraction, Indian participation was vital to its success. The city fathers of Pendleton, Oregon, advertised the first Pendleton Round-Up, begun in 1910, as "a frontier exhibition of picturesque pastimes, Indian and military spectacles, cowboy racing and bronco busting for the championship of the Northwest." The Pendleton event was closely modeled on the Cheyenne Frontier Days, already a decade-long success, and on Buffalo Bill's famous Wild West shows, just ending after thirty years of touring.

Rodeo competition and horse racing were essential to Pendleton's success, and so was the participation of the Indians—Umatilla, Walla Walla, and Cayuse—on the nearby Umatilla Reservation, who were famous for their horsemanship and who, before allotment, had been successful horse breeders. Roy Bishop, owner of the Pendleton Woolen Mills that manufactured Indian blankets, had built a solid relationship with tribal leaders, and he invited them to participate. In exchange for prizes and payments, the Umatilla leaders agreed to begin the Round-Up with an Indian horse race, to participate in daily races, and to provide a tourist attraction by creating the picturesque sight of a teepee-filled Indian encampment. (In fact, the Umatilla used tule mat shelters when they traveled, but thanks to Buffalo Bill's Wild West show, tourists expected teepees.) And so, every year, the Round-Up opens with the special flourish of an Indian horse race, followed by a week of rodeo events, an Indian pageant at the Happy Canyon encampment, and a powwow dance contest, all of which draw not only tourists but also Indian relatives and friends from other reservations as well.

Another Pendleton custom, the yearly selection of a rodeo queen, also included Indian women. In the early days, cowgirl athletes, both white and Indian, participated in all the broncobusting and other rodeo events. In fact, in 1914, Bertha Blanchett came within twelve points of winning the overall title, and photographs and articles about cowgirl athletes were a regular part of publicity for the Round-Up. However, in the mid-1920s, the newly formed Rodeo Association of America made rodeos all-male events by banning cowgirl athletes from competition on the grounds that it was too dangerous to them. Henceforth, rodeo queens became the only females active at the Round-Up.

To select the queen, the Pendleton Round-Up committee looked not to athletic cowgirls but to well-behaved local women to symbolize the city's gracious welcome to tourists. Over the years, the committee selected attractive daughters of Round-Up supporters without requiring outstanding horse(wo)manship, and they were always careful to select appropriately behaved women—"no bobbed-haired beauties need apply," the *Pendleton East Oregonian* joked. In 1926, the Round-Up board selected Esther Motanic, the attractive daughter of an active Umatilla family, to be the first Indian queen. Announcing her appointment, the local paper ran a photograph of Motanic dressed in traditional regalia mounted on a horse with beaded trappings, while at the same time stressing her middle-class attributes of beauty, education, and benevolence. The selection of Motanic showed the importance of Indian involvement in the Round-Up, within limits. Over the years, four more well-behaved young Umatilla women were selected to be Round-Up queens, and like Motanic, they exhibited commitment to their tribe in ways that whites deemed suitable. But for the Indian women themselves, the dual symbolism was even more meaningful. As historian Renee Laegreid recounted from her interview with the 1952 Umatilla queen Leah Conner, "the experience of riding into the arena, wearing her family regalia, and knowing she represented her people as a true all-American queen," Conner said, "was mind-bursting."

The fact that Pendleton designed the Round-Up as a tourist attraction points to the innovation that was to make mass tourism in the Greater Northwest possible: the automobile. The freedom and adventure that the automobile came to symbolize was presaged by, of all people, Sinclair Lewis. Before he became famous for *Main Street*, an astringent critique of Midwest culture, Lewis published a lighthearted road novel, *Free Air*, in which his intrepid heroine, Claire Boltwood, motors from Minneapolis to Seattle and finds romance along the way. As the novel opens, Claire and her father (who is a passive passenger suffering from "nervous exhaustion") have gotten their expensive Gomez-Deperdussin stuck in the mud, only to be rescued by the local hero, Milt Daggett, in his cheap Teal car, who thereupon decides to follow Claire west. As the two cars drive to Seattle, Claire is democratized by meeting "true" Americans, and good-hearted Milt learns how to dress, speak, and behave in ways acceptable to Claire's social class. For all the air of adventure, Lewis described a trip marked by an absence of good roads, frequently terrible food and lodging, and unfriendly hoteliers, as well as the daily need to patch punctured tires and change inner tubes—all of which Claire blithely accomplishes without complaint. Along the way, Milt repeatedly rescues Claire not only from road hazards but also from human ones, including one frightening hitchhiker who jumps on the running board next to Claire and refuses to leave. When they arrive in Seattle, Claire realizes that her socialite friends are vapid and pretentious and that her future belongs with Milt. In the final scene, the two of them, having figured out how to get their car out of a stream, "climbed back into the car, joyously raffish as a pair of gypsies," and motor off to their new home in Alaska.

Many of the details of this road trip were realistic, for Lewis and his wife actually took such a trip as newlyweds in 1916. It is doubtful that they enjoyed it as much as Claire and Milt, but Lewis fell in love with Washington place-names, including in *Free Air* an ode in their honor that begins with "Humptulips, TumTum, Moclips, Yelm" and ends, a rousing four stanzas later, with "Steptoe, Pluvius, Sol Duc, Twisp!"

With *Free Air*, Sinclair Lewis became one of the founders of a new American literary genre, the road novel, one that has mostly been associated with male heroes, as in Jack Kerouac's adventures in *On the Road*.

But Claire Boltwood came first, and it is perhaps not too fanciful to see her jaunty optimism as symbolic of the freedom young women sensed was theirs if they broke with the conventions that all but the most radical older women had accepted.

The 1920s has often been portrayed as the disappointing decade in which the suffragist dream of reshaping politics in female terms was rebuffed. But this interpretation fails to see the ways in which young women seized the opportunity to redefine female expectations in more realistic terms. Nearly all pre-suffrage women's groups had insisted that women's distinctive moral and domestic qualities entitled them to a special role in public affairs. Hence, for example, the notion of "municipal housekeeping," of protective legislation to preserve the reproductive health of working women, and even the notion that women's votes would clean up politics. The young women of the 1920s saw that an argument based on women's special qualities would restrict them to the traditional, appropriate roles, and so they experimented with behavior that fit their expectations of increasing equality between the sexes. But as they looked ahead, young women failed to anticipate the ways the Great Depression would rearrange their future.

SOURCES FOR THIS CHAPTER

Mary Murphy's insights in *Mining Cultures: Men, Women, and Leisure in Butte, 1914–41* (Urbana: University of Illinois Press, 1997) form the basis of this chapter.

For Rankin, see Norma Smith, *Jeannette Rankin: America's Conscience* (Helena: Montana Historical Society, 2002); and Joan Hoff, "Jeannette Rankin and American Foreign Policy: Her Lifework as a Pacifist," *Montana: The Magazine of Western History* 30 (Spring 1980).

For Seattle, see Anna Louise Strong, *I Change Worlds* (Seattle: Seal Press, 1979; reprint of 1935 edition by Holt, Rinehart and Winston); and Tracy B. Strong and Helene Keyssar, *Right in Her Soul: The Life of Anna Louise Strong* (New York: Random House, 1983). For labor politics, see Dana Frank, *Purchasing Power: Consumer Organizing, Gender, and the Seattle Labor Movement, 1919–1929* (Cambridge: Cambridge University Press, 1994); Helen C. Camp, *Iron in Her Soul: Elizabeth Gurley Flynn*; Sandy Polishuk, *Sticking to the Union: An Oral History of the Life and*

Times of Julia Ruuttila (New York and Amsterdam: Palgrave Macmillan, 2003); and Michael Helquist, *Marie Equi: Radical Politics and Outlaw Passions* (Corvallis: Oregon State University Press, 2015).

For the beginnings of consumerism, see Janice Rutherford, *Selling Mrs. Consumer: Christine Frederick and the Rise of Household Efficiency* (Athens: University of Georgia Press, 2003). For the under-studied topic of women's internationalism, see Leila J. Rupp, *Worlds of Women: The Making of An International Women's Movement* (Princeton: Princeton University Press, 1997); and, more recently, Kimberly Jensen and Erika Kuhlman, eds., *Women and Transnational Activism in Historical Perspective* (Amsterdam: Republic of Letters Publishing, 2010). For patriotic women, see Bruce Harding, "Lenna Baird: Mother to 200,000 Boys," in *Columbia* 13 (Spring 1990); and Kimberly Jensen, *Mobilizing Minerva: American Women in the First World War* (Urbana: University of Illinois Press, 2008), and her biography of Esther Pohl Lovejoy, *Oregon's Doctor to the World: Esther Pohl Lovejoy and a Life in Activism* (Seattle: University of Washington Press, 2012).

The standard source on the Sheppard-Towner Act, Robyn Muncy, *Creating a Female Dominion in American Reform 1890–1935* (New York: Oxford University Press, 1991), is too eastern, so I was especially grateful for the generosity of Katharine Nehls, "Red-Tape Fraternities: The Rise of Rockefeller Populism" (PhD dissertation, University of Georgia, forthcoming), and Jennifer Hills, "Midwives in Montana" (PhD dissertation, Montana State University, forthcoming), for sharing their research with me.

For political women, see Sandra Haarsager, *Bertha Knight Landes of Seattle: Big-City Mayor* (Norman: University of Oklahoma Press, 1994). For the political women in Umatilla, see the young adult book by Darleen Bailey Beard, *Operation Clean Sweep* (New York: Farrar Straus Giroux, 2004); Richard Cockle, "When Petticoats Ruled Umatilla," the *Oregonian*, March 7, 2012, p. B3; and Shelley Burtner Wallace, "Umatilla's 'Petticoat Government,' 1916–1920," *Oregon Historical Quarterly* 88:4 (Winter 1987), pp. 385–402.

For clerical women, see Margery W. Davies, *Woman's Place Is at the Typewriter: Office Work and Office Workers 1870–1930* (Philadelphia: Temple University Press, 1982); and for their new attitudes, Margaret Mead, *Blackberry Winter: My Earlier Years* (New York: Simon and

Schuster, 1972); but for the continuation of old behavioral expectations see Joan Sangster, *Transforming Labour*, p. 164.

For culture in the cities, see Mildred Tanner Andrews, *Washington Women as Path Breakers,* and her article, "Cornish School," HistoryLink. org,; and Ellen Van Volkenburg Browne and Edward Nordhoff Beck, eds., *Miss Aunt Nellie: The Autobiography of Nellie C. Cornish* (Seattle: University of Washington Press, 1964). Donna Evans unearthed the forgotten history of Mary Dodge, "Place Becomes Us: Kairotic Entelechy, Identification and Political Economy in Harney County, Oregon" (PhD dissertation, Washington State University, Pullman, 2011). Also Trudy Flores and Sarah Griffith, "Portland Junior Symphony," Oregon History Project, www.ohs.org/education/oregonhistory/historical_records/dspDo...; Paula Becker, "Photographer Imogen Cunningham opens her first portrait studio in Seattle in September 1910," HistoryLink.org; and "Emily Carr," The Canadian Encyclopedia, www.the canadianencyclopedia.com/articles/ emily-carr.

On farmers and homesteaders, see Walter Nugent, *Into the West: The Story of its People* (New York: Random House, 1999); Alice Day Pratt, *A Homesteader's Portfolio* (New York: Macmillan, 1922; reprint, with an introduction by Molly Gloss, Corvallis: Oregon State University Press, 1993); Barbara Allen, *Homesteading the High Desert* (Salt Lake City: University of Utah Press, 1987); Elaine Lindgren, *Land in Her Own Name: Women as Homesteaders in North Dakota* (Norman: University of Oklahoma Press, 1996); interview with Ione Adair by Sam Schrager, February 24, 1977, Latah County Oral History Project, Latah County Historical Society, Moscow, Idaho; and Carol Ryrie Brink, *Strangers in the Forest* (New York: The Macmillan Company, 1959). See also Molly Gloss's own imaginative recreation of the experience of a woman homesteader in *The Jump Off Creek* (New York: Houghton Mifflin Harcourt, 1989).

For Christine Quintasket, see Jay Miller, ed., *Mourning Dove: A Salishan Autobiography* (Lincoln: University of Nebraska Press, 1990); and Dee Garceau, "Mourning Dove: Gender and Cultural Mediation," in Theda Perdue, ed., *Sifters: Native American Women's Lives* (New York: Oxford University Press, 2001).

The Pendleton Round-Up story is in Renee M. Laegreid, *Riding Pretty: Rodeo Royalty in the American West* (Lincoln: University of Nebraska Press, 2006); also see Steve Wursta, *From Cheyenne to Pendleton: The Rise and Fall of the Rodeo Cowgirl,* DVD, Arctic Circle Productions, Bend, OR.

For automobile tourism, see Hal K. Rothman, *Devil's Bargains: Tourism in the Twentieth-Century American West* (Lawrence: University Press of Kansas, 1998); and Sinclair Lewis, *Free Air* (New York: Harcourt, Brace, Howe, 1919; Bison reprint, University of Nebraska Press, 1993).

Chapter 9
Home Fires 1930–1945

Preceding page: USO women and soldiers, 1940s (Tacoma Public Library, D14000-1A)

We are accustomed to thinking of the fifteen years from 1930 to 1945 as encompassing two separate and distinct events: first a long anxious Great Depression, followed by the powerful, united effort of World War II. Viewed through the eyes of individual women, however, the two events were more alike than different, connected as they were by anxiety and domestic concerns. The double blows of depression and war required most women, whatever their personal aspirations, to focus on the immediate needs of their own families. They suddenly were needed to meet the same responsibilities for household food production and emotional maintenance that had defined their grandmothers' lives. As the Depression deepened, women simply had no choice but to keep the home fires burning, as the popular World War I song had it. They were needed at home, and when Canada and the United States entered World War II, they were needed both at home and in the workplace. Even in the shameful case of the wartime internment of Japanese families living in British Columbia, Washington, and Oregon, women were called upon to fill a domestic role as best they could in hostile circumstances. Measured by the aspirations for freedom, autonomy, and political equality that some women had felt in the 1920s, these two decades were a step backward. But looked at another way, they exemplified a familiar female strength, the ability to adapt to meet an obvious need. Now what counted were their basic domestic skills: Could a woman feed her family?

As the United States slowly slid into the Depression between 1930 and 1932, families everywhere had to consider how to live. Hidden in the truism that farm families could feed themselves even in the worst of times were important implications for women's lives. William Robbins's study of Coos Bay, *Hard Times in Paradise*, gives a graphic sense of the effects of the Depression in one particularly verdant region of southwestern Oregon. Combining the bounty of farms and of the ocean with poached wildlife from the forests, there was enough for everyone to eat. As one resident, Eleanor Anderson, recalled, "People [read: men] went without work" as logging operations, sawmills, and commercial fisheries closed down, but, she said, "I don't think anybody starved." They worked hard for what they ate. To feed families that were often enlarged by city-dwellers returning home, women preserved the produce of large gardens and butchered and smoked or canned chicken, pigs, and cows. Coos Bay resident Cliff Thorwald vividly remembered the urgency to preserve sudden surfeits of bounty to last through the winter: "You can imagine the work—cut up and can, cut up and can." Women did most of this work, and organized the rest, and still had to find a way to buy flour, salt, and sugar at the store. Barter was common, and store-bought clothing a rarity. Women dug out their old treadle sewing machines to provide clothes for their families. But this was no rural idyll: life was hard and anxious, and the future uncertain.

During the Depression it was often said that farm people were better off than many urban dwellers because they could grow their own food. But what good was it to be able to feed yourself if you couldn't pay your taxes? As one desperate woman wrote to the governor of Montana after the local bank failed and wiped out their savings, "Can you advice me what to do we have always payed our honest debts when we could raise the money to do so, it was never spent for finery I am not to [sic] nice to wear cast off short and overalls of my husbands and work in the field. If only we could raise a crop again we could live."

Anxious as life was in the country, it was much worse in the cities. The Great Depression bore down hard on urban life. Before considering the special miseries of city life in the 1930s, one pertinent reminder is necessary: before the Depression, most Americans still lived close to the poverty line. As Robert and Helen Lynd discovered in 1924 when they investigated Muncie, Indiana (aka Middletown), fully 85 percent of workers paid no income tax because their earnings were so low. Now their lives suddenly became worse.

As early as 1930, Seattle and Portland suffered unemployment rates of 25 percent, and the traditional charities founded by women a generation earlier were overwhelmed by requests. In both locations, city and state responded with a range of bond-financed public works projects and stepped-up efforts to find jobs for unemployed men. These were substantial local self-help efforts, but their limits soon became clear as the economy continued to worsen.

Everywhere in the Greater Northwest the progression was the same: as women's private charities were overwhelmed, committees of civic leaders and businessmen stepped in, with their presumably superior organizing skills, to meet the growing need, only to be overwhelmed in turn. This led, in 1932 and 1933, to the frightening militancy of large numbers of men in marches and protests. Seattle's Unemployed Citizens League led a march of the unemployed on the state capitol at Olympia in 1932 and were only turned back from a second march in 1933 (the Depression's nadir) by a group of vigilantes. In Portland, a group of World War I veterans originated the Bonus March in the spring of 1932, eventually numbering twenty-five thousand by the time they reached Washington, where their request for an immediate bonus was voted down by Congress and their camp in Anacostia destroyed by the US Army.

In British Columbia, when unemployment hit 28 percent in 1931(the highest in Canada), the provincial government established relief camps for unemployed men to work on roads and other public works for $7.50 a month. The camps were built in remote locations, with the deliberate intent, as one planner admitted, to draw men away from Vancouver and Victoria where they might fall prey to "red" agitators. This strategy backfired, for unemployed married men and their wives responded with large marches and demonstrations in the cities to protest work that would require their enforced separation. And the protests continued. In May 1938 over a thousand unemployed men flooded the streets of downtown Vancouver and occupied the post office until evicted by tear gas. Still, relief continued to be inadequate, and there was never any provision for unemployed women at all. Female applicants were advised to go into domestic service or, as several women reported, rejected with the comment that "with their figures they shouldn't have to seek relief."

One consequence of this sorry record in British Columbia was the sudden rise of an avowedly socialist party, the Co-operative Commonwealth Federation, which elected three people to the Vancouver City Council and, a year later, added the first woman, the redoubtable Helena Gutteridge. In this capacity, Gutteridge continued fighting for working women as she had been since before World War I.

While all this was going on, individual women all over the Greater Northwest carried the burden of feeding and clothing their families with whatever resources were available. This was a vital role, but a nearly invisible one, consisting of many small economies: buying day-old bread or baking at home, using cheap cuts of meat or none at all, making clothes at home rather than buying from the store, doing the laundry rather than sending it out, taking in boarders or moving in with others. The credo was "Use it up, wear it out, make it do, or do without." Many women had always practiced some of these economies, but in the 1930s they did so with contrasting memories of the flood of new consumer goods of the 1920s. They were helped by, or helped to organize, food banks, soup kitchens, hand-me-down clothing distributions, and other relief efforts.

Often, the help of others was crucial. As a woman interviewed in Cheney, Washington, in the 1980s recalled: "Two winters my husband was out of work and Marion Bair [who owned the local IGA store] carried us through groceries for the winter. This day and age, you can't find any grocery store that will give you credit. . . . Thank goodness to Marion Bair, we made it through these two winters."

The Depression raised another, more private, issue for some women. As one Bellingham woman recalled, "If there was one tragedy that could befall a young married woman, it was to find yourself pregnant. Believe me, there was no help. I was in this position and I went to the welfare. They told me to go select a doctor. I said, 'How will I pay.' 'Don't pay.' What about the hospital? 'Have your baby at home.'" Another woman chimed in: "There were many woman who had abortions. They just couldn't afford to have children. . . . There were a couple of doctors here in town who would perform these abortions illegally, and in those cases the women were safe. But there were literally hundreds of abortions performed by unqualified people and there were deaths in this town of young mothers who had these abortions. But they had very little choice; these were the kinds of things that they had to face."

The experience of pregnant women in Bellingham was not unusual. As Diane Sands documented in a Montana oral history project, although abortions were illegal, they could be obtained either through referrals from one's family doctor or, as Rickie Solinger has shown, in the big cities such as Missoula and Portland, from abortionists who operated openly as the local police looked the other way. This was a predictable state of affairs in an era where contraception was rarely available or practiced. Birth control was still new and controversial. Some middle-class women used the diaphragm popularized by Margaret Sanger, but it required the extra expense of a visit to the doctor to have it individually fitted. Men rarely wore condoms, and they were not easily available.

Into this anxious time came the blast of optimism and innovation that characterized Franklin Delano Roosevelt's first term as president of the United States in 1933. New Deal programs, when they began to arrive that same year, were astonishing in their novelty, variety, and level of support. The range of public works projects—from the trail-building of the young men of the Civilian Conservation Corps (CCC) deep in the woods to the mural-painting and guidebook-producing efforts of the artists and writers of the Works Progress Administration (WPA)—was unprecedented, as were the amounts of money involved. At one point, it was estimated, a quarter of the residents of Montana were receiving some kind of federal payment, and in 1939, when the numbers were added up, the state had received more than $530 million in federal loans and grants, or almost one thousand dollars for every Montanan. There was no New Deal in Canada, which explains the continuing history of protest in British Columbia, which persisted until September 1939 when Canada, as a member of the British Empire, immediately declared war against Germany at Britain's side.

By their very nature, public works programs provided work to able-bodied men. There were many fewer programs for women; the most common were sewing rooms where women made uniforms and other simple clothing, and stuffed mattresses. Nurses and home aides found limited opportunities in federal health programs, and some professional women worked in libraries and other WPA programs. But nearly all New Deal work programs were for men, because the underlying assumption was that men worked and women kept house for them. Indeed, women with jobs were urged to quit them so that a man could be employed. Seattle school-teachers not only experienced several pay cuts, but also were admonished that if they married they would be forced to give up their job to a man. As a result, some teachers married secretly, needing the income to support an unemployed spouse.

In the Greater Northwest, the major occupations—mining, lumbering, fishing, and agriculture—had always been male-dominated. And it was also true that the loss of work—at one point, more than eight thousand Butte miners were laid off, and in other cities unemployment rates hit 25 percent—was a serious blow to male egos. Many men's identities were tied to the manly nature of their work and to their family roles as breadwinners. Thus the policy, from the federal level to the local one, of providing work for men was understandable. But efforts like Seattle's decision to fire women teachers were fruitless. Occupations had always been gender-segregated, and there was a clear line between "men's work" and "women's work." Firing women in a female-dominated profession like teaching was pointless, and many Seattle schools found themselves hiring substitute teachers from the very ranks of the married teachers who had been forced to resign. Equally striking were the contradictions in staffing relief programs at the federal and state levels. Social work was another female-dominated occupation, and all over the country young women with the appropriate degrees found themselves directing the programs that provided relief to older unemployed men, sometimes their own fathers and husbands.

As the Depression wore on, the jobs in the private sector that became available were not in manufacturing or other "men's work" but in office work and other female occupations. Women, married and otherwise, quietly took poorly paid and often part-time jobs, in offices and service industries, that could help support their families. Women in more visible positions often encountered discomfort or outright opposition at home. Unemployed men were embarrassed to have their wives work, and that could be a difficult pressure for a woman to resist. Montanan Eva MacLean, who got a job cooking for a WPA dormitory for rural schoolchildren, thrived as she went on to became a supervisor in a WPA recreation program until she realized how resentful her husband was of her success. Realizing that "I must either give up my 'career' or my family," she quit her position to follow her husband's uncertain job prospects in another state.

Perhaps Eva's husband left Montana to try his luck at Grand Coulee Dam on the Columbia River, the widely celebrated huge public works project that became the symbol of the New Deal in the Pacific Northwest. When construction of the dam began in 1934, men flocked to the site in north-central Washington, at first living in tents and shanties until the company built barracks and a giant mess hall. Most were single or left their wives behind, but there doubtless were women like Mary Clearman Blew's sister, Sylvia, who lived in a shanty with her husband on another big dam project at Fort Peck in Montana. They lived in a "boomer settlement" of tar-paper shacks. Soon there were more than enough children for a school, and Sylvia, a veteran rural schoolteacher, substitute taught one day a week. Otherwise, there were few jobs for women, except, of course, in the brothels that sprang up in the inevitable red-light district, which at Grand Coulee went by the name of B Street. Probably, as in the nineteenth-century gold rush towns, there were women owning or cooking in restaurants and running boardinghouses, but their activities appear not to have been recorded.

At Grand Coulee, more than three thousand people were moved because their farms and livelihoods would be drowned by the massive reservoir created by the dam. A number of them were Indians who lost not only their homes but also an important site of social and spiritual power,

Kettle Falls, a traditional gathering place for salmon fishing. Because the dam was built without fish ladders, from then on there were no longer any salmon on the upper Columbia.

On another front, however, the 1930s marked a major change in Indian policy. The shocking mortality rate on reservations demanded a response, which came first in 1928 when the US government published a research report by Lewis Meriam that was a wholesale condemnation of reservation health services and administration in general. In 1934, in the so-called Indian New Deal, the Indian Reorganization Act became law. Spurred at least in part by commissioner of Indian Affairs John Collier's own appreciation of Native culture, the act returned some autonomy and some Dawes Act lands to Indian peoples. Collier also moved to close Indian boarding schools and keep children at home and encouraged the US Public Health Service to begin programs on reservations. The Indian Reorganization Act marked the beginning of the reassertion of tribal sovereignty and cultural revitalization, but at the time, because it required tribes to vote on whether the new terms should apply to them, it precipitated bitter arguments and deep divisions between those who wanted to cling to the meager benefits available and those who wanted a fresh start. For example, in Oregon, only the Grande Ronde and Warm Springs tribes voted to accept Collier's plan. Significant as it was historically, the Indian New Deal had nothing to offer the Indians displaced by Grand Coulee.

Salmon and Indians were frankly not of concern at Grand Coulee in the 1930s. What was important was building the dam, then the largest concrete structure in the world, in the fastest possible time. Men worked day and night; pictures of the busy floodlit twenty-five-square-mile worksite were impressive, and the numbers were awe-inspiring: when the project finally ended in 1943, it was estimated that 152 million man hours had gone into Grand Coulee, and over twelve thousand men and women had worked on the dam, with seventy-four hundred employed at the same time at the height of the project. Built on a scale that matched the biggest he-man legends of the Pacific Northwest, Grand Coulee was, as Woody Guthrie celebrated in song, "The Mightiest thing ever built by man."

There were, of course, women who worked at Grand Coulee, in spite of the company's initial protestation that there were no "suitable quarters for female employees." The handful of women initially hired to do secretarial work grew as the project went on; women were hired as waitresses and cooks when the mess hall opened in 1935; they taught at the school in the company town of Mason City; and one woman, complete with hard hat, even breached the all-male construction zone in 1938 to operate a switchboard within the work area.

Originally, the rationale for Grand Coulee was the same as for other arid lands dams: irrigation for the vast interior of Washington state, which could not be successfully farmed without more water. But when Grand Coulee's turbines came online in 1941, their power was immediately harnessed for the war effort: power for the aluminum plants that supplied the materials for Boeing airplanes and for the mystery industry being built in central Washington that we now know as the Hanford Nuclear Reservation. Begun in top secrecy in 1943, Hanford produced the plutonium used in the first test explosion at Alamogordo in 1945, and for the second atomic bomb dropped on Nagasaki in August of that year.

The building of Hanford and of Grand Coulee Dam, a decade apart, had striking similarities. Both began by displacing settlers. At Hanford, fifteen hundred people were moved with a month's notice and no explanation; most were white farm families, for whom (as opposed to Indians) disregard of their wishes was a new and shocking experience. Following that, large crews of men performed heroic construction feats in record time, a process well documented in the Grand Coulee case and completely secret at Hanford, where most of the workers had no idea what they were working on. They lived in barracks with a communal mess hall, which provided some of the first jobs for women—and the first need for women's housing. Margaret Hoffarth, a widow with three children, was one of the first waitresses in the mess hall and one of the first to live in the quickly constructed women's barracks, which were surrounded by a barbed wire fence and had a guard at the gate. Another woman, Jane Jones Hutchins, who came with her sister by bus from Kansas in 1943 on the rumor of "these fabulous salaries they were paying," immediately got a job as a secretary. She too recalled the women's barracks, complete with a house mother and a fence: "I look back now and realize this was a free country, but we were living behind barbed wire at Hanford, all to protect womanhood." She vividly remembered why the protection was necessary: there were so few women that the pressure on them was enormous. "Hanford could either make you or break you. Gals who had never had male attention before were, you know, popular. You could either become a slut . . . or you could become very strong and be able to say 'No.'"

The Hanford men's camp had a rough reputation. The night life, Hutchins said, was "wild and woolly, for a 22-year-old kid who had lived in Kansas all her life." Because Hanford was so isolated and the need to retain workers so urgent, the management arranged entertainment nearly every night of the week of big bands, sporting events, and films. Still, every time the famous so-called termination winds blew into sandstorms, they lost hundreds of workers who quit (terminated) on the spot. As the residents could testify, dust storms were not just a Great Plains phenomenon.

Soon, in addition to the barracks, a huge trailer park with over four thousand privately owned trailers took shape. Opal Drum, who with her two daughters followed her husband Frank from Oklahoma to Hanford, remembers it fondly: "The Hanford trailer camp was wonderful. . . . It was policed, it was kept clean, they had great big bath houses. . . . The school was good. . . . It was a marvelous place to live." Then, beginning in 1943, the town of Richland was built to replace the original Hanford camp. Built army-style, with dormitories surrounding a hospital, a post office, and a small commercial strip, the town's residential areas consisted of one- and two-story prefabricated duplexes. Louise Cease remembered: "When we first came here, it was kind of wild. There was nothing here. The sand was knee-deep. . . .We had a lot of fun in that one-bedroom prefab. Everybody was from all over the country and didn't know anybody. So, you got acquainted real easy. The neighbors would come in for breakfast when Bill came home from the graveyard shift. They would come in at night when he was on the swing shift. We would have dessert together."

In striking contrast to the acclaim garnered by the gathering of workers at Grand Coulee and later at Hanford, Depression-era refugees from the Dust Bowl faced a chilly reception in the Greater Northwest. Washington and Oregon experienced an estimated in-migration of almost two hundred thousand people in the years 1935 and 1936, fleeing the Dust Bowl on the northern Great Plains. Less than a quarter of the new migrants were farmers, yet such was the power of the agrarian myth that at least half of them tried their hand at farming in the Pacific Northwest. Ironically, many of the new migrants tried to make a go of it on marginal land already abandoned by previous owners. In the Puget Sound area, migrants were lured by land companies and local boosters to establish "stump farms" on the cutover land left after timber companies had logged off the land, leaving stumps and debris behind. The quality of the soil was poor, and most migrants never made anything more than subsistence living out of the lands, if that. As Richard White caustically notes, "In practice, subsistence was synonymous with poverty, and most of these farms produced neither adequate food nor provided adequate shelter for their owners."

A popular book of the time, *Stump Ranch Pioneer,* told the story of one family's migration from arid Colorado to a new life amid the stumps of the great forest that had covered northern Idaho. As Susan Swetnam remarks in her introduction to its recent republication, "The book is full of cheerful hope, depicting a sort of populist paradise of pioneer workers without unions, a place where Edenic conditions exist [i.e., everything grows] . . . and resilient human beings rise to them." In reality, most Dust Bowl migrants found harsh conditions and hostile local people who were unwilling to welcome strangers. This was uncharacteristic for a region that viewed itself as underpopulated and had generally welcomed (white) newcomers.

The welcome mat had not been extended to nonwhite migrants before the Depression. In 1924, the United States Congress drastically changed the rules governing immigration. The National Origins Act heavily favored immigrants from northern Europe and imposed an "Asiatic Barred Zone" that ended all immigration from Asia. British Columbia completely prohibited Chinese immigration in 1923, a step beyond the restrictions that both countries had put in place in the 1880s. But in the eyes of many whites, the Asian menace had simply changed nationality and was now Japanese rather than Chinese. By the time of the 1924 Immigration Act, twenty-two thousand Japanese lived in British Columbia and another approximately twenty thousand in the Pacific Northwest.

Pioneered initially by single male migrants, the Japanese migration had better luck than the Chinese in creating communities of families. Although they too faced restrictions on immigration, their creative solution was to develop the "picture bride" system, in which traditional Japanese matchmakers arranged proxy marriages between women in Japan and their husbands in North America whom they knew only through photographs. Legally married by proxy in Japan, these women were allowed to immigrate to join their husbands, where they frequently found that their new husbands were older and less prosperous than they had claimed to be. Between 1909 and 1920, almost forty-five thousand Japanese women came to the United States to join their husbands. Another six thousand women joined their husbands in British Columbia before the practice was cut off in 1928. These Japanese families faced limited options: they could either farm marginal lands or operate a business in the Skid Row section of cities; they were not welcome elsewhere.

Seattle, Portland, Vancouver, and Spokane had sizable "Japantowns," but many Japanese were truck farmers who lived on the fringes of the region's cities. Prejudice against them, jump-started by earlier anti-Chinese feeling, grew rapidly. Japanese, classified as "aliens ineligible for citizenship," could not vote. All the Pacific Northwest states except Washington passed antimiscegenation laws forbidding white-Asian inter-marriage. Elsewhere in the nation these laws had been designed to prevent white-black marriages, but in the West the main targets had always been Asians—first Chinese, then Filipino, and now Japanese. In the cities, housing laws restricted Japanese to residence in Skid Row sections, while in the countryside the immigrant generation (known as Issei) was barred from owning land.

Within this restrictive framework, and clustered in their own communities, many Japanese nevertheless thrived. Monica Sone, whose parents began managing a "flophouse" in Seattle's Skid Row in 1918, remembers a rich, eventful, and confusing childhood in which she shuttled back and forth between the public school, where she played with her schoolmates like "a jumping, screaming, roustabout Yankee," to Nihon Gakko, the Japanese language school, where "I suddenly became a modest, faltering, earnest little Japanese girl with a small timid voice." Expecting to attend the University of Washington, as her brother had before her, Sone nevertheless bowed to her father's decision to send her to business school instead. Even this training was a gamble, for Japanese American women were barred from clerical jobs in prewar Seattle. Completing the two-year course in one year, Sone then unexpectedly found herself hospitalized for nine months in a tuberculosis sanatorium. Ironically, during this enforced stay she made her first close friends who were not Japanese. Recovering, and with a widened perspective, she looked forward to the future. But then came December 7, 1941.

In the farming community of Hood River, Oregon, the Yasui family lived a rural version of Monica Sone's Seattle experience. Masuo Yasui first came to the United States as a teenager in 1904 to join his father and brothers to work on a railroad crew. Later he worked as a houseboy in Portland, where he made it a point to learn English. In 1908 he moved to

Hood River, where he and his two brothers opened a general store catering to the hundreds of Japanese men who worked nearby in lumbering and in clearing the land for the apple orchards that were beginning to make Hood River famous. Soon some Japanese owned small plots of marginal land on which they practiced both orcharding and intensive farming. Strawberries did particularly well. Yasui, seeing opportunity, encouraged others to buy land, marry, and settle, and he followed his own advice. Although always a businessman, never a farmer himself, he began his own family.

In 1912, his wife-to-be, Shidzuyo, who had known Masuo in Japan, took advantage of the "picture bride" system to marry him by proxy in Japan and then sail to join him in Oregon. In the following years, the Yasuis had nine children, six boys and three girls, and Masuo became the acknowledged leader of the Hood River Japanese community. He was a land locater, a banker, a real estate agent, and a landowner himself. But the more successful he and the other Japanese were, the more alarmed some neighboring white farmers became. As one newspaper claimed in 1919, "Japanese farmers have swarmed into the Hood River valley like an army of conquest." Although in reality Japanese amounted to only 4 percent of the area's population, their high birthrates seemed to some to presage a demographic conquest yet to come. Thus not only Masuo's success as a businessman but also his thriving family were held against him. In 1923, the Oregon legislature passed an alien land law, preventing Issei like Masuo from owning land. But because his children were US citizens by birth, thenceforth he bought land in their names. The Yasui children were shaped to continue the family tradition of hard work: the boys worked as farm laborers during summer vacation from school, while the girls took over much of the domestic work from their mother. As the children grew, Shidzuyo increasingly helped out in the store and worked as a farm laborer herself (as did most of the other Japanese women). Weathering the Depression years by careful economizing, by 1941 the Yasui parents were looking forward to passing on their land to their children and to the professional success of some of them (one was a lawyer, two planned to become doctors).

For this successful family, the impact of Pearl Harbor was immediate. On December 12, 1941, the FBI took Masuo Yasui away. He was held incommunicado for two weeks, and his family did not know where he was. Then Masuo (and many other leading Japanese) were declared "potentially dangerous to the public peace and safety of the United States"

Fumiko Hayashida and daughter,
as they were evacuated from
their Bainbridge Island home
(Seattle Post-Intelligencer
Collection, Museum of History
and Industry, Seattle)

and interned for the rest of the war. Although he could write letters to his wife and family, they could not join him.

Shidzuyo and the two youngest children, Homer and Yuka, were interned at Tule Lake, California, along with older son Chop, with his wife and son. The conditions of the concentration camps—the harsh environment, the barbed wire fencing and armed guards, the crowding, the lack of privacy—were hard on everyone. As one internee later commented: "Evacuees ate communally, showered communally and defecated communally." For Shidzuyo the lack of privacy would have been excruciating and the enforced idleness unnatural. She could not even feed her own family, the most basic of her accustomed responsibilities. The mess halls were a daily reminder of a lost culture: there they were served unpalatable, un-Japanese food in such crowded and rushed circumstances that families could never eat together.

Much has been written about the devastating effect of internment on Japanese men, who were robbed of their customary patriarchal role. But the impact on women was surely as great. Deprived of her accustomed family role, Shidzuyo experienced "leisure" but a complete loss of purpose. Probably only her continuing responsibilities to her absent husband and to her children allowed her to keep functioning. Unable to keep the family together in the internment camp, Shidzuyo carefully broke it apart. She applied for educational leave first for Homer, who moved to join an older sister in Denver and enrolled in the university there, and later for Yuka, only fifteen, who followed him there to enroll in high school. A few months later, she applied for leave for herself, attaching four letters of recommendation from Hood River, all of which attested to the "excellent reputation" of this "good wife and cultured lady of high character." In May of 1943, after a year and a half of internment, Shidzuyo was allowed to go to Denver to join her children. On January 8, 1946 (almost five months after the end of the war), Masuo was released from detention. He never recovered from the experience of having his loyalty to the United States doubted.

Today the wartime incarceration of the Japanese who lived within 250 miles of the Pacific Ocean seems a barbaric violation of their civil liberties, but it seems wise to note how weak even our most vaunted institutions are in moments of popular fear. In 1943, one brave Japanese American, Gordon Hirabayashi, argued the legality of internment all the way to the Supreme Court—and lost.

The story was no better in British Columbia. There, all Japanese (two-thirds of whom were either Canadian-born or naturalized citizens) were rounded up and evacuated. The able-bodied men were sent to road-building and railroad maintenance camps, while wives and children went to old mining towns in the interior. More than two thousand were sent to work on sugar-beet farms in Alberta and Manitoba. One of the camps, the Lemon Creek Relocation Project, hired Helena Gutteridge as their welfare officer, where she fought officialdom (as she always had) to ease the plight of the incarcerated Japanese. The Japanese removal, Jean Barman reminds us, was "one of the greatest forced migrations in Canadian history, second only to the Acadians' expulsion from Nova Scotia" in the eighteenth century. The evacuation produced a classic of North American literature, Joy Kogawa's *Obesan*, a heart-wrenching novel that speaks to the emotional pain, anger, and confusion experienced by evacuees north and south of the international boundary. Following the war, the Canadian government refused to let the evacuees return to the West Coast until 1949, four years after the war's end. Japanese in British Columbia were offered the choice of settling east of the Rocky Mountains or repatriating to Japan. Over four thousand people, half of them Canadian-born, were deported to Japan. Originally, more had planned to follow, but the atomic devastation that ended the war in 1945—the bombs dropped on Hiroshima and

Nagasaki—changed their minds. One of those bombs was made in the Pacific Northwest at Hanford.

Today World War II is popularly called "the good war," and we honor the sixteen-million-strong "band of brothers" who fought for freedom all over the world. Doubtless the female relatives of those millions of men—the ones who survived and the ones who did not—shared the admiration and gratitude felt by the general public. But at the time, surely their main emotions were fear and anxiety: Will he be safe? Will he come home? What will I do if he doesn't? Indeed, there must have been more than one woman who saw the war as simply an extension of Depression anxieties by other and more drastic means.

The war years brought added domestic responsibility to many women. With their husbands overseas, women now bore sole responsibility for raising their young. Worries about food persisted, but in a new form: a national system of rationing for meat, flour, sugar, and milk. Every housewife had to figure out how to make the twelve ration points per person feed their family for the coming week. This kind of careful calculation was new and difficult. Urban housewives, encouraged by the government, found themselves growing their own food and canning the results, just as their rural sisters had done in the 1930s. Jean Barman describes wartime Vancouver as a place where "Victory gardens, war saving stamps, rationing cards and soldier's parcels became the motifs of everyday life." Shortages were everywhere: hemlines on women's skirts rose because of a shortage of fabric, but nylon stockings were unavailable, so pants (slacks) were somewhat more acceptable, although, of course, often home-sewn. Housing was in very short supply, and many found themselves "doubling up" with relatives or friends to save on rent. Money was in short supply too. In the face of shortages, the Depression habit of "making do" continued. The good news was that there were plenty of jobs available, if a woman could handle wagework on top of her domestic responsibilities. The bad news was that loved ones were no longer unemployed but in peril of their lives. One woman who found herself "roughing it," as her husband worked at Hanford, spoke for many when she said: "I didn't mind any of it, because Mac [her husband] was in this country, he was not overseas, I might not see him tonight but I at least would see him tomorrow night. So, I could take anything."

Nor were only men at risk. In an unprecedented step, women as well as men volunteered to serve in the military. Nationwide, nearly 350,000 US women served as nurses, as WACs (Women's Army Corps) and WAVES (Women Accepted for Volunteer Emergency Service) in the navy, and as WASPs (Women Airforce Service Pilots). All were originally described as auxiliaries, with members not full members of the military, entitled to less pay and fewer rights (especially pension rights) than servicemen. (This later changed for the WACs and the WAVES, but not until 1977 for the WASPs.) In British Columbia, an estimated twenty-six thousand women served in the equivalent Canadian military auxiliaries. The fear that had been so strong during the Depression, that women might claim male prerogatives, followed them into war. The persistence of this fear made the heavy recruitment of women into war industries all the more surprising. It was prompted by severe labor shortages.

The Greater Northwest was transformed by two basic wartime needs: massive military manpower and all-out defense production. Military forces flooded the region; in Washington alone, more than fifty army and navy bases were established or grew substantially. In Seattle, the Boeing Airplane Company, which had thirty thousand employees at the time of Pearl Harbor as it built B-17 bombers for Britain's Royal Air Force, grew another twenty thousand by 1944. As defense industries expanded, so did cities. Overall, Seattle's population nearly doubled, and Portland's the same. Five new aluminum plants, drawing on power from the Bonneville and Grand Coulee Dams, were built in the interior. In contrast to this massive urban growth, Idaho actually lost population during the war, as did other rural areas of the Greater Northwest. People were on the move—elsewhere.

Labor shortages soon developed; in response, West Coast war industries mounted nationwide recruiting campaigns. Kaiser Industries, with extensive shipyards in California and Oregon, targeted African Americans and other marginalized racial/ethnic groups as a labor source, sending almost two hundred recruiters to southern and Midwest cities and bringing thirty-eight thousand workers west on special "liberty" trains. As employment opportunity spread by word of mouth, the migration increased: eventually another sixty thousand workers made their own way to the sites of war industries. Among them were young men and women from the region's Indian reservations, who must have enjoyed the irony of actually being invited to *do* something, rather than disappear. Among their number were a young couple from Washington's Colville Reservation, John and Lucy Covington (she would later chair the tribal council), who worked in the Portland shipyards, and Adeline Skultka, a Haida woman from British Columbia who worked at Boeing and was a cofounder of the American Indian Women's Service League after the war.

Housing shortages were acute in Portland, site of major shipyards, and Seattle, home of Boeing, and in both cities, the small established black communities were overwhelmed by the newcomers. During the war years, the African American communities of both Seattle and Portland quadrupled, with consequences that took years to resolve. In Seattle, staid old-timers were shocked by blacks who had come straight from the segregated South and were heady with their escape from segregation and the prospect of good wages. As Melvina Squires summed it up: "These people were pretty conspicuous. They were loud, happy, and crude."

Recruitment of women into war industries was slow to get under way because of opposition from unions, which feared that women would undercut union salaries, and from owners, who objected to special training costs and refitting to adapt work routines to women's smaller size and strength. Managers at Boeing, for example, resented being caught between federal pressures for production and the resistance of male unions that were afraid that the "deskilling" required for mass employment of women would undercut union wage rates. As late as 1944, Boeing managers were still trying to limit the number of female employees, clearly agreeing with the sentiment voiced by Fortune magazine a year earlier: "We are a kindly, somewhat sentimental people with strong, ingrained ideas about what women should or should not do. Many thoughtful citizens are seriously disturbed over the wisdom of bringing married women into factories."

The recruitment of women was unprecedented, but it was also carefully calibrated to appear less radical than it really was. Already exhorted to do their part through domestic economies of all kinds, women were now encouraged to help their men by taking jobs in defense industries "for the duration." As one incentive, images of a well-groomed and remarkably clean Rosie the Riveter were suddenly everywhere: her overalls were tailored, her hair was protected by a neat bandana, and she handled her rivet gun easily while looking both attractive and determined. An even bigger incentive was wages at (nearly) men's rates, far above those available in traditional "women's work." Women flocked to welding jobs in the shipyards of Portland and Bremerton, Washington, and to jobs as riveters in Boeing plants. In 1944, the peak production year, women made up 46 percent of Boeing's fifty thousand workers, and in that same year they were nearly 30 percent of the workforce in the Kaiser shipyards of Portland, the highest percentage of any shipyard in the country.

Vancouver, British Columbia, was also an important site of wartime production, some of it "spillover" from Seattle. Vancouver had both shipyards and a government-financed expansion of Boeing-Canada that produced bomb bays for the B-29 aircraft being built in Seattle. Victoria and Vancouver suffered severe housing shortages as workers for defense industries poured in from rural areas and the prairie provinces. At the height of production, an estimated thirty thousand men and women worked in Vancouver and Victoria shipyards. Although the labor shortage opened doors for women in a number of British Columbia industries as well as in war industries, the numbers were not as great as in the Pacific Northwest, nor was there apparently a Canadian equivalent of the popular image of Rosie the Riveter. Perhaps because of a heightened Canadian awareness of the grim daily challenges of life faced by relatives on the British home front, Canadian war efforts had a sober tone missing from some US government war propaganda.

Nationally, in the United States, the female workforce increased by 50 percent, and, even more unusual, married women made up more than half of the new women workers. Still, almost 80 percent of married women remained at home, a testimony to custom and to the weight of the wartime domestic and volunteer responsibilities they bore. The Red Cross and other organizations counted on women, as they had in World War I, to send supplies to the troops. A Cheney, Washington, woman recalled: "During World War II, the women would do anything—like rolling bandages, tearing up their sheets, and all meet together at the church, or the school, or someplace and roll bandages and make slings and this kind of thing to send wherever—gloves and socks and a lot of things—to send overseas."

Most women took defense jobs because they needed the money. Soldiers were not particularly well paid, and although the government guaranteed a minimum of fifty dollars per family, this was not enough as wartime inflation inexorably nudged food prices higher.

So how did women fare in their unaccustomed jobs? Amy Kesselman's study of women in the Portland shipyards, *Fleeting Opportunities,* brings the experience of these Pacific Northwest Rosie the Riveters alive by using voices from an extensive oral history project undertaken in 1981 by the Northwest Women's History Project.

Etta Harvey had been working as a waitress, but when the Kaiser shipyards began to recruit and train women as journeyman welders in 1942, she, like others, found the wages "unbelievable," and signed up. Besides, she said, "I had a son to raise and I also wanted to prove that women were reliable and capable." Training took from ten days to four weeks, and then it was straight to the construction sites at Portland's Swan Island.

The first challenge was mastering the job. Sheer determination carried Edna Hopkins through training:

> One day my instructor, he comes along, and he took my stinger out of my hand and raised my [welding] hood, and the tears were just rolling down, you know, and he says, "Edna, what in the world are you crying for?" I said, "just look at all these burns." And he says, "Well, why don't you quit if it bothers you that much?" I said, "No, I'm bound and determined that I'm going to do this."

The work was cold, exhausting, and challenging. LuRayne Culbertson remembered:

> I think I cried myself to sleep the first week I was in the shipyards. "What have I done, how did I ever get into this mess? I didn't know it was going to be like this . . . " Physically, mentally, everything—that was tough for complete greenhorns to go out on large construction and not know what on earth you're getting into. You, I mean sure, you're going to be a welder, you get a little plate like this and you weld it, and all of a sudden you go out there and see a big ship with all these cranes and operations and what-not and noise—it's just hard to imagine.

An added pressure for African American women was that although they had been recruited to work in the shipyards, the Boilermakers Union balked at admitting them to the welding program. Most ended up working as helpers and sweepers, which were unskilled and especially dirty jobs that paid lower wages than those received by welders. Beatrice Marshall recalled: "Our first day at the shipyard, after we came out of the holes from the work, I really was embarrassed to get on the bus to go back home because of the condition of our clothes. We was just nothing but rust and dirt in our hair, just all over."

Almost all African American women experienced racial hostility, for few white Americans at the time had any experience with black people except as segregated and subordinate workers. An additional burden for black women was the disapproval they encountered at the same time from some members of the small and staid prewar black communities. Seattle's La Etta King might have been speaking of Marshall when she said, "I know I was quite ashamed of them. They looked so bad. Women wearing . . . jeans . . . and their heads tied up with a handkerchief." Before the war, always dressing well and looking respectable was one small way that African American women contributed to community pride. It must have seemed to King like an affront to community standards to see black women proudly wearing the practical clothing they needed for their wartime jobs, never mind that Rosie the Riveter dressed the same!

Another issue for all women was coping with men who were hostile to having women in the workforce or for whom the opportunity for a quick feel was irresistible. Sometimes the men got more than they expected: "This fellow came up and took hold of my ankle and without even thinking I just brought that hammer right down on his hard hat and knocked his glasses off and broke them. That was the only time anybody ever tried anything," Leona Ellis recalled, but some women had a much more difficult time and often found that complaints to supervisors were rejected. Frequently when a woman quit it was not because she couldn't do the job but that she couldn't find a way to stop the harassment. It is clear, from other accounts, that the harassment was worse than the Portland women acknowledged. Retrospective interviews from Boeing reported frequent harassment and sexism, as well as chauvinism: "Women were considered too stupid to know how to do anything," one woman remembered, and another said: "I had to work with a man who had never had a woman helper before. . . . He hated me."

Most frequently when women quit it was because they couldn't deal with the pressures of the double day, as LuRayne Culbertson recalled:

> A typical workday was getting up at six in the morning, fixing breakfast, taking the baby to the Fruit and Flower mission . . . catching the bus, going out to Oregon Ship, welding eight hours,

dashing home, Pap'd pick up the baby, I'd get cleaned up and take off for my waitress job at Nendel's and he'd take care of the baby. Then I'd come home at midnight and wash out the diapers and hang them up.

Marketing was a constant headache, because few grocery stores were open late enough for working women to shop. Child care was a constant worry, for on top of the problem of finding a reliable provider, common childhood illnesses, in a world before antibiotics, could mean either quarantine (for contagious diseases like measles) or long recovery times. Consequently, absentee rates for working mothers at the Kaiser shipyards at Swan Island were much higher than those of men (13.3 percent for women, 9 percent for men).

Concerned about these rates, in 1943 Edgar Kaiser announced plans for large, well-equipped on-site day-care facilities, open twenty-four hours a day (to serve all three shipyard shifts), complete with an infirmary for mildly ill children, an immunization clinic, and a take-home food service. Parents paid five dollars for six days of day care, about a third of the actual cost. The remaining costs were paid by the federal government. The excellence and novelty of the Kaiser facilities attracted national attention and praise, but at the time the Kaiser day-cares were controversial, because the idea that mothers of young children should work was opposed by many people, including most social workers, many of whom were themselves women. Official US government policy discouraged the employment of women with young children until 1943, and the idea of government funding for day care had never even been considered before the war. Only wartime necessity overrode these deeply ingrained notions of appropriate work roles for women who were mothers.

When the war ended, so did women's work in the shipyards, sometimes abruptly. As one woman recalled:

The day the war ended, every woman in there got it. The lead man came 'round and says, "Frances, tonight you can hang your torch up. Your job's done. The war's over." And on that day, I picked up a piece of scrap iron and lit my torch and wrote my name on it—my proof for my grandchildren and great-grandchildren that I really was a burner in the wartime.

War work had always been understood to be temporary, "for the duration," by the labor unions that carefully guarded the job rights of their
(male) members when they returned from the service. And women workers themselves knew that neither the government nor Kaiser Industries
planned to continue to build ships once the war ended. Many women were
glad to quit, eager for their men to come home and to enjoy with them
the pleasures of family life. Even the considerable number of women who
planned to continue working understood why *this* job would end, but they
hoped they could use their wartime skills to get other jobs at good wages.
They were wrong: the old division of "men's work" and "women's work,"
with its sharp difference in wage rates, reasserted itself with a vengeance.
In some cases, women's war work counted against them. One woman was
denied a job because, the personnel manager said, "I want a woman's work
record. You've never had a woman's job," he said, adding that her war
work was "to us like you have never worked."

For years, the heroic history of women's war work was all but forgotten. When the Northwest Women's History Project began their interviews
with former shipyard workers in 1981, one woman commented, "I thought
I'd die before someone remembered me." Today, these wartime women are
deservedly celebrated, but we must not forget all the other uncelebrated
women who stayed at home and kept the home fires burning. The story
of most of the Greater Northwest's women in the 1930s and 1940s was
a domestic one, with all of its anxieties and mundane detail. Once again,
women provided stability and continuity for their families and communities in uncertain and troubled times.

SOURCES FOR THIS CHAPTER

For a general narrative about the Great Depression, see William H. Mullins,
*The Depression and the Urban West Coast, 1929–1933: Los Angeles, San
Francisco, Seattle and Portland* (Bloomington: Indiana University Press,
1991). It is much harder to find accounts about women. Many of the details
of their Depression lives are in oral histories. See William Robbins, *Hard
Times in Paradise: Coos Bay, Oregon, 1850–1986* (Seattle: University of
Washington Press, 1988); Dixie Massengale, Norma Smith, and Gertrude
(Lee) Swedberg, eds., *Community Builders: Women of a Small College
Town* (Cheney, WA: Cheney Free Press, 1983); Phyllis W. Bultmann,
ed., *The Great Depression and Its Fifty-Year Shadow: Proceedings of a*

Conference Held at Western Washington University, November 1981
(Bellingham: Center for Pacific Northwest Studies, Western Washington
University, Occasional Paper #18, 1982); Diane Sands, "Using Oral History
to Chart the Course of Illegal Abortions in Montana," *Frontiers: A Journal
of Women Studies* 7:1 (1983); Rickie Solinger, *The Abortionist: A Woman
against the Law* (New York: Free Press, 1994); and Doris Pieroth, *Seattle's
Women Teachers of the Interwar Years: Shapers of a Livable City* (Seattle:
University of Washington Press, 2004). Jean Barman, *The West beyond the
West*, was my major source for British Columbia during the Depression.

For the New Deal, see Mary Murphy, *Hope in Hard Times: New
Deal Photographs of Montana, 1936–1942* (Helena: Montana Historical
Society Press, 2003); Mary Clearman Blew, *All But the Waltz: A Memoir
of Five Generations in the Life of a Montana Family* (Norman: University
of Oklahoma Press, 1991); Lawney L. Reyes, *B Street: The Notorious
Playground of Coulee Dam* (Seattle: University of Washington Press,
2008); Paul C. Pitzer, *Grand Coulee: Harnessing A Dream* (Pullman:
Washington State University Press, 1994); and S. L. Sanger, *Working on
the Bomb: An Oral History of WWII Hanford* (Portland: Portland State
University, 1995).

For Dust Bowl migrants, see John Blanchard, under the direction
of the Northwest Regional Council, Portland, Oregon, *Caravans to the
Northwest* (Boston: Houghton Mifflin, 1940); Richard White, *Land
Use, Environment, and Social Change: The Shaping of Island County,
Washington* (Seattle: University of Washington Press, 1980); and Nelle
Portrey Davis, *Stump Ranch Pioneer* (New York: Dodd Mead, 1942;
reprinted with an introduction by Susan Hendricks Swetnam, Moscow:
University of Idaho Press, 1990).

On Japanese immigration and internment, see Monica Sone, *Nisei
Daughter* (Seattle: University of Washington Press, 1953); Lauren Kessler,
*Stubborn Twig: Three Generations in the Life of a Japanese American
Family* (Portland: Oregon Historical Society Press, 2005); and Lise Yasui's
moving film, *Family Gathering*, which won many awards and was shown
on PBS as one of the American Experience series. Also Joy Kogawa,
Obesan (Toronto: Lester & Orpen Dennys, 1981; Boston: D. R. Godine,
1982); and Patricia E. Roy and John Herd Thompson, *British Columbia:
Land of Promises* (Toronto: Oxford University Press, 2005).

For World War II, see Richard W. Etulain and Michael P. Malone,
The American West: A Modern History, 1900 to the Present (Lincoln:

University of Nebraska Press, 2nd ed., 2007); "'Good Work, Sister!':
Women Shipyard Workers of World War II, an Oral History" (Portland:
Northwest Women's History Project, DVD, 2006), www.goodworksister.
org; Amy Kesselman, *Fleeting Opportunities: Women Shipyard Workers in
Portland and Vancouver during World War II and Reconversion* (Albany:
State University of New York Press, 1990); Quintard Taylor, *The Forging
of a Black Community*; Polly Reed Myers, "Boeing Aircraft Company's
Manpower Campaign during World War II," *Pacific Northwest Quarterly*
98:4 (Fall 2007); Karen Beck Skold, "The Job He Left Behind: Women in
the Shipyards during World War II," in Karen Blair, ed., *Women in Pacific
Northwest History: An Anthology* (Seattle: University of Washington
Press, 1988); and Karen Anderson, *Wartime Women: Sex Roles, Family
Relations, and the Status of Women during World War II* (Westport, CT:
Greenwood Press, 1981).

Chapter 10
Cold War Country 1950s

Preceding page: The promise of Columbia Basin farmland
(Oregon Historical Society, #bb012575)

When peace came in 1945, women in the Greater Northwest, like women elsewhere in North America, were ready to live the full family lives they had hoped for in 1929. Following the Great Depression and the dislocations of World War II, they looked forward to returning to normal at the war's end. Instead, they experienced some of the most rapid and wrenching changes in the region's history as progress, in the form of growth and development, reshaped urban and rural landscapes and expectations. At the same time that the Cold War remade the economy of the Greater Northwest, it also raised the fearful specter of nuclear war, fostering existential anxieties and suspicions that divided communities. Growth and development did indeed lead to widespread prosperity, but the underlying anxiety belied the apparent normality of the new forms of family and community life. Eventually, this paradox led some to question the nature of the domestic harmony of the postwar years.

After the delay caused by depression and war, the pent-up demand in 1946 for housing, consumer goods, and a chance to settle into personal life was overwhelming, and the federal government was ready to help. Following World War II, the Greater Northwest experienced the greatest population surge in its history: Portland doubled in size and Seattle tripled between 1940 and 1970, while the province of British Columbia grew 43 percent by 1955. Because almost all of the newcomers came not from other countries but from other states or provinces, much of the perceived remoteness of the region disappeared as the migrants themselves acted as a nationalizing force. At least part of the population growth in the Greater Northwest was caused by former servicemen who had seen the region for the first time during their military service and were attracted by the physical variety and beauty of the landscape, and the appealing outdoor life—camping, fishing, hunting—that it promised. No previous generation of young men (with or without their families) in the United States had been able to choose where they lived for leisure rather than work-related reasons. These former servicemen could, because they were supported at first by key national measures such as the GI Bill, which allowed seven million former soldiers to attend college, buy a home, or start a business, and provided a year of unemployment insurance to help them get on their feet. And they could afford to marry: the marriage rate, which had averaged a hundred marriages per thousand women in the 1920s and dropped to eighty-one in the 1930s now zoomed to 143. They could afford children, the famous baby boom cohort. In the period between 1946 and 1963, the fertility rate jumped from 2.0 to 3.8 children per woman. And men could find jobs in the region to support their families because federal defense spending generated by the Cold War turned out to provide more solid economic stability than the Greater Northwest had ever known before. With a few famous exceptions, such as the "Boeing recession" of 1970, defense-related spending has provided an ongoing economic base ever since.

The cities of the Greater Northwest, bursting with this new growth, sprawled outward into suburbs. Suburbanization was a national phenomenon, spurred by the inexpensive mass housing techniques used in Levittown and its many imitators, and by the automobile, which had been unaffordable or unavailable since 1929. The new suburbs attracted members of the new middle class, the families of veterans supported by the GI Bill and buoyed by postwar economic expansion. The suburbs were, however, initially closed to racialized groups such as African Americans or Asians. The Greater Northwest shared the national impulse toward suburban sprawl. By 1950, 40 percent of the residents of Seattle and Vancouver lived in suburbs; by 1980, two-thirds did. Portland's suburbs more than tripled in population in thirty years. Expanses of inexpensive tract housing provoked the instant scorn of old-time residents who deplored their architectural uniformity and lack of community. They were right about the first (although it didn't seem to matter to most of the residents) but wrong about the second. At this time of unprecedented affluence and anxiety, young couples sought a settled, secure, and traditional family life, and they worked together to achieve it in the new suburbs.

Young women were at the heart of suburban life. Working together with other young mothers like themselves, they built the networks that created a new kind of child-centered family life. As historians Rosalyn Baxandall and Elizabeth Ewen point out, "Women were the telephoners, organizers, and arrangers of community life," as indeed they had been in the community-building of Greater Northwest towns and cities in the nineteenth century. These customary female activities, albeit in a new setting, were apparently invisible to postwar critics, who claimed that Levittown and other much-studied suburbs were hives of uniformity and consumerism—that is, shaped by media forces, not by individual choices. Pacific Northwest historian Lorraine McConaghy did not make that mistake when she looked at the experiences of the young families who were the first occupants of the large unincorporated suburb named Lake Hills, across Lake Washington from Seattle.

The original residents of Lake Hills came from a variety of European ethnic backgrounds, but were overwhelmingly white. Most of the men were veterans, many with college degrees financed by the GI Bill, and three-quarters of them worked for Boeing, which, with federal defense financing, was expanding steadily. The women, 40 percent of whom were college graduates, were stay-at-home housewives with small children. The accepted breadwinner-housewife division of labor prevailed, with the important qualification that husbands and wives shared a commitment to building a new kind of community.

McConaghy's study, based on retrospective interviews with residents, described Lake Hills as a consciously child-centered community that "offered new opportunities for personal fulfillment and expression to men, women and children that the city and the country had not." Previously, in both city neighborhoods and in farming communities, these young adults would have grown up within existing adult networks, often inheriting a family identity whether it "fit" or not. In contrast, in the suburbs, as they met new people they were seen as individuals or (more likely) as "parents of," as they joined with others to create a new kind of community for their children.

The Lake Hills residents frequently thought of themselves as pioneers, believing, as the myth had taught them, that earlier western communities had been made up of random individuals rather than the family settlements that had actually been the Greater Northwest norm. These pioneers of the 1950s, surrounded by neighbors of similar age and economic circumstance, built community networks that expressed group norms. At the time, critics condemned suburbs as "conformist," but much of the conformity arose from the excitement of working together with like-minded people of one's own age for similar goals.

This postwar suburban community-building was fully as serious and permanent as that of previous generations, except for one new factor: mobility. In the early days, the new suburbs of mass-produced affordable homes (with mortgages guaranteed by the government) genuinely were democratic communities where social classes (although not races, and not poor people) and ethnicities mixed. But as historian Lizbeth Cohen has pointed out, increasing prosperity brought rising expectations, and the suburbs quickly stratified socioeconomically. Stable communities require permanent residents, but new job opportunities, or newer suburbs that offered larger houses or better schools, encouraged families to move up the social ladder, leaving their poorer neighbors behind. Ironically, the promise of a steadily expanding economy served to make each individual's commitment to each new community more temporary and encouraged them to view their houses as economic assets, not places of permanent residence. But in the immediate postwar years, when suburbs were new, the commitment to community-building was deep.

The suburbs provided a good home for new middle-class families that superficially resembled the traditional family, although their spirit was different. As family historian Stephanie Coontz points out, "The 1950s was the first time that a majority of Americans could even *dream* of creating a secure oasis in their immediate nuclear families" rather than looking to an extended family network. And, she goes on to say, the family of the 1950s was an *experiment* in family values: "For the first time, men as well as women were encouraged to root their identity and self-image in familial and parental roles." This commitment to family "togetherness" (to use a favorite '50s word) came closer to the fulfillment of the female dream of married life—a domesticated mother *and* father, secure finances, and healthy, well-tended children—than American families had ever achieved. And for women, the new consumer goods—first household appliances, later the flood of packaged foods—meant that domesticity no longer meant endless hours of household work, and left much more time for children than ever before. Thus, suddenly, the nature of domesticity shifted from the household production that had been so necessary during the Great Depression to consumption and child care.

The competing dreams that would spell the doom of "togetherness" and encourage personal and individual desires and ambitions were still only distant clouds on the horizon. Simone de Beauvoir's incisive analysis of discrimination against women, *The Second Sex*, was published in France in 1949 and translated into English in 1953 but was not widely read at the time. Most American women were unaware of sex discrimination until Betty Friedan published her own indictment, *The Feminine Mystique*, in 1963, but its instant popularity pointed to earlier, unnamed discontent. The year 1953 was important for another counter-dream: Hugh Hefner published the first issue of *Playboy* magazine, preaching the message that men could enjoy their greatest happiness as single men, enjoying the pleasures of sex and varied female companionship while escaping the "disaster" of marriage. Clearly, many men found *Playboy*'s message appealing, but widespread female willingness to join this male sexual fantasy had to wait until well into the 1960s, when the availability of contraception made intercourse less risky for them. In the meantime, marriage and many children were the overwhelming realities of the postwar years. Riding the wave of postwar economic growth and affluence, this was the promised "American way of life" that had to be defended against outside threat.

For however hopeful about the future these new postwar families might be, the Cold War years were also fearful ones. Real fears were generated by the possibility of nuclear war and the frightening "arms race" in nuclear weapons between the United States and the Soviet Union. This looming existential fear was fed by politicians, who warned of the internal threat from hidden subversives and from "deviants"—homosexuals, "communist sympathizers," free thinkers. The anticommunist hysteria we now call McCarthyism peaked nationally in the mid-1950s and deeply affected the Greater Northwest as well as the rest of the nation.

The most pervasive effect was on the young couples who were putting so much hope and effort into creating the new suburban families. According to historian Elaine Tyler May, Cold War anxieties led them to seek the security of their families all the more, and to shun individuals or ideas that seemed to threaten them. This included men and women who stepped outside the boundaries of standard sex role expectations as, for example, women who wanted to pursue careers instead of marriage. The popular idealization of domesticity and general social pressures deterred many young women from considering alternatives to marriage and motherhood. The first significant break in popular attitudes came in the mid-1950s, as mothers of high school–age children began entering the workforce as low-level clerical and office workers and educated middle-class women were encouraged to consider a career as a primary school teacher because it could be combined so easily with childrearing. Of course poor women had never stopped working, but media images were aimed at middle-class women, not at them.

If McCarthyism fostered family cohesion, it had a deeply divisive effect on community unity. In the suburb of Lake Hills, for example, a small number of members of the John Birch Society disrupted the school board and shattered the community consensus before their proposals were defeated. The academic community was seriously disrupted. When, for example, FBI director J. Edgar Hoover declared that college campuses were centers of "red propaganda," a wave of accusations, official hearings, loyalty oaths, and eventual faculty firings engulfed the University of Washington and other regional colleges as well.

The solidarity of some of the Greater Northwest's labor strongholds was shattered by anticommunist fears. Many unions were weakened by the anticommunist requirements in the Taft-Hartley Act of 1947 that stripped them of some of their best organizers and sowed suspicion about those who remained. In the mining town of Butte, Mary Orlich, president of the powerful Ladies Auxiliary of the International Mine Mill and Smelter Workers Union, was impelled to write to the *Saturday Evening Post* "I want to inform the women of America how their way of living is threatened. The commies are a common enemy, and the people don't know it." For questioning the loyalty of union men, Orlich was roundly denounced by a number of ladies auxiliaries, and union officials disparaged her, describing her as a "simple little housewife" who should not be "meddling in men's union affairs."

Julie Whitesel Watson remembered that as a high school student in Kellogg, Idaho, she joined an I Am An American youth group that very explicitly taught her the local dangers of subversion: "We believed it was the personal plot of Khrushchev and the Soviets to close down *our* lead and zinc mine and smelting operations in order to weaken our country. We believed the [local] union . . . , the International Mine Mill and Smelter Workers Union (Mine Mill) was infiltrated with Communists."

The result was a union election in which Mine Mill was replaced by a more compliant union just in time for contract talks with the Bunker Hill Company in 1960. The role of the company in whipping up anticommunist sentiment was never proved, but the fervor with which the youth group chanted "Better dead than red," surely played a role in the result.

The radical members of some other unions, among them longshoremen and cannery workers, were threatened by a provision of the McCarran-Walter Immigration and Nationality Act of 1952 that immigrants who had joined the Communist Party could be deported. Journalist Julia Ruuttila, who was then living in Astoria with her fourth husband, Oscar, immediately joined the Oregon Committee for the Protection of Foreign Born and was herself subpoenaed. Frustration still rises from the page as she recalled the House Un-American Activities Committee hearing in Seattle in November 1956:

> The hearings were all so ridiculous really. Part of the time you'd want to laugh—they were so hysterical, and meaningless, and senseless—and part of the time you'd want to swear and curse. . . .

I was on the stand for a day and a half. They asked all sorts of
questions. . . . I wanted to refuse to answer. You can answer a
question as to what your name is, but if you answer any other
questions you have to answer all questions or be found in contempt.

Because of that legality, Julia found herself taking the Fifth Amendment
(self-incrimination) even when only asked for her maiden name.

Characteristically, when Seattle activist and former Communist Party
member Hazel Wolf was arrested in 1949, accused of attempting to over-
throw the government by force and violence, she immediately cracked a
joke: "I must not have done a very good job!" Wolf fought deportation (to
Victoria, her birthplace) for fourteen long years, and finally won. Vindication
of a sort came unexpectedly in 1964 when, soon after she joined the Seattle
Audubon Society, she recalled that the very conservative president of the
organization called her and said, "I know you were in the Communist Party
and Communists are good organizers. I'd like you to come to board meetings." Wolf soon became the society's secretary, where she very effectively
organized environmental protests throughout the Pacific Northwest for the
next thirty years.

Although British Columbia never experienced a "red scare" like that in
the United States, it was gripped by its own brand of social conservatism.
The Social Credit Party, originally populist and vaguely socialist, turned
conservative under the leadership of W. A. C. Bennett, who first became
premier in 1952. Social Credit was uninterested in social reform. Instead,
Bennett promised residents "the good life" through development of natural resources and better transportation. His government built four dams
on the upper Columbia River and a huge dam (named after him) on the
Peace River in northern British Columbia. As in the United States, although
these projects involved both significant physical changes to the landscape
and relocation of people (usually Natives), they were justified by the belief
that increased energy production would lead to a higher standard of living
for everyone. These Social Credit policies were very similar to those of the
Eisenhower administration in the United States, with the difference that the
policies remained in place long after the 1950s, while the United States took
a different direction in the 1960s.

The transportation improvements of the 1950s throughout the Greater
Northwest facilitated the automobile tourism that was the hallmark

of what historian Susan Sessions Rugh tells us was the "golden age of American family vacations." Now that many people owned automobiles, the family road trip became possible, and touring the West's national parks and other wonders became almost a patriotic experience (along with the kids in the back seat asking "Are we there yet?"). Residents of the Greater Northwest hardly had to leave home to discover the pleasures of camping. All they needed was the right equipment: tents, sleeping bags, camp stoves, backpacks, fishing rods . . . the list goes on, and so did the small equipment companies who had catered to the small prewar market of climbers and mountaineers. This camping craze was one of the roots of the environmental movement, marking as it did the beginnings of a shift in viewing the land not as a source of work and income but as a site of pleasure, relaxation, and leisure.

It was partly to "put Seattle on the tourist map" that planners organized the successful Seattle World's Fair in 1962, demolishing entire city blocks to build gleaming white modernist structures, most famously the space needle, that still stand as city symbols. The world's fair was merely one of the plans to modernize the city. In common with cities all over the country, Seattle seized on the federal dollars in the Interstate Highway Act of 1956, first to build freeways that would bring suburbanites back to the city to do their shopping and then, in the process, to "redevelop" run-down and unsightly sections of the city where members of racial and ethnic groups lived. Usually "redevelopment" meant replacing substandard housing with roads, with little provision for alternative housing for the displaced.

In Seattle, some of these plans were stopped, or at least modified. Middle-class women and others who were members of the Audubon Society and historic preservationist groups coalesced into some of the first environmental protest groups. They came together first to oppose two projects in the heart of the city: the freeway that bisected downtown and a plan to demolish the Pike Place Market, where many of the produce vendors were members of racial/ethnic groups. They could not stop the freeway, but they "put a lid on it" by insisting on the public garden that now covers part of it, and they used historic preservation laws to save the Pike Place Market, now one of Seattle's main tourist attractions. The names of most of these early female environmental activists remain unknown, for the 1950s was a decade when male leadership of social protest groups was taken for granted even though women made up most of the membership.

Consequently, women's roles in the environmental movement (with the exception of famous national figures like Rachel Carson) are only just now beginning to be recovered. Equally, their limitations, in particular the failure to address the impact of redevelopment on racial/ethnic groups and the urban poor, are yet to be explored.

One Seattle woman might have been a member of these pioneering women's environmental groups had she not been otherwise engaged. Dorothy Stimson Bullitt was a member of a wealthy Seattle family. She probably expected to follow in the footsteps of her mother, Harriet Stimson, a cultural leader who had supported the Seattle Symphony, the Children's Orthopedic Hospital, the Seattle Art Museum, the Seattle Garden Club, and the League of Women Voters. Her daughter took a different path. Owing to the untimely deaths of her brother and her husband, Dorothy Bullitt became the head of the family and of the family property company in the early 1930s, in the depths of the Depression. At the time, wealthy businesswomen were rare indeed, and even more rarely treated seriously by men. As she recalled, "Sometimes I was treated as a strange animal. . . . Other times I was ignored, imposed upon, and disbelieved."

In response, Bullitt carefully honed a dignified, genteel persona, deliberately trading on her lack of experience by asking business contacts for information and advice in ways they found charming and unthreatening while effectively disguising her own determination and intelligence. In the 1950s, Bullitt's company published the *Seattle Magazine*, an influential monthly that expressed the new environmental concerns, so you might say that although she didn't walk in protest marches, she financed the talk. She directed company resources to FM radio in part because of her own love of classical music. Then, in the late 1950s, in a carefully prepared gamble, Bullitt pulled off the coup that stunned her male competitors, obtaining federal licenses that transformed her into the leading broadcaster in the Pacific Northwest, with five radio stations and three television stations in Seattle, Portland, and Spokane. Bullitt's hunch about the possibilities of television, still in its infancy, established KING TV as one of the key players that would transform Seattle from a provincial backwater to a fully modern city.

What did it mean to be a modern city? In contrast to Seattle, postwar Portland had no continuing defense contracts to sustain it. Instead, once the Kaiser shipyards closed, Portland found itself overcrowded, underemployed, crime-ridden, and corrupt. To clean up the mess, in 1948,

Portlanders overwhelmingly chose as mayor Dorothy McCullough Lee, only the second woman to be elected mayor of a major US city. The first had been Bertha Landes, mayor of Seattle from 1926 to 1928. Indeed, although Lee had a reputation as an able administrator, it was soon apparent that she shared Landes's by then outmoded belief in "municipal housekeeping," with its moralistic belief in social control that ill fit postwar notions of personal freedom. Like Landes, Lee attacked the visible signs of vice—shutting down brothels, burlesque houses, homosexual clubs, slot machines, and Chinese gambling dens—quickly earning the nickname of "Dottie-Do-Good." But she was attacking the symptoms, not the underlying economic cause, of Portland's stagnation. The real cause of Portland's troubles, the rising young politician Richard Neuberger argued, was that established businessmen rejected the modern belief in progress, growth, and development because they feared that rapid growth would attract racial/ethnic workers who would need low-cost housing and welfare measures that would add to the city budget and to taxes. Portland—or at least its businessmen—was hoping to return to a prewar "normal" that no longer existed. Lee's proposals—for a business tax, increased funding for schools, low-cost housing, and ending racial discrimination—were all rejected, not just by businessmen but by popular referenda as well. And so, in 1952, was Lee herself. Like Landes, she was a one-term mayor. As for all those workers who had flooded into Portland to work in war industries, some civic leaders hoped they would just go away.

In fact, the workers they feared were already there. During the war, thanks to vigorous recruiting by Kaiser Industries, the African American population of Portland had skyrocketed from two thousand to more than twenty thousand. The newcomers swamped the settled old-timers in the black community, often moving in with them because Portland's rigid housing laws restricted them to one small neighborhood. During the war, at Henry Kaiser's insistence, the federal government put up the money for a housing development to ease the overcrowding. Vanport, built quickly and cheaply on unincorporated land just north of the city, housed eighteen thousand people (blacks, in segregated units, were five thousand of the total), and alleviated the immediate housing problem. After the war, Vanport became a "catchall" residence for low-income people, including some returning Japanese. But in 1948 it was destroyed by a catastrophic Columbia River flood—fifteen people died—and the issue of housing discrimination could no longer be ignored.

The Portland African American community, vastly augmented by the wartime influx, demanded action. A Portland chapter of the National Association for the Advancement of Colored People (NAACP) dated back to 1914, just five years after the founding of the national organization. One of the founders of the Portland chapter had been Beatrice Morrow Canady, the editor of the weekly African American *Advocate* and the first black female lawyer in Oregon, who later organized a successful statewide referendum in 1925 to repeal the notorious clause in Oregon's 1857 constitution that denied blacks the right to enter the state. Although no longer enforced, this clause, "the shame of Oregon," as one newspaper called it, had become a symbol of persistent white hostility toward blacks.

Now, in the 1940s, the Portland NAACP, headed by longtime resident Marie Smith, and the Portland Urban League, founded in 1945 and directed by a newcomer, Edwin C. (Bill) Berry, joined together to challenge discrimination. Berry immediately launched a major outreach to white audiences, giving fifty-two speeches in the first four months after his arrival in Oregon. Meanwhile, as Berry was attracting most of the attention, Marie Smith and other female members were rebuilding the grassroots membership in the NAACP. According to historian Rudy Pearson, the two leaders did not always agree: Smith, for example, criticized the Urban League annual meetings as "fancy affairs" that attracted more whites than blacks. But slowly—painfully slowly—the combined efforts of both groups began to open up employment, then public accommodations, and finally housing.

The housing battle was the hardest. With Vanport destroyed and temporary wartime housing closed, black Portlanders lobbied hard for new construction and for the end of housing discrimination—to no avail. Despite Mayor Lee's support, voters rejected a ballot measure for low-cost housing and nondiscrimination in 1950. Population density in the restricted black neighborhood reached ghetto-like heights, and was exacerbated by urban renewal projects. The first, in the 1950s, demolished 476 houses to make way for a sports arena; the second, in the 1960s, displaced three thousand people to clear land for a major hospital expansion that, for lack of federal funding, never happened. In neither case were there funds for relocation. No wonder that residents bitterly joked that urban renewal actually meant black removal! Oregon was the last West Coast state to pass a basic civil rights bill in 1953, and did not pass a fair housing law until 1957. Even after that, much informal discrimination remained. As Berry pointedly told his white audiences, in words that are still relevant today, "Portland denies Negroes jobs, then calls them shiftless; segregates them under conditions which breeds delinquency, then calls them vicious; deprives them of incentive for education and self-improvement, then calls them ignorant and undesirable."

In contrast to the public protests that African Americans mounted to demand their civil rights, the Japanese who returned to their homes after internment did so quietly, often fearfully. Kay Sakai Nakao and her family returned to Bainbridge Island near Seattle in 1945. They were among the fortunate ones: their property was intact, and their white neighbors were welcoming. Still, as she said, "Everything was just fine, but, I don't know why, I just kept looking over my shoulder." Only a portion of the Japanese who were removed from Seattle, Portland, Vancouver, and smaller locations like Hood River, Oregon, returned. Most returnees had to begin all over again. Only a lucky few found their prewar property intact; when they sued to recover their losses they received, on average, ten cents on the dollar. The family of Masakazu and Teiko Tomita exemplified the process. The Tomitas had lived in the United States since 1921, farming in Washington first at Wapato on the Yakama Indian Reservation and then in Sunnydale just south of Seattle. They returned from wartime internment to find their formerly rural nursery business engulfed by suburban houses. Teiko Tomita went to work in a garment factory and, for the first time in her life, found herself working with women of many ethnicities with whom she could not communicate in Japanese. Her horizons broadened. A lifelong writer of tanka poems that served her like a journal, she wrote of her factory experience:

A German woman and I
Sewing together
Sharing the same feelings
Speaking of the war destruction
In each of our home countries

Other Japanese experienced similar dispersal from their close prewar Japanese communities. In Seattle, the combination of lower total numbers and large financial losses meant that ethnic businessmen never again reached their prewar prosperity, and the community as a whole was never as tightly knit. Some of the prewar cohesion, of course, had been caused by external discrimination; as that diminished, the Japanese community had less obvious need of internal supports and dispersed into the suburbs like everyone else. In Vancouver, British Columbia, the Japanese were granted the right to vote (for the first time) when they were finally allowed to return in 1949, but most found that they had to start over because their property had been destroyed or sold. Then in the 1970s the city planning department proposed to create a tourist attraction by creating a twentieth-century Japantown, complete with Japanese-theme light fixtures, banners, and street signs. A member of the Japanese citizen's committee responded, "I remember City staff saying you will return it into a Japanese village and have all the Japanese come back and live there, but that was never our goal. We want to be treated like everyone else. We don't want to be ghettoized."

The second-generation Nisei, many of them highly educated, cautiously took advantage of the mainstream jobs that were available as the economy expanded, and they were able to move beyond the segregation their parents had known. In time, the Nisei, who were native-born American citizens, mounted the movement to protest, commemorate, and demand reparations for the wrongs done to Japanese and Japanese Americans by internment during the World War II. Their protests, and those of Canadian Japanese, were finally successful in 1988.

Postwar change was not just an urban phenomenon: changes in agriculture were equally dramatic. In central Washington, the Columbia Basin Project opened up more than half a million acres of irrigated farmland to settlers, many of them veterans, in the 1950s. Quickly, the original 1930s plan for "family-sized" farms of forty to 160 acres was revealed as inadequate, for new economic pressures required farmers to cultivate more land. Federal farm price supports, first enacted in the New Deal in the 1930s, offered the nation's farmers an economic stability that encouraged them to make large investments in equipment. Although tractors, harvesters, fertilizers, pesticides, and improved seeds vastly increased productivity, they were expensive. Farmers found themselves on a treadmill that encouraged expansion to pay off the costs, further expansion to pay off those costs, and so on. In the Columbia Basin Project the trend was to larger and larger farm units: by 1970, the average farm size was 240 acres; by 1999, 500 acres. Another change was that this new agribusiness required large numbers of reliable seasonal fieldworkers to pick the row crops that grew so well there. The problem was answered by Mexican migrant workers who followed the crops while returning to their wives and families in Mexico and south Texas over the winter. The significance of their transition from transience to permanent residence, for themselves and for the Greater Northwest, will be a major topic of chapter 12.

The early Columbia Basic Project was a bellwether in another much-noted respect: farm women were acting strangely. In contrast to earlier homesteaders, these modern-day settlers were unwilling to live their initial years in poverty; as early as 1956, two-thirds were living in housing with refrigerators, running water, and indoor toilets and, further surprising the authorities, a considerable number were living in town and commuting out daily to their land. This insistence on sharing in the consumer culture of the 1950s was, the experts erroneously believed, all due to women, but in fact husbands also refused to live without basic consumer comforts. Furthermore, approximately 40 percent of farmwives, although they used the customary phrase "helping out," were working in the fields with their husbands, and perhaps another 20 percent had off-farm jobs.

Traditionally, farm women had been producers and savers: they fed their families and the hired help, thereby saving money that would have been spent on store-bought food; they sewed most of the family's clothing; and they managed in innumerable little ways to spend as little cash as possible. Until rural electrification in the 1930s (and in some places even later) they performed their daily work without benefit of labor-saving devices, aided usually only by their own children. Now, in the 1950s, all that had changed, and a farm's success depended more on investment in the latest technology and on knowledge of commodities markets than on domestic economizing. Judy Blunt, who grew up on a farm in Montana, remembered the transition: "Overnight, it seemed, the place I grew up on had fallen under the wheels of big business—big land, big lease, big machines, big debt. . . . And I had no place in the new dealings." This change left farm women with a real dilemma. For women, the deepest appeal of farming has always been partnership: it is a rare place in the modern world where the entire family works together, in complementary ways, for a common goal. But as the Columbia Basin Project was among the first to show, as agriculture modernized, farm women had to redefine their complementary role. The choice was clear: either work as "her husband's hired hand" (as one woman put it) or work in town, away from the daily activity of the farm, to bring in the money (or, increasingly, health benefits) to keep the farm going. As *Wallaces' Farmer* noted as early as the 1950s, "Practically speaking, it seems that mom has come to town so dad and the kids can stay on the farm." In the twenty-first century, as the proportion of farmers and ranchers has shrunk to approximately 2 percent of the population of the Greater Northwest, farm women are still searching for the best ways to fulfill the promise of partnership.

In the 1930s, Grand Coulee Dam in Washington had been widely regarded as a unique and colossal achievement, but in the Cold War era, grand dam building on the Columbia River became almost routine. Between 1954 and 1971, eight additional dams were built on the Columbia, followed by four more dams on the lower Snake River built by the Army Corps of Engineers in the decade between 1962 and 1972. As promised, the dams provided flood control, hydropower, and irrigation, and fostered commerce. They achieved those purposes by changing the river: today, the Columbia River is largely a series of placid lakes, enabling barges to carry large cargoes 340 miles from Lewiston, Idaho, to Portland and thence to worldwide commerce. The environmental damage caused by the changes in river flow and temperature soon became apparent, and one of the largest consequences of dam building has been the millions spent to prevent the genuine risk that Columbia River salmon might become extinct.

The damming of the Columbia was a potent Cold War demonstration of the belief that progress and prosperity required large-scale development and displacement, whether it took the form of urban freeways and redevelopment or of massive irrigation projects or the physical transformation of the Columbia River. Most people, even the farmers whose riverside fruit orchards were flooded, accepted the argument that the dams were a necessary price of progress and essential to national security. But one immediate and devastating example, the drowning of Celilo Falls by The Dalles Dam in 1957, showed the disregard in which the federal government held Indian people. Celilo had been the hub of trade, socializing, and ceremony for Plateau and river people for at least ten thousand years. Now it was to be submerged below the waters of the Columbia. The Yakama, Warm Springs, Umatilla, Nez Perce, and smaller tribes were unable to prevent this disregard of Native history; instead, they unwillingly accepted monetary compensation.

On March 10, 1957, the gates of The Dalles Dam closed, and the rising waters of the Columbia slowly crept up the Long Narrows to Celilo Falls

Maggie Jim and her daughters watch as the Columbia River floods Celilo Falls (Collection of the Maryhill Museum of Art, 1997.10.1790)

as groups of Indians, many in ceremonial dress, lined the banks of the river to watch. Rosita Wellsey, then a child, vividly remembered: "As the little islands disappeared, I could see my grandmother trembling, like something was hitting her. . . . She just put out her hand and she started to cry."

As Katrine Barber points out in *Death of Celilo Falls*, there were no significant non-Native objections to the drowning of Celilo. Serious planning for The Dalles Dam began in 1945, too early for organized environmental protests. Aside from the Indians themselves, opposition came from white fishermen and, belatedly, from a few religious and women's groups supporting Indian rights, who urged the relocation of the dam so that the falls would not be flooded. But overwhelmingly, public opinion supported the notion that the damming of the entire Columbia River system would bring progress and prosperity to the entire Greater Northwest (British Columbia built four dams on the upper Columbia as part of the overall effort). A handful of people were, however, concerned about the plight of the thirty-six Indian families who lived in Celilo Village. Barber's spotlight on the relocation activities of two women—Flora Cushinway Thompson and Barbara MacKenzie—sheds light on this devastating decision.

Flora Cushinway Thompson opposed The Dalles Dam and equally vehemently demanded relocation and reparations. She was the spokesperson and liaison for her husband, the venerable Tommy Thompson, who had been Salmon Chief of the Wy'ams at Celilo since the late nineteenth century. In that position, he had allocated fishing sites, mediated disputes, and regulated fishing hours and conditions at Celilo Falls since he was a young man. Flora, a Warm Springs Indian, married Thompson in the 1940s (he was in his eighties, and she about half his age) and inevitably, as discussions with federal authorities about the dam began, Flora slid into a familiar role for Indian women, as cultural intermediary and spokesperson. When it came to dealing with Army Corps of Engineers officials, the discussions were very straightforward. As Flora recounted it, when the last engineer, Colonel Parker, came asking Thompson to sign a contract,

> Chief was lying in the bed over there. He says, "May I ask how old you are?" Colonel Parker, he says, "forty years." "Oh you just a little boy Now you want to buy my fishing? I'm not going to sign." . . . I was standing right there and I says, "Well Colonel Parker, there's your answer. You're not going to make him negotiate with you and I'm not going to persuade him either. . . . You tell your engineers, colonels, to never come to interfere with him no more. That's the last big word he gave you—no, I'm not going to negotiate. So you remember that."

Tommy Thompson was in a nursing home by the time Celilo Falls was flooded; he died two years later. More than a thousand people attended his funeral in the Celilo Village longhouse, where they watched Flora Thompson ceremonially wrap his body in white buckskin and ten Pendleton blankets and put a single eagle feather in his hands before placing him in a cedar coffin and burying him in the Indian cemetery close to the place where the falls had been.

Barbara MacKenzie was the person employed by the Bureau of Indian Affairs (BIA) and Wasco County to relocate the residents of Celilo Village, in other words, to destroy the community that had existed before the dam. MacKenzie, who had trained as a teacher (a common choice for middle-class women) had by the 1950s become an experienced social worker, thanks to extensive volunteer and professional work with the American Red Cross during and after World War II (volunteer work was common for middle-class women of her generation, but MacKenzie's level of professional responsibility was unusual). She brought some unusual sensitivities to what was basically a coercive process. She decided to form an advisory committee composed of both Indians and non-Indians to help implement the policy that was decided by another all-white official committee. To make it work, she had to convince the Celilo residents that she was not simply another BIA agent but genuinely wanted their cooperation, which she did by renting a trailer and living in it full time on the outskirts of Celilo Village. She made it clear, by her opened curtains, that she welcomed visitors. Then she waited several weeks until one day Flora Thompson came to her door and the two formed a partnership to help the villagers through a difficult process. Still, owing to requirements concerning sanitation, availability of utilities, schooling, and welfare that MacKenzie was required to follow, only four of the original thirty-six families moved to the new village. She helped the rest move elsewhere, some to reservations, some to The Dalles and even to Portland. Praised for her successful efforts, she said, "I didn't do anything anyone else couldn't have done," but the fact was that many white residents of The Dalles would *not* have done it, claiming that MacKenzie's limited efforts were a denial of progress, and of the need for complete Indian assimilation. And after all, they reasoned, there was no point in staying once the fishing was gone. Only, one might argue, ten thousand years of history and heritage.

The shock of the loss of Celilo was one factor strengthening the determination of Pacific Northwest tribes to break free of continued dependence on the BIA and to develop their own advocates who would fight for them. A second crucial reason for self-reliance was a sharp shift in federal policy from the limited sovereignty of the Indian Reorganization Act of 1934 to a new policy of termination. The fiscally conservative Eisenhower administration of the 1950s decided that the costs of the reservation system were too high and that Indians, at least those in the economically stronger tribes, could manage on their own. In exchange for a lump sum payment, tribes would relinquish all of their land and throw it open for sale, and the individual payments would allow tribal members to "live like white men." The timber-rich Klamath tribe of southern Oregon was one of the first to be terminated, followed by various groups of western Oregon Indians, including the Grand Ronde, Siletz, and Coos. A much longer list of Greater Northwest tribes was thrown into nearly twenty years of argument, dissention, and effort as they tried to agree on policies to avoid or reverse termination.

Termination had consequences that went far beyond individual reservations. Displaced Indians flooded into the cities of the Greater Northwest, joining former war workers and returning veterans. Many of them did not fare well; it soon became a sick joke that, as one Colville Indian remarked, "If you wanted to see an Indian in Seattle you'd jump in the car and go down to Skid Row." In response, a group of Native women decided in 1958 to establish the American Indian Women's Service League in a storefront Indian Center located just a few blocks from Seattle's Skid Row. As founding president Pearl Warren said, the center was intended to be "a friendly Indian meeting place." Like her six cofounders, Warren, a member of the Makah tribe, had first come to Seattle for a job in wartime industry and had stayed and married an ethnic non-Native man; similarly, cofounder Adeline Skultka, a Haida, married a Filipino. Given the poverty and disorganization of much urban Indian life, these founding women represented the stable middle class, and they were in a position to help, which they did so successfully that historian Coll-Peter Thrush, in *Native Seattle,* called the service league "Seattle's leading urban Indian organization . . . for almost two decades." The league offered immediate assistance in housing and employment to Indians of all tribes whom they found, for example, by looking for Indian newcomers at the Greyhound bus station.

Health was always a major concern: the center housed an Alcoholics Anonymous group and fostered the creation of an Indian Health Clinic that grew into the very successful Seattle Indian Health Board. Many of the center's activities would have been familiar to the benevolent middle-class women of the early twentieth century, but with one big difference: it was fine to help Indians find jobs and housing, but their survival *as Indians* was equally important. As the inaugural issue of the service league's newsletter said, "To those who can see a way of picking up and straightening out the threads from the tangle of Indian affairs, there is the opportunity of doing a real service to the Indian community—locally, statewide, or even nationally." To that end, the center fostered Indian pride by offering crafts classes, dance instruction, and the telling of traditional legends and, later, a gift shop and gallery and annual powwow. The center also fostered, all unknowingly, a new, more militant Indian activism, led by Bernie Whitebear, a Colville Indian who had been a center volunteer and dance leader.

Throughout the 1960s, members of the Seattle Audubon Society (Hazel Wolf prominent among them) had been negotiating with the city and the US military for 534 acres of the decommissioned military post called Fort Lawton to become urban open space and bird habitat. In March 1970 this genteel lobbying was upstaged by the dramatic predawn takeover of the site by a group calling itself the United Indians of All Tribes (UIAT). Bernie Whitebear grabbed the headlines when he claimed to "re-claim the land known as Fort Lawton in the name of all American Indians." This dramatic gesture had widespread support in Seattle's Indian community, including several Service League "old ladies" who scaled the fences with sandwiches and thermoses of coffee for the demonstrators. Because so many of the demonstrators were young people, this athletic support from the elders was much appreciated. Some (but not all) members of the Service League, and some (but not all) members of the Seattle Audubon Society supported Whitebear in the subsequent discussions about the future of Fort Lawton. Today Seattle's Discovery Park (as Fort Lawton is now called) houses the Daybreak Star cultural center where Head Start programs for Indian children and Indian art displays and cultural events are held in a park that embodies the Audubon Society's notion of an urban open space and natural habitat.

Elsewhere, however, the reservations of the Greater Northwest continued to be places of poverty and despair. Salish Indian author Debra Magpie Earling captured the mood in her 2002 novel, *Perma Red*, based on the life and death of her aunt Louise White Elk on the poverty-stricken Flathead Reservation in northwest Montana in the postwar period. While dreaming of a meaningful, loving life, in reality young Louise is trapped among the desires of three men, one a traditional Salish man, another a lazy and predatory white businessman, and another a tribal policeman who cannot protect her. With these three forces—traditionalism, white exploitation, and weak tribal control—against her, Louise could not survive. Her fate, Earling implied, symbolized the larger realities of reservation life.

And what, finally, of the greatest symbol of the Cold War in the Greater Northwest, the Hanford Nuclear Reservation on the Columbia River? When its existence and deadly purpose were revealed at the end of World War II, Hanford quickly became a regional symbol of mixed pride and awe. As John Gunther observed in 1947, "The bomb is, in truth, a kind of apocalyptic, demonic child of the Columbia." Momentarily, in 1945, Hanford workers wondered whether their jobs had come to an end, but in fact the Hanford saga was just beginning. The initial operation of three reactors was augmented with six additional reactors and five plutonium-processing plants as

Hanford produced bombs for the Cold War and, as regional residents later learned, contaminated the air, ground, and water with radioactivity in the process. The last reactor was shut down in 1987 amid a clamor of health claims from "downwinders," and Hanford remains today the largest toxic waste dump in the United States. Ironically, federal funding for cleanup costs exceeds the former weapons budget, so the local economy is thriving.

In the postwar period, the old Hanford camp, which at its height had housed fifty thousand people, was abandoned, and an entirely new city of Richland was built to replace the dormitories and prefabricated wartime duplexes. As urban historian Carl Abbott has explained, the new Richland was a carefully planned, government-owned town that embodied the new suburban values of the era. That is, it was built for white, middle-class Hanford families clustered in school-centered neighborhoods and dependent on automobiles for access to jobs and to shopping. Construction workers and members of racial/ethnic groups found housing outside of Richland or in the nearby towns of Pasco and Kennewick. Richland itself, which had twenty-five thousand residents by 1955, was a hive of civic activity, supporting twenty-five churches, 250 civic groups of all varieties, yearly community events like the Atomic Frontier Days and high school sports teams, who were named, almost inevitably, the Richland Bombers, with a mushroom cloud as their symbol. Richland was a typical suburban community with two exceptions: first, it remained a company-owned town run by the Atomic Energy Commission until 1958, and, second, residents had to ignore the very real risks of working and living there. Privately, residents were perfectly well aware of both facts. As a Richland woman wrote to Senator Henry Jackson in 1955, "This is not a normal community and never will be. . . . The truth is that people are here for one reason only, the job. . . . I have never felt that this is anything but temporary and look forward to the time we can move to a normal community." This middle-class Richland woman might have been shocked to realize that she shared the circumstances of working-class women like the Butte miners' wives, who kept house while knowing that the great open and toxic Berkeley pit was gradually expanding westward toward their homes, or the mothers in Kellogg who learned in 1975 that their children risked permanent impairment from lead emissions from the company smelter.

In 2000, Teri Hein published a disarming memoir, *Atomic Farmgirl*. In it she tells an appealing story of growing up on a small farm in a wheat producing region in eastern Washington. The reader soon notices, however, that the customary rural activities of this established farming neighborhood are shadowed by death. Our awareness grows as Hein's does, and we realize that their farm is downwind from Hanford, where, as residents finally learned, a series of unannounced radiation emissions occurred in the late 1940s, after the wartime "secret" of Hanford was known but before officials thought it necessary to warn civilians. When the information became public in the 1990s, Hein's mother promptly joined the "downwinders" lawsuit, in spite of the disapproval of some of her neighbors, who argued that *if* the land and its occupants had been contaminated it was a regrettable but necessary civilian price to pay for winning the Cold War and besides, going public might adversely affect land prices. But as Hein's mother said at a government hearing, the price was too high. As she said, "This square-mile neighborhood I have just described has only ten families living in it. Of the ten farms, seven have had at least one, if not multiple, cases of cancer in the last thirty years." As of this writing (2015), the downwinders lawsuit is still in court.

As promised, postwar government spending on defense and dams brought unprecedented prosperity to the inhabitants of the Greater Northwest, but it did not bring ease. Middle-class suburban women lived out a domestic dream in the postwar period, but they could not ignore its limits and underlying anxieties. In the films, books, and television shows of the time, women are usually depicted standing quietly on the sidelines, looking pretty, as the men take action. That passive appearance was inaccurate. In the 1950s women were active community-builders and improvers, advocates for equality and for social welfare and for the environment. And as a youthful president inaugurated a turbulent decade of activism, young women began to look for lives that reached far beyond the domestic role that many of their mothers had embodied in the 1950s.

SOURCES FOR THIS CHAPTER

It proved surprisingly difficult to excavate the story of women's activities from the overwhelmingly negative literature on suburbs contained in classics such as Kenneth Jackson, *Crabgrass Frontier* (New York: Oxford University Press, 1985), and others. The books I found useful were Rosalyn Baxandall and Elizabeth Ewen, *Picture Windows: How the Suburbs Happened* (New York: Basic Books, 2000); Stephanie Coontz,

The Way We Never Were: American Families and the Nostalgia Trap (New York: Basic Books, 1992); Lizabeth Cohen, *A Consumer's Republic: The Politics of Mass Consumption in Postwar America* (New York: Alfred A. Knopf, 2003); and especially Lorraine McConaghy, "No Ordinary Place: Three Postwar Suburbs and Their Critics" (PhD dissertation, University of Washington Department of History, 1993). McConaghy's was the only intensive study of Northwest suburbs I found. For the impending changes, see Simone de Beauvoir, *The Second Sex* (New York: Knopf, 1953); and Barbara Ehrenreich, *The Hearts of Men: American Dreams and the Flight from Commitment* (New York: Random House, 1983). For the connection between the Cold War and suburban families see the influential study by Elaine Tyler May, *Homeward Bound: American Families in the Cold War Era* (New York: Basic Books, 1988; rev. ed. 1999).

For McCarthyism, see "University of Washington Sees Red and Fires Three Faculty Members on January 22, 1949," www. historylink. org, essay 1482; Laurie Mercier, "'A Union without Women is Only Half Organized': Mine Mill, Women's Auxiliaries, and Cold War Politics in the North American Wests," in Elizabeth Jameson and Sheila McManus, eds., *One Step Over the Line: Toward a History of Women in the North American Wests* (Edmonton: University of Alberta Press, 2008); and Julie Whitesel Weston, *The Good Times Are All Gone Now: Life, Death, and Rebirth in an Idaho Mining Town* (Norman: University of Oklahoma Press, 2009). Sandy Polishuk tells Julia Ruuttila's encounter with HUAC in *Sticking to the Union*. Unsurprisingly, Hazel Wolf has her own oral history: see Susan Starbuck, ed., *Hazel Wolf: Fighting the Establishment* (Seattle: University of Washington Press, 2002), and Starbuck, "Crossing Boundaries: Hazel Wolf Inside the Environmental Establishment," *Pacific Northwest Quarterly* 96:2 (Spring 2005).

For automobiles and recreation I used Susan Sessions Rugh, *Are We There Yet? The Golden Age of American Family Vacations* (Lawrence: University Press of Kansas, 2008).

On British Columbia and Bennett's Social Credit development policy, my sources were Barman, *The West beyond the West*; and Robbins and Barber, *Nature's Northwest*.

For postwar Seattle, see Jeffrey Craig Sanders, *Seattle and the Roots of Urban Sustainability* (Pittsburgh: University of Pittsburg Press, 2010); and Delphine Haley, *Dorothy Stimson Bullitt: An Uncommon Life* (Seattle: Sasquatch Books, 1995). For Portland in the same period, see David Peterson del Mar, *Oregon's Promise: An Interpretive History* (Corvallis: Oregon State University Press, 2003); Meryl Lipman, "Dorothy McCullough Lee (1902–1981), *Oregon Encyclopedia,* www.oregonency-clopedia.org/entry/view/ lee_dorothy_mccullough/; and for a detailed look at the black experience, Rudy N. Pearson, "African Americans in Portland, Oregon, 1940–1950: Work and Living Conditions—A Social History" (PhD dissertation, Washington State University Department of History, 1996 electronic resource). On housing, see Stuart McElderry, "Building a West Coast Ghetto: African-American Housing in Portland, 1910–1960," *Pacific Northwest Quarterly* 92:3 (Summer 2001), pp. 137–148; and "The History of Portland's African American Community (1805 to the Present)," Portland Bureau of Planning, February 1993, www.portlandoregon.gov/bps/article/91454.

Detailed study of the Japanese return and postwar employment is just beginning. I found the following helpful: Lane Ryo Hirabayashi, "Community Destroyed? Assessing the Impact of the Loss of Community on Japanese Americans during World War II," in Josephine Lee, Imogene L. Lim, and Yuko Matsukawa, eds., *Re/collecting Early Asian America: Essays in Cultural History* (Philadelphia: Temple University Press, 2002); Linda Tamura, *The Hood River Issei: An Oral History of Japanese Settlers in Oregon's Hood River Valley* (Urbana: University of Illinois Press, 1993), and *Nisei Soldiers Break Their Silence: Coming Home to Hood River* (Seattle: University of Washington Press, 2012); Gail Nomura, "Tsugiki: A Grafting: A History of a Japanese Pioneer Woman," in Karen Blair, ed., *Women in Pacific Northwest History: An Anthology* (Seattle: University of Washington Press, 1988); Masumi Izumi, "Reclaiming and Reinventing Powell Street: Reconstruction of the Japanese Canadian Community in Post-World War II Vancouver," in Louis Fiset and Gail Nomura, *Nikkei in the Pacific Northwest: Japanese Americans and Japanese Canadians in the Twentieth Century* (Seattle: University of Washington Press, 2005); and the beautiful and heartbreaking novel by Julie Otsuka, *When the Emperor Was Divine* (New York: Knopf, 2002). Finally, there is the large Seattle-based Densho (legacy) Project of more than seven hundred oral history videos largely about internment but with a few fine recollections of return as well.

The Columbia Basin Project and the changing role of farm women is covered in Brian Q. Cannon, *Reopening the Frontier: Homesteading in the Modern West* (Lawrence: University Press of Kansas, 2009); and

Corky Bush, "'He Isn't Half So Cranky As He Used to Be!': Agricultural Mechanization, Comparable Worth, and the Changing Farm Family," in Carol Groneman and Mary Beth Norton, eds., *"To Toil the Livelong Day": America's Women at Work, 1780–1980* (Ithaca: Cornell University Press, 1987), pp. 213–229. Judy Blunt is quoted in Sandra K. Schackel, *Working the Land: Stories of Ranch and Farm Women in the Modern American West* (Lawrence: University Press of Kansas, 2011), and her autobiography, *Breaking Clean* (New York: Vintage Books, 2002) tells her experience of changing sex roles in vivid detail.

For the story of Celilo Falls, the primary source is Katrine Barber, *The Death of Celilo Falls* (Seattle: University of Washington Press, 2005). There is rich material also in the *Oregon Historical Quarterly Special Issue: Remembering Celilo Falls*, edited by Barber and Andrew H. Fisher, *OHQ* 108:4 (Winter 2007). The lively oral history excerpt by Flora Thompson is in the *OHQ* special issue. Barber and Janice Dilg conducted an oral history with Barbara MacKenzie and wrote an illuminating biographical essay, calling her both an extraordinary and representative woman of her time: "'I Didn't Do Anything Anyone Else Couldn't Have Done': A View of Oregon History through the Ordinary Life of Barbara MacKenzie," *Oregon Historical Quarterly* 103:4 (Winter 2002), pp. 481–510. Special thanks to Kathleen MacKenzie Hunter of Wallowa, Oregon, for the opportunity to read the family history she wrote based on her own oral history with her aunt. For an illuminating article about how Cold War anxiety and affluence shaped white attitudes toward Columbia River dams, see Bob H. Reinhardt, "Drowned Towns in the Cold War West: Small Communities and Federal Water Projects," *Western Historical Quarterly* 42 (Summer 2011), pp. 149–172.

For urban Indians and the American Indian Women's Service League, see Jeffrey Sanders, *Seattle and the Roots of Sustainability*; Susan Lobo, "Urban Clan Mothers: Key Cities Households," in Susan Applegate Krouse and Heather A. Howard, eds., *Keeping the Campfires Going: Native Women's Activism in Urban Communities* (Lincoln: University of Nebraska Press, 2009); and Coll-Peter Thrush, *Native Seattle: Histories from the Crossing-Over Place* (Seattle: University of Washington Press, 2007). Debra Magpie Earling's novel, *Perma Red*, was published by Penguin Putnam in 2002.

On Hanford, see Carl Abbott, "Building the Atomic Cities: Richland, Los Alamos, and the American Planning Language," in Bruce Hevly and

John M. Findlay, eds., *The Atomic West* (Seattle: University of Washington Press); John M. Findlay and Bruce Hevly, *Atomic Frontier Days: Hanford and the American West* (Seattle: University of Washington Press, 2011); and Teri Hein, *Atomic Farmgirl: The Betrayal of Chief Qualchan, the Appaloosa, and Me* (Golden, CO: Fulcrum Press, 2000). Published too late to be incorporated into the analysis was Kate Brown's searing study, *Plutopia: Nuclear Families, Atomic Cities, and the Great Soviet and American Plutonium Disasters* (New York: Oxford University Press, 2013).

Chapter 11
The Noisy and Quiet Revolutions
1960s–1980s

||||||||||||||||||||||||||||||||||||||||||||||||||||||||||||||||||||||||||||||||||||||||||||||||||||||||||||||||||||||||||||||||||

1908: Socialist working women in New York city led a demonstration against garment industry sweat shops, against the brutal conditions and exploitation of children workers, and for women's right to vote.

1910: The socialist Second International commemorated this action by setting aside March 8 as International Women's Day. This was in recognition of the special oppression of women and of the dynamic role women had played in the struggles of working people.

1917: Women textile workers in Czarist Russia went out on strike on International Woman's Day, thus sparking the revolution

INTERNATIONAL WOMEN'S DAY

that ended Czarist rule.

1970: Women are coming together to fight against their second-class status, their low pay, the discrimination they face in every area of their lives.

WOMEN'S LIBERATION TEACH-IN

MONDAY / MARCH 9 / 7:00 P.M. / University of Washington / Husky Union Bldg. (HUB) 25 ¢ donation / men welcome / speakers: Janet McCoud, INDIAN RIGHTS & INDIAN WOMEN / Alice Spence, BLACK PANTHER PARTY / Clara Fraser, WOMEN & SOCIALISM / Margaret Benston, THE ECONOMICS OF THE FAMILY / Sue Shinn, THE SUPER-EXPLOITA- TION OF WORKING WOMEN / WOMEN IN THE UNION MOVEMENT / THE STRUGGLE FOR WOMEN'S LIBERATION - PAST & PRESENT / child care will be available at the Teach-In / sponsored by Women's Liberation - Seattle / office: 5224 - 19th NE / LA 5-2711

We are still living with the repercussions of the women's revolutions of the 1960s and 1970s. At the time, noisy, exuberant, and angry public protests of the largely student Women's Liberation Movement attracted intense media attention while other feminists more quietly enacted major legislative changes intended to benefit women of all races. In this time of change, most of the women of color of the Greater Northwest—African American, American Indian, and Latina*—gave their first priority to the liberation struggles of their own communities, not to women alone, but some of the new legislation affected them as well. The peak of well-publicized feminist activities occurred in the mid-1970s, leaving a mixed legacy of change and controversy. But that was only the beginning, for then came what economists called "the quiet revolution": the steady, persistent, and irreversible movement of women of all races, ethnicities, and economic classes into the labor market, until by 2009 they made up half the workforce in the United States and nearly that in Canada. This was fundamental change.

The force that catalyzed the many social movements of the 1960s was the civil rights revolution, brought to public notice by the 1954 Supreme Court decision ending segregated schools in *Brown v. Board of Education*, the Montgomery bus boycott of 1956, and the Little Rock High School crisis of 1957. A mass movement quickly grew in the South to protest the systematic segregation and discrimination faced by African Americans there (and, many whites were surprised to learn, throughout the nation). The civil rights struggle galvanized black communities and white sympathizers in Portland, Seattle, and smaller cities throughout the Greater Northwest. As the 1960s progressed, black communities moved ever more forcefully to demand the end of housing discrimination and access to employment opportunities. Combining new tactics of direct action with older lobbying techniques and backed, for the first time, by the force of federal law on their side, African Americans demanded the chance to participate in a world of greater opportunity. Women were deeply involved in these struggles, but many of their activities were invisible outside their own communities. As the four female authors of *Seattle in Black and White*

---

* Terminology: "women of color" is the term currently used to denote what were earlier called "minority women." "Latina" is an umbrella term used to indicate all Spanish-speaking women of Central or South-American origin or descent; in the Greater Northwest, it primarily denotes Mexican and Mexican American women (born in the United States of Mexican descent).

(their personal histories of CORE, the Congress of Racial Equality) noted, "Although Seattle CORE was in the forefront of civil rights activity in the early 1960s, it was in other ways a reflection of its time." Routinely, women were elected as secretary but never as chairman, in part because "CORE's male leaders assumed—probably correctly—that they would be speaking to white male businessmen who would not take women seriously." The long and continuing civil rights battle for full equality in employment, housing, and education has taken many different forms and consumed the ongoing efforts of African American women and men for many decades, long after the hopeful mood of the 1960s dissipated. For most of the region's African American women, today as in the past, the needs of their own racial community have been primary. Likewise, Latinas in the Pacific Northwest, galvanized in the 1960s by the United Farm Workers movement led by Cesar Chavez, have been engaged since then in efforts to achieve economic justice for farmworkers and in the larger struggle for immigrant rights.

Community needs always came first for American Indian women. Frank's Landing, home of the Nisqually tribe on Puget Sound, became a famous site of the "fish-in" protests demanding the fishing rights guaranteed by treaties but since denied by white governments. In contrast to the almost complete lack of white support in the fight against dams and termination in the 1950s, the "fish-ins" attracted widespread celebrity participation and media attention. The protests began in 1962, when state police arrested Native fishermen for catching too many fish. Billy Frank, a Nisqually fisherman, soon became the media symbol of the protests, but as he said himself, "I was not a policy guy. I was a getting-arrested guy." His sister, Maiselle Bridges, became a major strategist and publicist, aided by her three daughters and other tribal members. The Fish Wars spread to the nearby Puyallup tribe, where tribal council member (later chair) Ramona Bennett was an active participant in local protests and a cofounder in 1964 of the Survival of American Indians Association (SAIA), which helped gain national attention to the "fish-ins." The SAIA newsletter, *Survival News*, was edited by Janet McCloud, a Tulalip woman married to Billy Frank's stepbrother. She remembered that she found an old mimeograph machine and brought it home and recruited her children to help. Her daughter, Sally McCloud recalled, "All us kids would be all right here, sorting and stapling all the papers together, late into the night." The newsletter was a major source for the Indian side of the story during the decade-long Fish Wars.

The fish-ins were community-wide cooperative efforts, involving men, women, and children. The three women acted as Native women have always done, updated to fit modern circumstances, for their community. Legal scholar Charles Wilkinson summed up the importance of Frank's Landing: "[It] lay at the moral center of the tribal sovereignty movement nationally, as tribes began to climb up out of the termination abyss of the 1950s."

The Fish Wars ended with victory in the Boldt decision of 1974 that affirmed Indian treaty rights to fish in "usual and accustomed places," giving Pacific Northwest tribes a vital legal foothold from which to reclaim their rights. The decision came soon after President Richard Nixon's 1972 announcement of a historic change in federal Indian policy. As he said, "The time has come to break decisively with the past and to create the conditions for a new era in which the Indian future is determined by Indian acts and Indian decisions." This was truly new. This principle, embodied in the 1975 Indian Self-Determination and Assistance Act, coupled with other acts guaranteeing Indian child custody rights, religious freedom, adherence to treaty rights and return of Indian grave goods, reversed assimilationist policies such as the Dawes Act that had done so much harm.

At Frank's Landing, after the 1974 Boldt decision, all three women redirected their activism to help their people. Maiselle Bridges founded an Indian-run school, the Wa-He-Lut Indian School in Olympia. Ramona Bennett, whose social welfare concerns had been nurtured by Seattle's American Indian Women's Service League, went on to become a coauthor of the 1978 national Indian Child Welfare Act. Janet McCloud turned in a spiritual direction, founding the Sapa Dawn Center in Yelm, Washington, where in 1985 three hundred women met to found the Indigenous Women's Network that championed Native women, families, and tribal sovereignty throughout the hemisphere.

The national women's rights movement began far from the Greater Northwest, in Washington, DC, where a group of longtime female federal workers seized the opportunity of John F. Kennedy's election in 1960 to raise some new questions: Why were there so few women in the professions? For that matter, why were so few women seeking college degrees? Why were the wages of working women so low? And why were they clustered in so few occupations? To most people, these were genuine and puzzling questions, demonstrating, many thought, that women were innately domestic and unambitious. The President's Commission on the Status of Women, when it reported in 1963, swept away these misconceptions by documenting a widespread and systematic pattern of employment discrimination against women and consequent lower wages—on average, white women earned 60 percent of what men earned, while black women earned only 42 percent. This report and those of similar state commissions set out a clear agenda to achieve full equality for women. In Canada, the Royal Commission on the Status of Women reported similar findings in its 1970 report.

As the civil rights movement in the South unfolded in the 1960s, white women reformers were quick to grasp the new opportunities it created. In Congress, women's groups joined forces with civil rights activists to ensure the passage of the landmark Civil Rights Act of 1964, which prohibited employment discrimination on grounds of race, religion, national origin—and sex. They formed a group, the National Organization for Women (NOW), directly modeled on the powerful National Association for the Advancement of Colored People (NAACP), to lobby for enforcement of equal access to occupations and professions. In the subsequent cascade of federal laws, executive orders, and lawsuits of the 1960s and 1970s that swept away discriminatory labor laws and mandated equality in education, the greatest immediate beneficiaries in employment were not African Americans but white middle-class women, who had economic and educational advantages that most African Americans—men and women—did not. NOW, originally formed in 1965 as a small Washington, DC, lobbying group, burgeoned in the 1970s into a mass middle-class women's organization of a size and scope not seen since the beginning of the twentieth century.

Other women's groups took action in other ways. As controversy over US actions in the Vietnam War convulsed college campuses, student-based women's liberation groups began to emerge from mostly male antiwar groups such as Students for a Democratic Society (SDS). Historian Barbara Winslow, herself a participant in the student protests at the University of Washington, credits Seattle's radical tradition as the initial catalyst for women's actions there. Seattle Radical Women, formed by students and community women in 1967 and led by Gloria Martin and Clara Fraser of the Socialist Workers Party, was the first to offer classes in the new topics of women's history and socialist feminism. Radical Women made the news when members protested the objectification of women at an appearance by a hapless Playboy bunny, only to have the event turn into a mini-riot when female members of the audience turned on the protesters. Soon student women split from Radical Women over issues of Marxist politics and formed Women's Liberation Seattle (WLS), which supported the causes of the African American and Chicano student groups (including the Black Panther Party and Eldridge Cleaver, whose sexism they never publicly questioned). They were very active in Students for a Democratic Society, joining protests against the war in Vietnam, but definitely not in favor of the infamous slogan coined by the draft resister movement: "Girls say yes to boys who say no."

Tensions between feminist concerns and the increasingly militant masculine bravado of the antiwar movement escalated as WLS turned to long-term institution-building on the University of Washington's Seattle campus, working to establish a free day-care center and a women's studies program. Finally, the antiwar movement itself imploded with a violent month of protests in May 1970 that led to the arrest and eventual trial of the "Seattle Seven." Susan Stern, the lone woman among the Seven, projected, one observer said, "a miniskirted and leather-jacketed image of tough sexy femininity." Whatever unity had existed among different Seattle antiwar groups did not survive this welter of violence.

Canada did not send troops to Vietnam. Consequently, Vancouver's youth movement exemplified the other, more peaceful, rebellion of the era, the counterculture that had first flowered in San Francisco in the "Summer of Love" in 1967. The initial intent of the counterculture was to live peacefully and communally, rejecting both materialism and political engagement. Drugs (marijuana and LSD, both of which were illegal), sexual freedom, and music became both the strengths and the weaknesses of the counterculture, for increasingly adherents joined for the thrills, not for any deeper purpose. Hippies, as they were called, were distinctive in their appearance as well as lifestyle, identifiable by long hair, unisex and colorful clothing, and a tendency toward nudity. In 1968, more than six thousand gathered in Vancouver's Stanley Park for a peaceful Be-In; their numbers forced the city's comfortable mainstream to deal with them. The Vancouver city government worked constructively with local churches to provide food, clothing, housing, and counseling support to nearly thirteen thousand visitors by 1969. When, a few years later, police reacted harshly to a public mass demonstration of illegal drug use, Vancouverites tended to place the blame on the American draft resisters living in the city, and they may have been right.

As many as ten thousand Americans fled to British Columbia to avoid the draft (out of a total fifty thousand who fled to Canada as a whole). One little-noticed fact was that half of them were women, who, as sociologist John Hagen has shown, were often the ones who urged the flight to Canada in the first place. In almost every case, Hagen says, the decision to seek refuge in Canada was a joint one and so was the decision to stay in Canada that some took after the United States declaration of amnesty in 1977 offered a choice.

American draft resisters were also prominent in the back-to-the-land movement that clustered in the beautiful and remote Slocan Valley in southeast British Columbia. The Christian pacifist sect called the Doukhobors, who had lived in the valley since the turn of the twentieth century, helped the newcomers, who were mostly urban and suburban kids, learn the rudiments of farming. Unlike the popular "drop-out" image of the hippies gathered in cities, many of the back-to-the-landers seriously hoped to develop a new kind of society. Most of these back-to-the-land experiments of the 1970s failed, for the economic and personal (usually sexual) reasons that most communal efforts have failed. The experience may have gone bad for women faster than it did for men, according to the memoir of Melissa Coleman, daughter of back-to-the-landers in Maine. What she remembered as a child was constant fear of hunger: "Despite the appearance of bounty, we were always on the verge of not having enough." And she remembers that the cycle of growing, cooking, and preserving fell hardest on her mother: "Mama was doing the kinds of housework many women believed they'd left behind with their virginity in the 1960s."

Young women growing up in the 1960s and 1970s were understandably confused by the range of female roles represented in all these movements, ranging from violent, sexy activist women to dreamy flower children to militant asexual feminists to overall-clad farmers, to name just a few. The general public was disturbed by the new gender-blurring unisex clothing and the fact that both young men and women wore jeans and had long hair. Female activists who did not dress or style their hair in fashionable ways were quickly branded by the media as lesbians, while young women who gladly abandoned the girdles, torpedo bras, and pointy-toed shoes of the 1950s were popularly branded as "hippie chicks" and therefore assumed to be sexually available. Thus for young women, from the very beginning, questions of sexuality were tied up with all the other events. For one thing, lesbians, many of whom had long been quietly living in the region's cities and supporting women's issues for decades, now participated openly in the women's movement. Lesbian history in Seattle, for example, dated to the 1920s, when some lesbians looking for other like-minded women frequented a few openly gay bars that had opened in Pioneer Square. Some of these bars featured flamboyant drag queens, clearly an act of defiance by gay men at a time when homosexuality was both illegal and defined as a mental illness, and when police harassment was common. Like the drag queens, some lesbians adopted the exaggerated sex stereotypes known as femme and stone butch, but others disparaged these displays and sought to live more quietly but, in consequence, often in isolation.

By the 1950s, at a time when homosexuality was still almost exclusively defined as male, two women, Del Martin and Phyllis Lyon, who first met in Seattle, founded the Daughters of Bilitis in San Francisco. Originally intended as a secret social club, they soon began to publish a newspaper, the Ladder, hoping to foster community and challenge the facts of lesbian invisibility. In another step toward visibility, Daughters began holding annual conventions in 1960. A sign of the times at the first convention was the attendance of two policemen, investigating a rumor that some women were wearing men's clothing. Forewarned, all the attendees were decorously dressed in skirts. For lesbians, the women's movement was a welcome location where they could find like-minded others and where they could engage with both gay and straight women in intense discussions of topics that ranged from sexuality to motherhood, from spirituality to separatism. And for straight women, the presence of lesbian women opened many eyes to new possibilities of thought and action. The same kinds of discussions also galvanized gay men, later taking dramatic forms in the 1980s as the AIDS epidemic spread. From these open discussions of sexuality that shocked so many observers grew the gay, lesbian, bisexual, and transgender movement that exists today and that has led to substantial changes in public attitudes.

In the 1950s, young women who were sexually active had often been forced, by parental and community pressure, to marry if they became pregnant, or to give birth secretively in special clinics and give their babies up for adoption. In the early 1960s, the birth control pill became available and was popularly believed to have caused the sexual revolution. Elaine Tyler May has shown that the immediate beneficiaries of the pill were married women; single young women were deterred by medical requirements and expense. Nonetheless, there *was* a sexual revolution in the 1960s, and unprotected sex in a society with limited access to safe and reliable contraception was one of the reasons that abortion was such an issue for young women. The main reason, of course, was that illegal abortions put women in physical danger and in danger of possible arrest as criminals. For many women in the 1960s, abortion became the hated symbol of male control over female bodies and of the enforcement of demeaning stereotypes that they rejected.

Pro-abortion activity took an especially dramatic turn in British Columbia. In 1969, the Canadian Parliament in Ottawa passed an omnibus bill that legalized contraception, abortion, and homosexual acts between consenting adults. It was a stunning victory by Prime Minister Pierre Trudeau's Liberal Party over formidable conservative opposition. Still, the bill contained the crippling restriction that abortions had to be approved by hospital-based therapeutic abortion committees (TACs) of physicians. Few hospitals established TACs, and those were mostly in urban areas, leaving vast stretches of rural Canada unserved. The newly formed Vancouver Women's Caucus, composed largely of students at Simon Fraser University, was outraged by this paternalistic law and determined to take action. In the spring of 1970, the Vancouver Abortion Caravan left Vancouver, bound for Ottawa. Leading the cavalcade of cars was one carrying a coffin filled with coat hangers to symbolize the deaths of women from illegal abortions. The caravan made many stops as it traveled east, meeting with local women's groups and, very much in the spirit of women's liberation, mobilizing opinion by performing guerilla theater skits dramatizing the unfairness of the new law.

The caravan arrived in Ottawa, as planned, on Mother's Day, and a group of approximately three hundred women marched on Parliament Hill, waving placards and chanting slogans demanding repeal. One group of protesters broke off, carrying the coffin, and demanded to see Prime Minister Trudeau at his residence. Conveniently, the prime minister was out of town. The protesters left the coffin, with appropriate speeches, and temporarily retreated, but not before the prime minister's aide had a chance to chastise them for not being "nice" because they called the police officers "pigs" (very much the protest language of the day). Two days later the protesters struck again by infiltrating Parliament and staging a protest that shut down the Canadian House of Commons for the first time in its history. Borrowing a tactic from the militant British suffragettes of the early twentieth century, the protesters wore decorous dresses to escape detection and, armed with fake passes, locked themselves to seats in the visitors' gallery and shouted out their protest. They caused a very satisfying pandemonium before security guards carried them off. Nevertheless, it took nearly twenty more years before the abortion issue was finally settled in Canada by a Supreme Court decision in 1988. Although there have been attempts at restriction since then, none have been successful. The same is not true in the United States, where antiabortion groups have successfully enacted restrictions in many states and, at the national level, prohibited federal funding for women seeking abortions. Idaho, the most restrictive of the Greater Northwest states, currently (2015) prohibits abortions after twenty weeks, denies funding except in cases of rape, incest, or danger to the life of the mother, and requires parental notification and consent for minors, counseling, and a twenty-four-hour waiting period. Defeated by constant picketing and harassment of clients, only four abortion clinics remain in the state.

In the United States, three national measures enacted in 1972 epitomized the strengths and the vulnerabilities of the women's movement. First, Congress approved the Equal Rights Amendment (ERA) to the Constitution: "Equality of rights under the law shall not be denied or abridged by the United States or by any State on account of sex," contingent on its approval by thirty-eight states within six years (as required for all constitutional amendments). Second, the US Supreme Court, in *Roe v. Wade*, legalized abortion during the first trimester of pregnancy; and third, Title IX of the Education Amendments Act mandated equality in education. The ERA gave a focus to liberal women's groups in the Greater Northwest, which worked together to lobby their state legislators on behalf of the measure. The Supreme Court decision on abortion, which at first seemed uncontroversial, mobilized the Christian right into a powerful antiabortion political force. In some ways, however, Title IX, the least noticed of the three 1972 measures, has had the greatest long-term impact on young women, easing their access to higher education and opening the door of competitive sports and athletic physicality to them.

Galvanized by the flood of federal equal rights legislation, chapters of the National Organization for Women formed throughout the Pacific Northwest in the early 1970s. Members often formed consciousness-raising groups wherein they came to realize that many personal inadequacies were caused by systematic discrimination against women, thereby popularizing the term "the personal is political." In Portland, a moment of awakening came for one women's group in 1971, when the all-male City Club rebuffed a motion to admit women with joking comments such as, "This club has too much cleavage already." Thereupon the women, led by the media-astute housewife Gretchen Kafoury, armed with a rolling pin, picketed the City Club at their weekly meetings until they changed their vote.

Shocked by new awareness of the extent of the casual sexism (as it came to be known) of the City Club members and other men, women began to enter politics in record numbers. Many chose to be political by creating and staffing new "alternative" institutions (as they were called) such as women's health clinics and rape crisis centers and providing counseling for "displaced homemakers," as older married women venturing into the workforce were known. But a considerable number of women decided, for the first time, to directly enter politics themselves. Some of these women were longtime members of the League of Women Voters (LWV), the organization first established in the 1920s to educate newly enfranchised women about politics. In subsequent years, the determinedly nonpartisan LWV had evolved into a significant fact-finding and watchdog group. The LWV was the natural home for women who were interested in politics but who had been discouraged from becoming active politicians themselves. Now a number of LWV members, schooled by years of observation in local politics, began to step forward for election to their city councils and as mayors. Many younger women, such as the Portland group that took the name Politically Oriented Women (POW), were children of the suburbs; many were at home with activism, having grown up watching their mothers organize their new communities. They were likely to be members of newer women's organizations and to move directly into local politics from college or graduate school; a few of them ran for statewide office. When enough of them won, change could happen rapidly.

As always, someone had to lead the way. In Oregon in 1962, Betty Roberts, then a schoolteacher and divorced mother of four, contemplated her options: "Just in the past seven years, I'd been told by a male registrar that I couldn't major in physical education; by my [ex] husband that I couldn't teach; by a male minister that I should never have gone to college; and by a male academic advisor that I should be happy being a housewife."

Instead, Roberts decided to go to law school and to run for the Oregon State Legislature. When she was elected in 1964, she was one of only seven women in the House; four years later, she was the sole woman elected to the Oregon Senate. In 1977, she became the first woman appointed to the Oregon Court of Appeals and the first female Oregon Supreme Court judge in 1982. No wonder she subtitled her memoir *Breaking Trails in Politics and Law*.

There had been female legislators in the Greater Northwest since the enactment of suffrage in the early twentieth century, but they had been solitary, token figures. Roberts was a trailbreaker because she actively mentored the women who followed immediately after her and shared her desire to reshape the law to reflect women's new expectations and social roles. Their political efforts produced the single most dramatic change in the legal status of women in the history of the Greater Northwest.

The 1973 session of the Oregon State Legislature showed what was possible. Mentored by Betty Roberts, who had been in the legislature since 1965, and in close coordination with outside women's groups represented by lobbyist Gretchen Kafoury, female legislators of both parties agreed on an agenda of bills to serve the needs of the maximum number of Oregon women of all races and classes and then worked closely together to pass eleven of them. (Betty Roberts noted that the total would have been twelve, had not male legislators, apparently in a fit of pique, balked at a bill allowing a woman to keep her own name if she chose rather than automatically taking that of her husband when she married.)

The 1973 Oregon legislators, urged on by their charismatic governor, Tom McCall, approved the national Equal Rights Amendment by large majorities in the first month of the session. Then came the test for the small female caucus (only 12 percent of the total legislature) to pass laws to make equality a reality. One was a sweeping civil rights bill forbidding discrimination on the basis of sex or marital status in public accommodations, housing, and education. Another bill was the first to provide public funding for child care. Two other bills concerned contraception: one made condoms more available (not hidden behind the pharmacist's counter) and another improved access to voluntary sterilization (not to be confused with the widespread practice of involuntary sterilization of Indian women and the mentally ill, an abuse activists were determined to stop). Five bills addressed small but vital issues affecting employment, including insurance, enforcement, nonsexist language, and equality in job classifications. Another bill even addressed equity in prostitution by requiring that purchasers (i.e., the johns) be as criminally liable as the prostitutes themselves. This package of measures became law not just because the women cooperated across party lines but also because they could count on the help of moderate Republican and Democratic legislators, and they knew they had widespread public support. Another reason, perhaps more clearly seen in retrospect, was the fact that all the bills addressed obvious inequities. In subsequent years, as controversial issues divided the parties, legislative change became more difficult.

While all this was happening in Oregon, female legislators in Washington, who amounted to 30 percent of that state's legislature, were also enjoying success. Prescient members of women's groups in that state, fearful that a national ERA would not pass, mobilized to pass a state Equal Rights Act, the first in the four states of the Pacific Northwest (now two: in 2014, Oregon voters approved a state ERA). Interviewed years later about the law, state senator Karen Fraser emphasized its comprehensiveness:

> A really good way to look at the differences the State ERA made in women's lives would be to see what laws the Legislature changed in order to implement [it]. . . . They related to equal employment opportunity; elimination of various restrictions on working conditions for women that served mainly to block them from getting better paying jobs; marriage and divorce; parental rights and responsibilities; equal treatment in business, credit, insurance, and real estate transactions; pensions; unemployment insurance; rape; state contracting with women and minority owned businesses; child care; and re-wording many statutes to make them gender-neutral.

One popular goal was to change the laws that seemed to blame the woman in criminal cases involving rape, domestic violence, and other crimes against women. The existence of the state ERA later made possible such important victories as the landmark lawsuit *Blair v. Washington State University* (1987), initiated by female athletes and coaches for equity in intercollegiate sports. Change came more slowly in Idaho and Montana, where there were few female legislators, and women's rights activists were on the outside looking in. Nevertheless, one index of the spirit of the times was that both the Idaho and Montana legislatures voted in favor of the national Equal Rights Amendment, although later, when the climate changed, Idaho rescinded its vote.

In British Columbia, the protesters of the 1970 Abortion Caravan are credited with "kick-starting" the feminist movement in Canada. They certainly had an impact on their home town, Vancouver, where the growth of women's groups was exponential: from two in 1969 to more than a hundred in 1974. As in the United States, women's activism took a variety of forms, from the customary steps of joining unions, political parties, and lobbying groups to newer forms such as the establishment of women's centers, feminist bookstores and publishers, women's health centers, hotels, and even music festivals. They operated, however, under a particular handicap: the conservative Social Credit Party still dominated provincial politics, except for a three-year break from 1972 to 1975. In that brief period, the liberal New Democratic Party (NDP) enacted a flood of pent-up social legislation, including a civil rights bill banning discrimination in housing and employment, a reorganization of the social services, and a raft of labor legislation. And in contrast to Social Credit, which had never supported more than a handful of female legislators, the NDP welcomed them, providing the party base that BC women had lacked. Defeated in 1975, the NDP did not regain control of the BC legislature until the 1990s, but now more than a third of its legislators are women.

The overwhelming successes of the 1973 legislative session were never again repeated in either Oregon or Washington, but on the other hand, women's issues were never again completely ignored. Indeed, it is likely that the presence of female legislators ensured that education, children's issues, and social welfare—the perennial "women's issues"—became permanent parts of the political agenda. In Washington, a strong women's lobbying organization, Washington Women United, often working in concert with public employees unions, kept these issues on the table. In 2010, Washington became the first state in the nation to boast the simultaneous office-holding of a woman governor and two female senators, as well as several female representatives in Congress. Regionally, Washington has had two female governors, Dixie Lee Ray and Christine Gregoire; Oregon two, Barbara Roberts and Kate Brown; and Liberal Christy Clark became premier of British Columbia in 2013. No woman has as yet been elected governor of Idaho or Montana. Over the years, women's representation in state legislatures has reached as high as 40 percent but settled back into the 25 to 30 percent range in Oregon, Washington, Idaho, Montana, and British Columbia. And in contrast to the successes of 1973, the passage of some legislation was drastically slowed. As Kate Brown, former legislator and current governor of Oregon, found, it took sixteen years—her entire legislative career—to get a bill passed requiring health insurance companies to cover the costs of contraception. As she ruefully told a reporter in 2011, "If somebody told me it would take that long to pass the bill, I would have said, 'You're nuts.'"

The rapid legal and social changes for women in the early 1970s quickly provoked opposition, skillfully stirred by Phyllis Schlafly, already a prominent figure in the national network of Republican Women's Clubs and quickly supported by conservative politicians everywhere. The focal points were the Equal Rights Amendment and the legalization of abortion. Schlafly began organizing a STOP (Stop Taking Our Privileges) ERA campaign as soon as the amendment was approved by Congress. Within a year there were active committees in more than half the states, insisting that equality threatened the American family, defined as nuclear, heterosexual, and made up of a breadwinning father, a housewife mother, and their children. Aside from the alarmist soundbites that now seem absurd—unisex bathrooms, women in the military—Schlafly and her supporters zeroed in on a fundamental issue. The classic marriage "bargain" assured the authority of the man in exchange for his commitment to support and protect his dependent wife and children. Independent women who insisted on competing equally in the male realms of employment and politics, Schlafly argued, broke the bargain and thus encouraged men to shirk their responsibilities to their families. The STOP ERA message thus was crafted to alarm the nation's many housewives who wished to be full-time wives and mothers, or who doubted their own ability to manage on their own. Warning that the ERA meant that "men were off the hook," Beverly Hubbert of Seattle, who had been recruited personally by Schlafly, spoke widely and publicly against the ERA, saying, "Women have enjoyed special privileges by law in this country because of the value that this country placed on the family, and the women who had the children and raised them. . . . Equality is a detriment to the woman in society." Coupled with the concerns of religious denominations who opposed abortion, anti-ERA forces forged coalitions to defend "family values" and, increasingly, to defend traditional heterosexual marriage.

In Washington state, the "pro" and "anti" forces collided at a conference in Ellensburg in the summer of 1977. To mark International Women's Year (IWY), every state held an open meeting to discuss women's issues and to elect delegates to a national convention. At Ellensburg, months of careful planning were disrupted by the unexpected arrival of an estimated two thousand women motivated by Schlafly and mobilized by the Mormon church (and, at least according to some observers, directed how to vote by Mormon men). The sudden appearance of this formidable opposition came as a surprise to most feminist activists, who simply assumed that all women would agree. Similarly, the national IWY conference in Houston, which had aspired to speak for all women, was confronted by a counter-conference organized by Schlafly on the same weekend. More seriously, there was a protest within the IWY convention itself, organized by the handful of delegates who were women of color (then called "minority" women) who claimed that their issues had not received adequate attention from white participants. These unexpected outcomes shattered the feminist faith in their inevitable march toward equality, a belief further weakened by the final defeat in 1982 of the Equal Rights Amendment, which died for lack of enough favorable votes of the states. Since that time, the position of women, increasingly symbolized by the issues of abortion and gay rights, has become a key divider between the major political parties. In the Pacific Northwest, gays and lesbians have faced two distinct waves of legislative hostility, first in the 1990s when they rallied to defeat anti-gay referendum measures in Washington, Oregon, and Idaho, and again in the early 2000s when all four state legislatures, following a national trend, passed "defense of marriage" (DOMA) laws limiting marriage to a man and a woman. Since the 2013 Supreme Court decision invalidating the national DOMA, the Pacific Northwest states are following suit, some more slowly than others, and antigay groups have not given up the fight. In British Columbia, protection of gay rights has been included in the national Constitution since the 1980s, and gay marriage was legalized in 2005.

One sign of the new antifeminist mood was the election of Idaho's Helen Chenoweth to Congress in 1994. Chenoweth, slim and attractive, well-groomed and fashionably dressed, was a new kind of female politician. Stridently conservative, relentlessly antifeminist (she insisted on being called congress*man*, for example), Chenoweth quickly became the darling of the reactionary right when, among other things, she claimed that white men were "an endangered species." Before Chenoweth, female politicians of both parties had always taken care to dress modestly and speak carefully. But Chenoweth spoke out, voicing the then-new rallying cry: "We want things to be the way they used to be," as she advocated unregulated gun ownership, abolishing the Environmental Protection Agency and the departments of education, energy, commerce, and housing, and unlimited development of natural resources. She attracted media attention not so much for her views (which were considered irresponsibly radical in the mid-1990s) as for her clever challenge to the image of the responsible female politician. Somehow, because she was so conservative, she could say things that other female politicians could not.

In retrospect we can see that Phyllis Schlafly's anti-ERA movement was fortunate in its timing. Her emphasis on the need for special protection for housewives was belied, five years later, by the number of mothers of young children flooding into the labor market. From 1970 to 2010, as the percentage of women in the total workforce inexorably climbed from 43 percent to 60 percent, sociologists kept saying it was temporary, or that it would surely stop rising. However, the rise reflected fundamental changes in the economy as well as new social circumstances. For some women, the reason was rising career aspirations and the need to accept the customary (read: male) career path whether they had children or not. For others, high divorce rates and single motherhood were important factors. But increasingly, even families who disapproved of working mothers and who deeply believed in family values were making the decision that the wife had to work to help maintain household income as men's wages stagnated.

Three crucial innovations enabled mothers with young children to combine family and work responsibilities. Thanks to effective and accessible contraception, for the first time in history women had control over their own reproductive lives and could plan their births in ways that helped them combine their family lives and careers. Once the children were born, vaccines kept them from contracting childhood diseases like measles and chickenpox that had once required quarantine of the child, and usually its mother, often for several weeks; and antibiotics assured that a sick child would recover quickly. Day care was another vital support, although it was often more expensive than many families could afford. And last but far from least was the willingness of young fathers to take on a share of caring for sick children and of housework. Cumulatively, each of these changes created new expectations for young families and for single mothers.

Several different streams of women entered the workforce. The most visible was the entry of women into the professions. Prior to the new laws of the 1970s, all of the nation's professional schools for graduate training had informal "quotas" for women; once they were removed, women flooded into law, medicine, academic life, and business. They were rarely welcomed by their new colleagues. Accustomed to regarding women as inferior, many men were scornful or fearful—or both. The first woman in every field repeatedly found her competence questioned: as Washington senator Karen Fraser remarked about her reception in the legislature, "There seemed to be curiosity as to whether the first woman could really do the job." Most women did the job very well indeed, but acceptance often remained grudging, prompting Charlotte Whitton, the first female mayor of Ottawa, Canada, to say in a famously flippant remark, "For a woman to get half as much credit as a man, she has to work twice as hard, and be twice as smart. Fortunately, that is not difficult." Betty Roberts responded to such treatment by adopting the attitude of "Get used to it, guys, I could be here a long time." She was right: census figures showed that in 2011, American women held 51 percent of all professional and managerial positions. Within the Greater Northwest, the percentages vary. As of 2009, Washington had the highest percentage—40 percent—of women in managerial and professional positions, followed by Oregon at 38 percent, and Idaho, Montana, and British Columbia at 35 percent.

On another employment front, the story was very different. As protective legislation for women, in force since early in the twentieth century, was dismantled, working women naturally looked to enter the skilled trades that paid so much better than "women's work." These heavily unionized occupations were not easy for anyone, male or female, to enter. Typically one had to be first accepted into a training program and then to an apprenticeship on the job before fully qualifying to be an electrician, a machinist, or a firefighter, for example. Physical strength was a requirement for many of these jobs, so only some women qualified. Yet learning the skills turned out to be the least of the challenges women faced. Whatever the equal employment laws might have said, throughout the nation all-male trades greeted female entrants with such hostility, harassment, and outright violence that one woman likened it to trench warfare. In the male-dominated industries of the Greater Northwest, men had always opposed female workers, whom they feared would lower wages. These fears were redoubled in the 1970s, as unions declined and owners increasingly found ways to eliminate or automate jobs.

In 1974, Seattle became one of the first cities in the country to initiate a special training program in the electrical trades for women and minorities at the municipal utility, City Light. In spite of the care that administrator Clara Fraser, a well-known socialist feminist, took to design the program and meet union concerns, the program was a disaster. In the first seven years of the program, only one woman qualified to be a lineman, and she commented bitterly that "there is no way to prove yourself except by changing your sex." Other women complained that coworkers had unhooked their safety straps, dropped heavy objects on their heads, and electrified lines on which they were working. In self-defense, the Seattle (now Washington) Women in Trades organization formed in 1978 to network among women and provide information via a career fair, which is still held yearly. In spite of improved information and stronger laws, the Women in Trades website in 2008 admitted that the percentage of women in the construction trades "is still dismal," although the percentage of female firefighters in Seattle had risen to 9 percent.

A different encounter with men's work occurred elsewhere in the region at the same time as the City Light fiasco. The conjunction of lesbian separatism and the back-to-the-land movement led to a network of lesbian communes, collectively called Women's Lands, in rural southern Oregon in the 1970s. Among the many commitments women made in these communes was one to challenge the customary gendered division of labor by building their communities entirely themselves. They determined to confront their own beliefs about appropriate women's and men's work, learn the skills of traditional male crafts like carpentry and mechanics, and then do even the heaviest "men's work" well enough to provide basic shelter, all without outside male help or advice. The Women's Lands communes accomplished their goals by the classic methods that farming communities in the West have always used, information-sharing and cooperative work, but this time solely among women. What emerged was a division of labor based on each woman's skills and preferences, not on her gender, thus demonstrating that men's work and women's work were not based on innate, inherent skills.

Women of color benefitted from the new equal employment laws of the 1960s and 1970s. In the Greater Northwest, African American and Japanese American women, who had faced blatant discrimination and exclusion in the past, now had wider work opportunities. Black women with high school degrees left domestic service jobs to earn higher wages as secretaries and clerical workers, and those with college degrees found employment as managers, especially in the public sector. As the virulent prewar anti-Asian sentiment waned, Japanese American and other Asian American women faced few formal racial barriers. Much informal discrimination remained, but for women with appropriate credentials (usually a college or professional degree) there was more opportunity than before—but not for those without. While some women of all races and ethnicities (but especially white women) fared very well in the job market, the majority of women did not. In the 1980s and 1990s, as corporations moved overseas and reshaped the US economy, more and more women entered the workforce only to find themselves in low-paying retail or service jobs. The result was that by 2007, 43 percent of employed women in the United States were still clustered in female-dominated occupations (the professional positions of teaching, nursing and social work, clerical work, and jobs in retail and service industries) with average median earnings of less than $28,000 a year. The "gender gap" in wages meant that women earned seventy-seven cents for each dollar earned by men—an improvement over the sixty cents of 1960, but still far from equality.

A 1993 study from the University of Oregon confirmed these national trends. As of 1990, half of Oregon women were in the labor force, and many of them were mothers of young children, as the proportion of working mothers doubled from 30 percent to 60 percent in a decade. The good news was that half of the new workers were in professional and managerial jobs; the bad news was that because mid-range clerical jobs were declining, women were pushed into lower-paying technical and service jobs. And 14 percent of the female population of Oregon was in poverty, with the highest rates for Indian women (27 percent), African American women (29 percent), Latinas (25 percent), and Asian and Pacific Islander women (20 percent). The rate for white women was 12 percent.

What was particularly striking about this study was the way it presaged trends for male workers very much in the headlines nearly twenty-five years later. Growth in the professional and managerial ranks marked real gains for women with higher education degrees. But elsewhere, women remained clustered in a number of low-paying "women's occupations," just as they had at the beginning of the twentieth century. Moreover, the figures showed that women made up two-thirds of all minimum-wage earners. Thus, for women, the "hollowing out" of employment opportunity started a long time ago, with openings at the top and at the bottom and a decreasing number in between. For all of its activism, advocacy, and legislation, the women's movement had not been able to improve employment possibilities for the majority of working women. Nor had it been able to make much of a dent on the gender division in the workforce, largely because of fierce resistance by private employers to wage equalization measures such as comparable worth, which was partly implemented in Washington in 1985, but only for public employees.

As with the issue of abortion, the most striking aspect was the class division: affluent women had made substantial gains, but poorer women had not. Social movements are rarely long-lived, because the demands of daily life gradually wear down the energy required to protest. So it was with the women's movement, which had subsided by the 1980s, helped along by conservative backlash. Many once-vibrant women's organizations declined, died, or shifted focus from large-scale to more limited concerns. Much remained undone, but those who eagerly declared the "death of feminism" failed to realize how much had changed. For example, a century before, the thought that women's issues might dominate the political agenda would have been laughable (witness the repeated rejection by nineteenth-century state legislatures of the issue of votes for women); now they became key points of difference between the political parties.

Changes in the regional economy further underlined women's changed position. In the 1980s, in one of the most dramatic reversals in the economic history of the Greater Northwest, two of the region's oldest male-dominated natural-resource industries simply collapsed. First, the mines shut down: the Anaconda smelter in Montana stopped operations in 1980, and the next year the Bunker Hill Company closed its mines in the Coeur d'Alene district in northern Idaho. Then, in 1983, the once-unthinkable occurred: the copper mines in Butte closed. At the same time, another traditional stronghold of male industry began to give way. The timber industry underwent changes that culminated in the famous "timber wars" of the 1990s that pitted loggers against environmentalists who wanted to save old-growth forests. As the men's jobs vanished, mining and timber families and their communities were thrown into crisis because it was obvious, unlike in the Great Depression of the 1930s, that the jobs would not come back. These industries were gone—mining companies to foreign holdings and lumber companies to the American South—and the men's skills were no longer needed. Jean Barman notes that in British Columbia in 2005, just

3 percent of the population was employed in the traditional male occupations of forestry, mining, fishing, trapping, and agriculture combined.

When, as in mining towns, the company simply left, there was not much community recourse. But in timber country, there was someone to blame: environmentalists using an endangered species, the spotted owl, to demand protection for its old-growth habitat. Much media attention focused on public meetings full of angry speeches about whether spotted owls and their protectors were better boiled or fried, and there was much genuine distress about the loss of a way of life. But the real changes were happening, less publicly, within families.

Timber towns were communities in which the classic male role as breadwinner had survived: men worked hard in a physically demanding industry, and they expected the traditional care and gratitude from the wives and children they supported. Now they had no jobs. Sociologist Jennifer Sherman carefully studied the result in one timber town near the California-Oregon border. Many men could not adapt; they deserted, became addicted to drugs or alcohol, or exploded in episodes of domestic violence. Others refused to let their wives work and tried to get by on temporary jobs. But in the most common adaptation, wives quietly added a low-paying and part-time clerical or sales job to their ongoing domestic work as they figured out how to feed their families on less money. They had become, to use Stephanie Coontz's telling phrase, "co-providers." They did not demand that their husbands share the housework or visibly take on the role of "house husbands." But, Sherman found, women were no longer willing to accept the domestic violence and substance abuse that had been tolerated as one of the costs of men's jobs in the timber industry. In some timber towns a new community ethos took shape in which a good man was valued not for his income but for his ability to be a "family man," committed to good parenting and nonviolent, addiction-free behavior. That these communities were poor was evident, but the men in them took pride in their commitment to their own families and to helping other families overcome abuse. And they all, men and women alike, were angry at a society that talked so much about family values but did nothing to stem the tide of drugs or to provide jobs at decent wages.

In 2009, *Time* magazine reported that "The Argument About Women Working is Over." Their survey showed that three-quarters of the American public viewed the fact that women were full-time members of the paid workforce as a positive for the economy and for society. At the same time, however, the survey showed that a majority of both men and women believed that the traditional nuclear family—father as breadwinner, mother as stay-at-home housewife—was best for the children. But because that was economically and socially impossible, *Time* described daily life for couples with children as one of constant adjustment and negotiation as both parents figured out how to balance their own job needs with those of the household and children.

Picking up on this theme, former journalist Maria Shriver pointed out, "Quite simply, women as half of all workers changes everything," not just for women but for their families, their workplaces, their communities, and the wider society. As her team of researchers argued, "We as a nation have not come to terms with what this means," because "government and business are out of touch with the realities of how most families live and work today." The families in the former timber community studied by Jennifer Sherman would certainly agree.

A look back at the lives of women in the Greater Northwest since the 1960s invites us to take stock of the obvious and more subtle changes that have occurred. The noisy revolution—the explosion of women's rights activism and legislation in the 1960s and 1970s—questioned everything: women's sexuality, psychological and health needs, motherhood, "women's work," men's rights and responsibilities, power issues within the nuclear family, and the priorities of politics itself. While most of these issues have been resolved on broadly feminist terms, some remain unsettled today, engendering unease and outright controversy. On the other hand, the quiet revolution of women in the workforce has, by a more subtle kind of change, altered our daily lives. As historian Joan Sangster has pointed out, fundamental, permanent change is usually slow and incremental rather than sudden and dramatic. As working mothers learned to adjust their daily lives to the schedules, timetables, and hours of employment, so too their consciousness changed. Following that, and often much more slowly, their family members also adjusted. We are still living out these changes; we will all carry them with us into our political and social choices in the future. For now, however, what is obvious is that the doubts that women "could do the job," so widespread in the 1960s, have largely dissipated.

SOURCES FOR THIS CHAPTER

The Greater Northwest sources for this chapter, with a few exceptions such as Betty Roberts's sparkling autobiography, are scarce and scattered. I have patched together what I could from regional sources on women's politics that tilt heavily toward Washington and Oregon (with apologies to Idaho, Montana, and British Columbia) and from national data on women that don't fully take account of regional variations. To fill out the regional picture I consulted several national sources on women's issues, in particular the historical overview by Ruth Rosen, *The World Split Open: How the Modern Women's Movement Changed America* (New York: Viking, 2000; rev. ed., Penguin, 2005); and, for women in the workforce, Claudia Goldin, *The Quiet Revolution that Transformed Women's Employment, Education, and Family,* Working Paper 11953, January 2006, National Bureau of Economic Research, http://www.nber.org/papers/w11953.

Two recent books have begun to document the activities of African American women in the civil rights struggle: Joan Singler, Jean Durning, Bettylou Valentine, and Maid Adams, *Seattle in Black and White: The Congress of Racial Equality and the Fight for Equal Opportunity* (Seattle: University of Washington Press, 2011); and the biography of a pioneering African American female legislator in Oregon, Avel Louise Gordly, with Patricia A. Schechter, *Remembering the Power of Words: The Life of an Oregon Activist, Legislator, and Community Leader* (Corvallis: Oregon State University Press, 2011).

Charles Wilkinson's eloquent and intimate portrait of the Fish Wars, *Messages from Frank's Landing: A Story of Salmon, Treaties, and the Indian Way* (Seattle: University of Washington Press, 2000), has been a major source for my awareness of the activities of Maiselle Bridges, Ramona Bennett, and Janet McCloud, supplemented by http:indigenouswomen. org and Wikipedia, http://en.wikipedia.org/wiki/Janet_McCloud (on McCloud), and the Seattle Civil Rights and Labor History Project biography of Bennett, www.depts.washington.edu/civilr/bennett.htm.

For the Women's Liberation Movement, see Barbara Winslow, "Primary and Secondary Contradictions in Seattle, 1967–1969," in Rachel Blau DuPlessis and Ann Snitow, eds., *The Feminist Memoir Project: Voices from Women's Liberation* (New York: Three Rivers Press, 1998), and her interview with Kate Weigand on May 3–4, 2004, for the *Voices of Feminism* project, Sophia Smith Collection, Smith College, online resource. For lesbians, see Gary L. Atkins, *Seattle: Stories of Exile and Belonging*

(Seattle: University of Washington Press, 2003); Marcia M. Gallo, *Different Daughters: A History of the Daughters of Bilitis and the Rise of the Lesbian Rights Movement* (New York: Carroll & Graf Publishers, 2006); and Cameron Duder, *Awfully Devoted Women: Lesbian Lives in Canada, 1900–1965* (Vancouver: University of British Columbia Press, 2010), a history focused on stories of individual consciousness. On 1950s reproductive issues, see Rickie Solinger, *Wake Up Little Susie: Single Pregnancy and Race Before* Roe v. Wade (New York: Routledge, 1992), and her critique of the strategies of abortion advocacy, *Beggars and Choosers: How the Politics of Choice Shapes Adoption, Abortion, and Welfare in the United States* (New York: Hill and Wang, 2001); and Elaine Tyler May, *America and the Pill* (New York: Basic Books, 2010).

One basic source for the national women's movement is the contemporaneous collection by Robin Morgan, ed., *Sisterhood is Powerful: An Anthology of Writings from the Women's Liberation Movement* (New York: Random House, 1970). For Canada, see Dominique Clement, *Canada's Rights Revolution: Social Movements and Social Change, 1937–82* (Vancouver: University of British Columbia Press, 2008); Christabelle Sethna and Steve Hewitt, "Clandestine Operations: The Vancouver Women's Caucus, the Abortion Caravan, and the RCMP," *Canadian Historical Review* 90:3 (September 2009), pp. 363–495; and Judy Rebick, *Ten Thousand Roses: The Making of a Feminist Revolution* (Toronto: Penguin Canada, 2005).

For the antiwar movement in Seattle, see "Seattle Liberation Front Clashes with Police during Protest at Federal Courthouse on February 17, 1970," HistoryLink.org, essay 2129, www.historylink.org.

For Vancouver in the 1960s, see Lawrence Aronsen, *City of Love and Revolution: Vancouver in the Sixties* (Vancouver: New Star Books, 2010). John Hagen, *Northern Passage: American Vietnam War Resisters in Canada* (Cambridge: Harvard University Press, 2001), focuses on Toronto, not British Columbia, but is still a thorough and convincing study. There is little as yet on the large back-to-the-land movement in the Slocan Valley, though one dissenting woman's perspective is offered in Melissa Coleman, *"This Life Is in Your Hands": One Dream, Sixty Acres and A Family Undone* (New York: Harper Perennial, 2011).

Memoirs by women active in politics in the 1970s and 1980s are just now beginning to be published. Betty Roberts, *With Grit and By Grace: Breaking Trails in Politics and Law: A Memoir* (Corvallis: Oregon State

University Press, 2008), was the first of several political autobiographies published by the Oregon State University Press. See especially, Barbara Roberts, *Up the Capitol Steps* (Corvallis: Oregon State University Press, 2011). For the remarkable 1973 session of the Oregon legislature, see the fine article by Tara Watson and Melody Rose, "She Flies with Her Own Wings: Women in the 1973 Oregon Legislative Session," *Oregon Historical Quarterly* 111(1), pp. 38–63; Marian Yeates, *Gretchen: The Story of Gretchen Miller Kafoury* (Salt Lake City: Marian Yeates, n.d.); for Helen Chenoweth, see Timothy Egan, "Politics: A New Populist; Idaho Freshman Embodies G.O.P.'s Hope and Fear in '96," *New York Times,* January 15, 1996, http://www.nytimes.com/1996/01/15/us/politics-a-new-populist-idaho.... . The Washington Women's History Consortium (www.washingtonwomenshistory.org) has extensive interviews with Senator Karen Fraser and many others on the campaign for the state ERA and the Ellensburg conference of 1976.

For women entering the workforce, I consulted Rosen and my own unpublished research for the entry of women into the professions, and the following for working-class women: Nicole Grant, "Challenging Sexism at City Light: The Electrical Trades Trainee Program," Seattle Civil Rights & Labor History Project, http://depts.washington.edu/civilr/; Seattle Municipal Archives, Women in the Trades, www.seattle.gov/cityarchives/Exhibits/Women; Washington Women in Trades, www.wawomenintrades.com; Susan Eisenberg, "Women Hard Hats Speak Out," *The Nation,* September 18, 1989, p. 272; Shelley Grosjean, "A 'Womyn's' Work is Never Done: The Gendered Division of Labor and the Creation of Southern Oregon Lesbian Separatist Communities," University of Oregon History Department, undergraduate thesis, 2009), http://hdl.handle.net/1794/11043; and Margaret Hallock, Sandra Morgen, and Karen Seidel, *Women in Oregon: A Profile from the 1990 Census* (Eugene, OR: Center for the Study of Women in Society, 1993).

On women in former timber towns, see Jennifer Sherman, *Those Who Work, Those Who Don't: Poverty, Morality, and Family in Rural America* (Minneapolis: University of Minnesota Press, 2009); and Beverly A. Brown's book on the topic of low-paying jobs for women, *In Timber Country: Workingpeople's Stories of Environmental Conflict and Urban Flight* (Philadelphia: Temple University Press, 1995).

Several important publications directed their attention to issues for women in 2009, among them "What Women Want Now: The State of the

American Woman," *Time* magazine, 2009, www.time.com/specials; *The Shriver Report: A Study by Maria Shriver and the Center for American Progress*, 2009, www.shriverreport.com; and Madeline M. Kunin, *The New Feminist Agenda: Defining the Next Revolution for Women, Work, and Family* (White River Junction, VT: Chelsea Publishing, 2012). Finally, Joan Sangster's reminder about slow change in *Transforming Labour* seemed like an appropriate way to end this chapter.

Chapter 12
This Land We Call Home 1990s–2010s

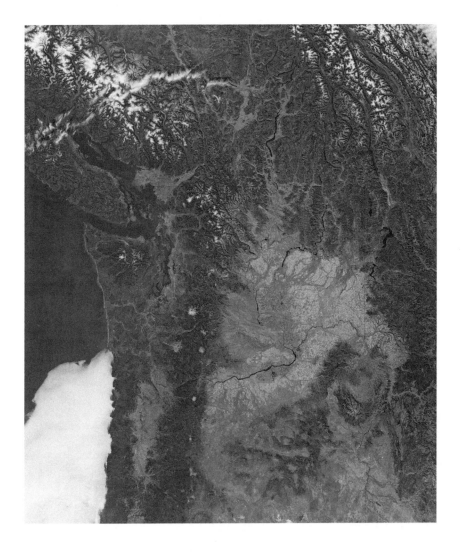

As residents of the Greater Northwest entered the twenty-first century, they faced two new challenges: several large and culturally distinct migrations, and pressures to redefine the land itself. The presence of migrants was not new, but their diversity, numbers, and cultural expectations were. In both Canada and in the United States, immigration laws liberalized in the 1960s led to the large-scale migration of "visible minorities" (the Canadian term for non-European migrants identifiable by the color of their skin) that changed the population balance and required existing residents to recognize new viewpoints and cultural practices.

At earlier times in North American history, immigrants were expected to quickly assimilate and abandon their "foreign" ways. These earlier migrants *did* assimilate, either by forgetting their original languages and cultural traditions or by preserving them for use within their own ethnic communities while presenting an assimilated face to the outside world. Today's migrants are determined to remain bicultural, and to make their own choices about how to blend parts of their own heritage with North American ways. This is new.

Similarly, environmentalists and urban migrants to rural areas in the Greater Northwest hold attitudes toward the land that conflict dramatically with rural ones. In many ways, they share with the new immigrants a disinclination to assimilate by conforming to local codes of behavior. Taken together, these two challenges asked longtime residents of the Greater Northwest to rapidly adjust some of their basic beliefs about the rules of social interaction and the nature of the region itself. It is obvious that there can be no single overarching solution to these two challenges; each community has to find resolution in its own way. Women and men today are working together, sometimes in old ways, sometimes in new, to find their footing in this changed landscape.

The migrant challenge was most dramatic in British Columbia, where as late as 1970, people of British descent amounted to almost 60 percent of the population and, historically, excluded Asians were less than 4 percent. By 2001, however, Asians had shot up to nearly 20 percent of the British Columbia population and the British proportion had shrunk by a third. Vancouver was the locus of this abrupt transition in the 1990s, as over one hundred thousand Hong Kong Chinese moved to the city, seeking a safe haven within the British Commonwealth from which to assess Hong Kong's uncertain future. These Hong Kong Chinese families were wealthy, well-educated, and spoke English. Thanks to laws favoring wealthy migrants (the United States has similar laws), they did not have to stand in line to be admitted: they could buy their way to permanent resident status. Thus they were different from most previous immigrants to the Greater Northwest, who had been poor and expected to work their way up. "They weren't going to start out as pizza delivery men and working in Chinese laundries," historian Henry Yu remarked. Rather, "they expected to be first-class citizens, they wanted to live in the best neighborhoods, wanted the best schools for their kids." Vancouver was a safe place for their families and their money—"the Switzerland of the Pacific," the city was soon nicknamed—while they waited to see what the reversion of Hong Kong to China in 1997 would mean.

The effects on Vancouver were dramatic. Hong Kong Chinese invested in real estate. As new skyscrapers altered the city's skyline, entire suburbs underwent rapid change as Chinese families bought property, tore down existing homes, and built large inward-focused Chinese-style houses— "monster houses," objectors called them—and patronized new shopping malls where the shops and the signage were Chinese. Sociologists began calling such new locations "ethnoburbs." Real estate prices tripled, and local universities experienced a wave of applications from young well-educated Chinese. Then, after 1997, the Hong Kong Chinese began an unusual, possibly unique accommodation to their new country.

When Chinese rule turned out to be more benign than had been feared, these Chinese Canadians adopted a distinctive family strategy. Today, a number of Hong Kong Chinese businessmen (and some women) are popularly referred to as "astronauts" because they work in Hong Kong and fly in once or twice a month to see their wives and children in Vancouver. This behavior is the reverse of earlier migrations when the men ventured to the new country for work while leaving their wives and families at home, the pattern the Chinese themselves had followed in the nineteenth century. Then, most Chinese men who came to North America left their wives— "Gold Mountain widows," they were called—in China. This time, however, it was the women, not the men, who bore the stresses of immigration and the challenge of anchoring the family in a new place. In an odd way, then, the situation of the Vancouver wives of contemporary Hong Kong businessmen was the precise opposite of the nineteenth-century women left behind in China. Removed from the traditional supports of friends, family, and employment, many Hong Kong Chinese women in Vancouver were at first isolated and lonely, bearing major responsibility for childrearing and housekeeping (they had servants in Hong Kong), while wondering whether their husbands would find new sexual partners (as indeed some men, especially rich merchants, did in the nineteenth century, with one family in China and another in North America). Time has eased many of these strains as women have found new friends and activities, only to realize that their husbands have not changed and expect to be as much in charge during their flying visits as if they had been there full time. As one woman bluntly put it, "When my husband is here I don't have my freedom." One thing that is clear about this under-studied reversal of customary migration patterns is that today's female migrants bear much greater responsibility for the future of their families than "Gold Mountain widows" did a century ago. Over time, they surely will change the traditional family dynamics by insisting upon more equal decision-making power.

More recently, as many families decided to return to Hong Kong, wealthy mainland Chinese have applied for residency, seeking shelter for their money and higher education for their children. Their numbers have precipitated a new real estate boom and predictions that a quarter of Vancouver's population will be Asian by 2030. Following the earlier family pattern, the wives and children live in Vancouver while the husbands continue to work in China. It will be interesting to see whether these women, like those from Hong Kong, begin to demand autonomy to match their new responsibilities.

Moving from these personal strategies to a wider perspective, Vancouver is now, almost two decades after the initial migration from Hong Kong, larger, richer, and more global than ever before. Once described as "a beautiful city on the wrong side of Canada," Vancouver is now Canada's gateway to the Pacific and the booming trade with Asia. Although native-born Canadians complained about the abrupt change, the economic benefits to the city were undeniable. As local populations always do—sometimes with great reluctance—they adjusted. With its large multicultural population and its thriving Pacific trade and financial networks, once-staid Vancouver is well on its way to becoming what geographers call a world city (only San Francisco and Los Angeles are currently so classified on the Pacific Coast of North America).

In the Pacific Northwest, Mexicans were the largest and most "visible" group of recent immigrants. In one sense, the term "recent" is an insult:

as far back as historical records exist, men of Spanish Mexican origin had been explorers, fur trappers, miners, and cowboys, but the first sizeable migration of families to the Greater Northwest occurred in the 1920s, when they were heavily recruited to work in the irrigated sugar-beet fields of southern Idaho. Because Mexicans were exempt from the 1924 immigration restrictions, they moved freely in seasonal migrations across the Rio Grande and were highly sought, first as agricultural workers and later as railroad workers, replacing the Chinese and Japanese workers who were barred in 1924. Indeed, by 1929, it was estimated that Mexican-origin men made up 60 percent of the track workers on the Idaho sections of the railroads. In contrast to fieldwork, railroad work was year-round, and Mexican families began to "settle out" in Idaho cities like Pocatello and other railroad hubs. In some other locations, like Idaho Falls and Nampa, agricultural families did the same.

In 1942 the federal government enacted a temporary wartime contract labor system known as the bracero program, in which approximately fifty thousand men migrated yearly to work the fields in western states, leaving wives and families behind in Mexico. Although Pacific Northwest growers did not officially participate in the program after the war, their dependence on Mexican labor, and its seasonal pattern of migration, had been established. And as labor-intensive agriculture developed in the Columbia Basin Project and elsewhere, the need for workers grew.

Settling out in the Pacific Northwest was a big step for migrant families, for unlike California or other Southwest states, there were no existing historically rooted Mexican American communities to ease their way. Among the first to take the step were families of seasonal workers living in south Texas who were US citizens. In the postwar years they wanted more for their children than the yearly migrant cycle of exploitation, discrimination, and poverty.

That was the thinking of Irene Castañeda in 1946 when her husband José, newly returned from contract labor in a Vancouver shipyard, could not find a decent job in their hometown of Crystal City, Texas. Lured by the (as it turned out) false promises of a labor contractor, the Castañedas, their five children, and five other families, "packed in like sardines" in a truck, made the long trip north to Washington's Yakima Valley. The Castañedas never returned to Texas, choosing to live year-round in old army barracks in the Yakima Valley that had become a labor camp. They were unusual in their decision then: most of their relatives and friends, unwilling to leave their family and community connections, continued the seasonal journey that took them from Texas to California, then to Oregon or Idaho and back to Texas or Mexico for the winter.

More than fifty years later, as historian Antonia Castañeda remembered and analyzed her own and her parents' journey, the rhythm of fieldwork dominated her narrative:

> Under reclaimed desert skies, rows of fields, patches, orchards, vinyards, and hop yards stretched before us, waiting for our contracted bodies: cotton, spinach, potato, beet, tomato, melon, hop, cucumber, lettuce, beans, asparagus, berries, apple, grape, grape, peach, plum, lemon, and cherry. Walking, bending, crouching, straddling, crawling, dragging, climbing, stretching, lugging sacks, pails, baskets, baskets, boxes, and crates, and wielding knives, hoes, cutting forks, and shears, we worked from March through October. "Jalando parejo" working at an even pace, we ebbed and flowed—a sea of humanity moving up and down the rows chopping, hoeing, weeding, cutting, topping, twining, tying, thinning, pruning, picking, harvesting—in keeping with the season and the crop. From dawn to dusk, the tide of bent bodies was visible in fields.

As a child working in the fields, Castañeda learned about power relations: Mexican families were the stoop labor, but Anglo men were the foremen, crew bosses, and tractor drivers. Anglo women had indoor jobs in canneries and fruit-packing houses. "Women were paid less than men, Mexicans were paid less than Anglos, and Mexican women were paid the least of all." The lesson was about more than economics. It was about race: "What I understood growing up in the fields of Washington State was that nonwhite bodies were despised." Thus, for the Castañedas, and for subsequent Mexican settlers, achieving justice in the fields and respect for their ethnicity became dual community imperatives.

In the 1960s, farmworkers in the Pacific Northwest were galvanized by the successes of the United Farm Workers, founded by Cesar Chavez and Dolores Huerta, in California, who organized a nationwide grape boycott to demand better wages and working conditions in the field and respect for Mexican culture and values. Following the UFW model, an Oregon organization, PCUN (Pineros y Campesinos United de Noroeste) of farmworkers and reforestation workers was formed in 1985 in the Willamette Valley, while a large UFW chapter was established in Washington's Yakima Valley. Organizing among farmworkers who were so poor and so vulnerable because of their immigration status was a difficult challenge. One of the most effective organizers was Rosalina Guillen, a Mexican American who grew up in western Washington. She led a seven-year UFW boycott that resulted in a contract with the Chateau Ste. Michelle (CSM) winery in 1995. Her success was due, at least in part, to her attention to women, who made up between 30 and 40 percent of the winery workforce but who at first were absent from organizing meetings. Guillen recognized that women were key participants in the tight family networks that already existed among CSM worker families, who shared a common migrant base in Michoacán. Guillen's careful attention to conditions on the ground slowly transformed a fearful, defensive network of worker families into a group that was proud of its skills and ready to work with growers from a position of strength, not of weakness. When the CSM contract was signed in 1995, it was recognized as exceptional not only for better wages but particularly for basic rights like health benefits, pension rights, grievance procedures, and concern about pesticides. Unfortunately, it remains the exception rather than the rule. Most Pacific Northwest growers refuse to sign UFW contracts with fieldworkers. Thus, although wages and working conditions are not as scandalously wretched as they were in the 1960s, today's farmworkers are still engaged in a constant struggle for justice in the fields.

Away from the fields, young Latinas, like previous immigrants, try to hold on to many cultural traditions while trying at the same time to fit into mainstream society. And they have trouble finding a balance. As Dora Sanchez Trevino, whose family settled in Quincy, Washington, in the 1960s recalled,

> I started school in the middle of the school year, and there was a clear stereotype of Mexicans who came in later than usual. No matter what the circumstances were, you were labeled a "migrant." And many of the white students look down on migrant school children. Unlike some of the other Mexicans, I attempted to get along with everyone. I told myself I was there to get one thing done and that was to finish high school. Some of the other Mexican students did try to put me down, especially when I was trying to get involved in school activities and I had white friends.

She felt the tension sharply: "Most of the time you were either a Mexicana or someone trying to act like a gabacha [white-identified]." As an adult, Trevino continued to try to find that balance, working as a bilingual specialist for a state agency and becoming deeply involved in local politics (she was the first woman of color on the Quincy City Council). In recent years, after her son, an innocent bystander, was killed, she has become a leading advocate for measures to control gang violence.

In another example Eva Castellanoz, a former migrant worker and *curandera* (healer) in Nyssa, Oregon, recounted a story about her daughter Chana, who fulfilled her mother's hopes by moving from the fields to a white-collar position in a local bank. When Chana, who had recently been promoted to a supervisory position, helped a local customer, he said (presumably joking), "How did a little Mexican girl like you grow up to be so smart?" to which she replied, "My mother raised me to always do the best I can."

Many Mexican farmworkers might have preferred to continue the customary migrant cycle to the Greater Northwest, had it not been, ironically, for the Immigration and Control Act of 1986. Famous for granting "amnesty" (legal residence) to three million farmworkers, the act also dramatically tightened control of the border. Consequently, many Mexican women and children moved north to join the men who had earlier made the yearly journey alone. They and subsequent migrants who are officially illegal are forced to live in confused and perilous circumstances. Many individual families today contain both legal and undocumented members, and they must devise ways to protect them. Even if they themselves are "legal," they cannot participate fully as American citizens if their actions imperil other family members. Because undocumented members are denied recognition, their status complicates the efforts of the wider Latino community to achieve the basic civil and social rights to which they are entitled as US citizens.

Today, Mexicans and Mexican Americans make up 11 percent of the populations of the states of Washington, Oregon, and Idaho. (British Columbia has an active contract labor system that brings Mexican men north to pick fruit but discourages them from settling.) They are the essential workforce in the region's most prosperous agricultural areas and the majority population in many small farm towns. And many Mexican Americans live in the region's cities, where they fill low-level jobs such as hotel maids and construction workers and where a growing number have middle-class professional occupations. In a very familiar immigrant saga, they hope that their children will get more education and opportunities to move up to the next rung of the employment ladder. But they will not do it at the price of denying their origins or their cultural values.

Many among them, especially in the first immigrant generation, believe that their family-based cultural values hold a lesson for the wider society. As Butte resident Lula Martinez, migrant field worker, organizer of farm-worker health clinics, and advocate for low-income residents, said, echoing organizer Rosalinda Guillen: "We're all *familia*. We're all one big family. Until people realize that . . . we come from the same tree of life, until they realize that, we'll never be able to relate to each other or really love each other the way we should because people don't relate that way. But we're all one big family."

Unlike the Hong Kong Chinese, most of the Mexicans who migrated to the Pacific Northwest were poor and still occupy the lowest rungs of the economic ladder. But they have demographic power: in the long term they will have the power of numbers to force politicians to listen. Today, many Mexican Americans would consider Martinez's hope for one *familia* as naïve, yet the women mentioned in this section—historian Antonia Castañeda, activists Rosalinda Guillen, Dora Sanchez Trevino, and Lula Martinez, and healer Eva Castellanoz and her daughter—all reach across the racial and cultural divide and ask us to do the same.

A third major group speaking up for recognition in the Greater Northwest comprised the region's oldest inhabitants, Indian peoples. Their most recent battle to claim their voice and their land began in the 1950s when the Eisenhower administration decided to "terminate" Indian reservations, thereby throwing the nation's tribes into turmoil, as described in an earlier chapter. Three nationally recognized women emerged as leaders of the fight against termination in the Greater Northwest. Lucy Covington of the Confederated Tribes of the Colville Reservation of northern Washington held to the deeply traditional belief that if her people gave up their lands they would be giving up their soul. But at first, as Laurie Arnold's *Bartering with the Bones of Their Dead* has shown, she had to battle the majority on her own Colville tribal council, which, eager to be free of restrictions imposed by the Bureau of Indian Affairs (BIA), initiated the request for termination in 1956. They thereby precipitated almost twenty years of dissension among the Colvilles, a confederation of twelve different bands, a number of whom (like Chief Joseph's band of Nez Perce) were initially placed on the reservation against their will. Thus the fact that Covington could claim her own lineage as a great-granddaughter of the famous Chief Moses and granddaughter of the legendary Yakama chief Kamiakin impressed some outsiders but not all Colvilles from other bands. First elected to the tribal council in 1956, Covington battled until 1971 before she obtained a majority on the council. Highly regarded in Washington as a lobbyist, she was described as "smart, frank, dignified, selfless, beautiful and a commanding presence." Her persistent and effective advocacy was credited with influencing federal officials to end the policy of termination in the 1970s. However, Arnold's account shows clearly that divisions within the Colvilles, and the abject failure of termination elsewhere, were at least as important in changing federal policy as even the persistent efforts of this one outstanding woman.

If Covington garnered widespread admiration in Washington, Esther Ross of the Stillaguamish tribe was widely regarded as a pest. "Oh God, here comes Esther Ross," one member of Congress was heard to complain, as she appeared, yet again, to lobby for federal recognition of the scattered Stillaguamish, who were among the numerous different groups of Puget Sound Indians. Of mixed Norwegian-Stillaguamish heritage, Esther grew up in California, only vaguely aware of her Indian heritage until she moved near maternal relatives in Washington in the 1920s. But then, when asked to organize legal efforts to sue for lost land and services, she spent the next fifty years fighting for recognition, which was achieved in 1976. After that, she fought with tribal members, for as a result of all her years of almost single-handed efforts, Esther was used to being in charge and was impatient with opposition.

The Grand Ronde tribe of western Oregon was terminated in 1954. Kathryn Harrison, later tribal chairwoman, recalled that the termination payment worked out to thirty-five dollars apiece. One of her children bought a bicycle with his payment; another bought school clothes. Harrison, mother of ten children, left her alcoholic husband in the 1960s and went on welfare, where she received training as a practical nurse. From the early 1970s to 1980, she worked for the closely related Siletz tribe in their alcohol treatment program and helped them regain recognition. When the Grand Ronde decided to apply for restoration, Harrison returned home, which at that point consisted of a six-acre tribal cemetery, a small caretaker's building, and an outhouse. Harrison scoured the surrounding countryside to draw up a list of members with the necessary Grand Ronde blood quantum, compiling an initial list of one thousand, which later rose to five thousand when the requirement was dropped to one-sixteenth (one great-grandparent). Then, when asked to show that the Grand Rondes had local non-Indian support for restoration, Harrison scoured the countryside again, asking for support from city and county governments, business people, civic groups, and members of other tribes.

In September 1983, Harrison led off the testimony for restoration before Congress, but the star witness was her sixteen-year-old daughter, Karen, who said: "All my life I have known only termination. People ask me what tribe I am and when I tell them, they've never heard of it. . . . Becoming restored is important to all of the young people of the Grande Ronde tribe. . . . [It] will make us one again, a whole, a people, to be known again by our government as Indians."

Officially restored in November 1983, the Grand Rondes planned to support themselves by lumbering but unexpectedly became rich by building the Spirit Mountain Casino in 1995. Casino profits have funded tribal housing, college scholarship funds, a medical clinic open to non-Indians as well as tribal members, and a large community development fund. When Kathryn Harrison retired in 2001 after twenty-seven years on the tribal council, including three terms as chairwoman, she could look back with satisfaction on a job well done.

The Indian Gaming Regulatory Act of 1988 gave many Indian tribes, such as the Grande Ronde, the economic base they had always lacked. The gaming act was one of the measures that followed the Indian Self-Determination and Education Assistance Act of 1976. It, along with other acts guaranteeing Indian child custody rights, religious freedom, adherence to treaty rights, and return of Indian grave goods, gave American tribes a firm legal basis on which to reassert their cultural identities. Since then, many Pacific Northwest tribes have taken vigorous measures to regain land, revive languages, and sponsor significant cultural revitalization efforts.

In British Columbia the picture was not so bright, for Natives (or First Nations, as they were now called) did not have the legal basis for land claims that US Indians had in their treaties with the federal government. After World War II, Canadian federal authorities slowly began to abandon their long-standing policy of enforced assimilation. In the 1960s they began to close the hated boarding schools (later still, apologizing for their abuses and, in 2007, offering reparations) and repealed the laws against potlatching. After nearly two decades of protests, the Canadian Museum of Civilization returned six hundred ceremonial pieces that had been seized from the Kwakiutl in the 1920s. Since then, other First Nations peoples have recovered some of their cultural artifacts and, like US Indian groups, have demanded the return of the bones of their ancestors held in museums. In 1985, a serious gender inequity was removed when the law was changed to permit First Nations women to retain their band status when they married a man not from that band (as increasingly Natives and Indians of all tribes were doing).

But the most important change derived from contestation over land rights, which was a matter for provincial, not federal, authorities. In British Columbia, only a handful of the two hundred separate bands had ever concluded treaties with the provincial government. Most band members lived in small reserve villages and led a marginal existence, combining hunting, fishing, and wagework when it was available. The Social Credit Party, which governed British Columbia from the 1950s into the 1980s, rejected all pressures to negotiate, arguing that it was economically unfair to ask the province to bear the costs of settling the claims of so many individual bands. By the 1990s, the new and more liberal NDP government realized that the issue could no longer be evaded. First Nations groups began to realize that, in the absence of formal treaties, their claims to the land *had* to be considered by provincial and federal authorities in any plans for large-scale projects like lumbering and the building of pipelines, a pressing issue once the extensive oil sands lands in northern Alberta started to produce enough oil for export. Negotiations began in the late 1990s and have been, as one commentator put it, "glacially slow" and controversial. Now, in the twenty-first century, treaty-making discussions with more than fifty bands in British Columbia are under way, and the position of First Peoples is slowly improving, but there is a long way to go.

Hopeful as these changes are, the success of current revitalization efforts in the Greater Northwest is far from assured. The younger generation may not be as enthusiastic about the reintroduction of tribal languages as their elders hope. It may not be possible to reconcile the beliefs of tribal traditionalists with the actions that other tribal members believe are necessary to live in the modern world. Efforts to establish tribal policing authority over reservations checkerboarded with white holdings frequently fail. The process of buying back land is slow and expensive, and the effort to expand the tribal economic base beyond casinos is similarly slow and difficult. Forty years after the Boldt decision, the assertion of tribal fishing rights still encounters resentment and occasional violence from white sportsmen. And, as in so many other aspects of contemporary life in the Greater Northwest, the gap between the "haves" and the "have-nots" is wide: tribes that have income from successful casinos are thriving, while those without them are nearly as poverty-stricken as ever.

On one particular topic, the environment, the concern and expertise of Indian people has met a listening ear. After the Boldt decision, Nisqually activist Billy Frank stopped getting arrested and became a leader in the cooperative effort to restore the lands and habitat of the Nisqually River, quickly gaining respect on all sides for his fairness in often-difficult negotiations. He voiced the concerns of many in his eloquent statement:

> I don't believe in magic. I believe in the sun and the stars, the water, the tides, the floods, the owls, the hawks flying, the river running, the wind talking. They're measurements. They tell us how healthy things are. How healthy we are. Because we and they are the same. That's what I believe in.

Increasingly, residents of the Greater Northwest are listening to the Native voices that bring millennia of experience and careful observation to the environmental issues that are of growing concern throughout the region. As extractive industries have declined or died, new attitudes toward the land have begun to replace the former heroic images of loggers, miners, and fishermen, who, seen through environmental eyes, were despoilers of the land and depleters of the waters. Urban dwellers, many of them initially attracted to the Greater Northwest because of its landscape and recreational opportunities, have increased their demands for clean air, clean water, unmarred wilderness, and healthy wildlife. Because most of the region's population is concentrated in its cities, these environmental beliefs often prevail, even when, as in the case of restoring salmon to the extensively dammed Columbia River, the effort is immensely difficult, expensive, and not very successful.

Many of the rural people in the Greater Northwest who still make a living from the land do not like the change in attitudes toward it. Not only are many of their customary farming and ranching operations under fire, but they have recently been confronted with an unexpected invasion as well. As one example, when the logging industry collapsed in the 1980s, the timber towns of southern Oregon experienced another onslaught: the invasion of urban and suburban migrants. One of the first sizable migrations in the 1980s was of affluent Californians to southwest Oregon, northern Idaho, and parts of Montana. Motivated in part by a desire to escape soaring house prices and population pressures, a number of urban migrants also exhibited large admixtures of "white flight" and reactionary and libertarian politics.

Everywhere, the new migrants broke accepted rural codes of behavior. In the past, when newcomers moved to town, they knew they had to conform to local ways if they wanted to find jobs and friends. The legendary cohesion of rural towns had been built on homogeneity, adherence to local customs, and the discouragement of open dissent. But these newcomers came with money and with the urban belief that they should be able to live their lives on their own terms. They often did not realize that residents expected them to adapt to established community norms. Instead, they brought their urban ways and money with them. They wanted new amenities and a greater selection at the grocery store, parks and recreational opportunities, better policing and public services. Most seriously in local eyes, they bought what had been open land and built on it, fenced it, and marked it with "No Trespassing" signs. The new residents often possessed the land with as little regard to previous custom as pioneer settlers had shown toward Indians on their seasonal rounds 150 years before.

Historian William Robbins has noted the similarities between this urban "invasion" of rural areas and gentrification in the cities; certainly it causes the same kind of economic dislocation and resentment among rural people as it has among the displaced residents of urban neighborhoods. The difference in these urban and rural viewpoints is not easily bridged. At a profound level, this current gentrification of the rural Greater Northwest has the potential to change attitudes toward the most basic resource, the land itself. Historically, the land was the source from which people derived their living, but the new urban ethic at its best favors limitation of extractive uses of the land and the restoration of habitat for the benefit of wildlife as well as people. At its worst, the urban impulse is to simply use the land, as Robbins says caustically, as a playground in which to build second homes and golf courses. If history is any guide, urban interests will simply ride roughshod over the community values of rural people. Invaders have done that before.

Women are on both sides of this urban-rural tension, and in many of the rural towns affected by the new economy they are working to create businesses catering to tourists or to urban markets that will keep themselves and their communities alive. But rarely these days are they doing it alone. Today the cooperative efforts involve both women and men as equal partners and spokespeople. Some are working on a change of understanding, one that asks the urban migrants to understand diverse viewpoints and different cultural values. One example of this approach was explained by Diane Josephy Peavy, who has lived on a sheep ranch near the resort towns of Sun Valley and Ketchum, Idaho, for twenty-five years. An urban-dweller before she married third-generation rancher John Peavy, Diane Josephy admits it took her quite a while to adjust to rural ranch life and to realize the tremendous gap between urban and rural viewpoints. Faced with a barrage of attacks from environmentalists opposed to continuing the grazing permits on public lands on which many small ranches depend, the Peavys puzzled about how to react. They tried to find a way to enact the "conviction that if we share our ranching lives with those who know little about living on the land, even those hostile to us, we will make friends for rural and ranching communities." When a local controversy pitted a new bike path against a traditional stock route for sheep, the Peavys found a creative solution: they invited the neighbors to help them herd the sheep from summer to winter pasture. Meeting beforehand over coffee, John Peavy talked about the history of his family's sheep business and then invited everyone out to help herd fifteen hundred sheep alongside a section of the bike path. This small local overture has since grown into a weekend event, the Trailing of the Sheep Festival, that annually attracts as many as ten thousand people and their tourist dollars. The Sun Valley-Ketchum Chamber of Commerce is pleased. More to the point, the Peavys are pleased. As Diane said, "From the beginning the festival was a kind of challenge to the community to learn about the history and culture of its landscape, to listen to the stories of this place they call home."

There are many other efforts under way, in other places in the Greater Northwest, to reconcile past and present ways of living with the land and the hopes and dreams of past and present occupants. Women are part of these reconciliation efforts, as they always have been, but the gap is wide. The Greater Northwest today is not the same place it was a century ago. William Robbins and Katrine Barber remind us that in the early twentieth century more than half the population lived in communities of one thousand people or less. Today, only 2 percent do. And there are many more of us. The combined population of the Greater Northwest in 1900—a little over a million people—has multiplied to over nine million, and, as has been noted, it is substantially more racially diverse. Nor is the land the same, connected as it now is by roads, dammed rivers, telephones, and Internet connections in ways literally unimaginable a century ago. It is farmed and logged and mined differently and, paradoxically, more of it is devoted both to housing (suburbs) and to recreation (national parks, national forests, ski resorts, and designated scenic and recreation areas, to name a few). Yet in spite of all the changes, the sense of living in a distinctive region persists. We live here, not somewhere else. Today we are, as the Schitsu'umsh (Coeur d'Alene) people said long ago, "the ones that were found here." Their descendants and those who have migrated here either recently or long ago need to agree on what that means today. As has always been the case, the Greater Northwest is both unique and changing, and women are a vital force in understanding the past and shaping the future.

SOURCES FOR THIS CHAPTER

Chapter 12 has been the hardest chapter of all for which to find good women's stories, mostly because the events are so recent in historical terms. But examining the sources closely made me realize that the apparent neglect of women stemmed, at least in part, from the fact that women were equal participants in community activities.

On the changing face of Vancouver, see David W. Edgington, Michael Goldberg, and Thomas Hutton, "The Hong Kong Chinese in Vancouver" (Vancouver: Vancouver Centre of Excellence, Research on Immigration and Integration in the Metropolis 2003), at www. Canada.metropolis. net/; "Chinese Vancouver: A Decade of Change," *Vancouver Sun,* June 30, 2007, at www. Canada.com/vancouversun/story.html; Henry Yu, "Global Migration and the New Pacific Canada," *International Journal* (Autumn 2009), viewed at www.history.ub.ca/documents/faculty/Yu_APF_essay. pdf.; and Johanna Waters, "The Flexible Family? Recent Immigration and 'Astronaut' Households in Vancouver, British Columbia," Vancouver Centre of Excellence Working Paper No. 01-02 (January 2001), and the shorter version in *Social and Cultural Geography* 3(2), pp. 117–134.

For Mexican migration and immigration, see the excellent study by Erlinda Gonzales-Berry and Marcela Mendoza, *Mexicanos in Oregon: Their Stories, Their Lives* (Corvallis: Oregon State University Press, 2010), that combines interviews with thoughtful analysis; also Jerry Garcia and Gilberto Garcia, eds., *Memory, Community and Activism: Mexican Migration and Labor in the Pacific Northwest* (East Lansing: Michigan State University, 2005), especially the essay by Maria Cuevas, "'As Close to God as One Can Get': Rosalina Guillen, a Mexicana Farmworker Organizer in Washington State," pp. 277–308; Mario Compean, "Historical Overview: Mexican Americans," in *Columbia River Basin Ethnic History Archive*, http://archive.vancouver.wsu.edu/crbeha/home.htm; Antonia Castañeda, "'Que Se Pudiera Defender (So You Could Defend Yourselves)': Chicanas, Regional History, and National Discourses," in *Frontiers: A Journal of Women Studies* 22:3 (2001); Jerry Garcia, "A Chicana in Northern Aztlan: Dora Sanchez Trevino," in Karen Blair, ed., *Women in Pacific Northwest History* (Seattle: University of Washington Press, rev. ed., 2001); Eva Castellanoz and Joanne Mulcahy, *Remedios: The Healing Life of Eva Castellanoz* (San Antonio, TX: Trinity University Press, 2010); and Laurie Mercier, "We're All *Familia*: The Work and Activism of Lula Martinez," in Janet Finn and Ellen Crain, eds., *Motherlode*.

For Indian termination and revival, see Roberta Ulrich, *American Indian Nations from Termination to Restoration, 1953–2006* (Lincoln: University of Nebraska Press, 2010); Laurie Arnold, *Bartering with the Bones of Their Dead: The Colville Confederated Tribes and Termination* (Seattle: University of Washington Press, 2012); Alexandra Harmon, "Lucy Covington," in Susan Ware, ed., *Notable American Women: A Biographical Dictionary Completing the Twentieth Century* (Cambridge: Harvard University Press, 2004); Robert H. Ruby and John A. Brown, *Esther Ross, Stillaguamish Champion* (Norman: University of Oklahoma Press, 2001); and Kristine Olson, *Standing Tall: The Lifeway of Kathryn Jones Harrison* (Portland: Oregon Historical Society Press, 2005). For British Columbia see Barman, *The West beyond the West;* and Patricia Roy and John Herd Thompson, *British Columbia: Land of Promises* (New York: Oxford University Press, 2005), which, although much less comprehensive than Barman, offers succinct information on the position of First Nations people in the province.

On rural life, see Beverly A. Brown, *In Timber Country*; and William G. Robbins and Katrine Barber, *Nature's Northwest: The North Pacific Slope in the Twentieth Century* (Tucson: University of Arizona Press, 2011). See also Diane Josephy Peavy, "Confronting Fear," in Laura Pritchett, Richard L. Knight, and Jeff Lee, eds., *Homeland: Ranching and a West that Works* (Boulder, CO: Johnson Books, 2007), pp. 26–33. For British Columbia and the Canadian West, see the more academic Roger Epp and Dave Whitson, eds., *Writing Off the Rural West: Globalization, Governments, and the Transformation of Rural Communities* (Edmonton: University of Alberta Press, 2001).

Conclusion

It has been almost one hundred years since Virginia Woolf, in *A Room of One's Own* (1929), pointed out, "We think back through our mothers if we are women," yet most of us have never considered the notion of a distinct female historical tradition. Surely the many women's stories in the preceding pages amount to just that. My purpose in braiding all these lives together into a continuous story is to dispel any lingering notion that only a few extraordinary women made brief appearances at important events. Women were and are everywhere in the history of the Greater Northwest as active participants.

Since the moment of European contact, Native women have been engaged in a continuous effort to defend and sustain their customary ways of life in the face of unrelenting white incomprehension, hostility, and efforts to "civilize" them. That they and their communities are still here at all is a sign of their success. The fur trade flourished only briefly in the Greater Northwest; it would not have been possible at all if Native women had not been willing to provide a bridge between cultures. Beginning in the 1840s and continuing for nearly half a century, the Greater Northwest was gradually settled by farm families that were physically and emotionally sustained by women. Repeatedly, they used the cooperative skills at the heart of the farm partnership to build the family and neighboring relationships that supported communities. In the 1880s, the Greater Northwest was transformed as its natural wealth—minerals, trees, fish, soil—was exploited by corporations and their armies of transient workers. Women banded together in groups, clubs, unions, and social movements to establish civic institutions to serve their communities and to help poor and immigrant women and children who were casualties of the new economic order. Their achievement of woman suffrage in the early years of the twentieth century is one sign of their success, but of equal importance was their insistence that it was the responsibility of city and state governments to provide basic social services to everyone. In effect, even before women had the vote, they created the framework of the modern welfare state. At the same time, immigrant women from both Europe and Asia faced the challenge of adapting themselves and their families while saving as much as they could of their home cultures. Then, in the 1920s, came a pause as the reform impulse waned. We will never know what women might have done next, for the double blows of depression and war required women to take up their most basic role: keeping their families together. In the postwar period, women's community-building in the new suburbs was vital, as was their part in the beginnings of the environmental movement. Had these activities been acknowledged at the time, perhaps the sudden eruption of activist women in the 1960s would not have been such a surprise.

Today, women are in more visible positions than ever before, as TV actors and anchors, doctors, lawyers, politicians, and astronauts, and as members of police and fire departments and of symphony orchestras, to name just a few. They are also where we have come to expect to see them: as teachers, nurses, social workers, office workers, housewives, and mothers, as well as most of the workers in banks, offices, shops, and restaurants. Women are everywhere in Greater Northwest history. Their activities represent a continuous history of activism on behalf of families and communities. Their efforts have taken different forms at different times, but the intent has remained the same. And of course the story continues.

Some parts of this Greater Northwest female historical tradition have been easier to see than others. For example, the story of the efforts of Native women to save their families, communities, and culture from the devastation of conquest has just barely begun to be told. Most versions of our regional history portray European contact and settlement as quickly successful and largely untroubled, with the exception of a few brief Indian wars. This is not accurate: the cost to Native communities, both immediately and over the next two centuries, was catastrophic. Until the full story of Native women's resistance to conquest is fully told, our regional history will be incomplete. Before then, the example of the American Indian Women's Service League, with its distinctive mix of social welfare and cultural affirmation described in chapter 10, seems one to keep in mind.

The domesticity so essential to the survival of the Oregon Trail pioneers of the 1840s is a world apart from the skills a modern-day housewife needs today. Yet because the basic purpose—taking care of the needs of one's family—remains, we haven't fully realized how completely women's domestic activities have changed. The Applegate women of the 1840s (chapter 3) needed a full day to do the family's washing; their present-day descendants need only press two buttons, one on the washer and one on the dryer. Likewise, pioneer housewives were too busy to pay much individual attention to their children, whereas child nurturance is today's domestic priority. That probably explains why, when recently polled, respondents overwhelmingly said that the needs of young children were best served by a nuclear family consisting of a male breadwinner and a full-time female housewife, even as they acknowledged that today's families require two full-time wage earners (chapter 11). The traditional domestic division of labor is so familiar, and so emotionally comforting, that it is difficult to abandon. But the lesson of the 1950s (chapter 10) is clear enough: unless domesticity makes an important contribution to the family's economic well-being, as it did until 1945, it is not enough. Today, while remaining committed to their children's welfare, women have sought ways to use their abilities in the workforce.

Women's efforts to fulfill their responsibilities both at home and at work are made much harder by the continuing gender segregation of the workforce. Unequal pay was a major target of women's rights advocates in the 1970s (chapter 11), but their efforts have been undercut by the failure to raise wages in the so-called women's professions of teaching, nursing, and social work and by the clustering of women in low-paid service jobs. Gender segregation in the workforce has a long history and clearly is difficult to change, but it is clear that pay equity is essential to a truly equal society.

In addition to these recurring themes, one more characteristic of women's activism must be underlined: women rarely acted alone. The theme of collective action and collaboration that runs through these accounts is too strong to ignore. And, it must be pointed out, cooperation is not just a female prerogative. What this account repeatedly shows is that people—men as well as women—don't act alone. They migrate together in groups, or they join a chain migration. They work together in an occupation, or they consciously join together, as in clubs and community-building. New immigrants are not the only people who cluster: as a general rule, we all seek commonality at work, in leisure, and in politics. We all operate within social networks. In the past they would have been immediate—family and local community—whereas today they might be social media that connect us around the world.

Shall we blame Hollywood and the figure of the lone gunslinger for the way we have overstressed the individualism of western history? Or the failure of past historians to include enough people in their stories? Or the hastiness with which a regional image of the Greater Northwest was built on the heroic figure of the laboring man in logging, mining, and fishing? Regardless, we must correct it, because misunderstanding our past leads us to underestimate the urgency of the need for people of diverse interests to work together to build our common future. A history of women such as the present volume is one way to open up our sense of the past, but only one of the ways. Other historians with other perspectives are already contributing their efforts to this common cause.

Aside from adding to our sense of the past, what shall we conclude about women in the Greater Northwest? First it must be said that a general overall survey such as this book can only be the beginning of an answer. Nearly every woman mentioned in the previous pages deserves further study, and we cannot hope to have a full answer to the question until then. Further, as I suggested earlier, the story is ongoing. But for now, an interim answer might be that this is best seen as a history of the continuous adaptations that women in the Greater Northwest have made to changing social and economic circumstances. They have largely done so with the welfare of their families and communities in mind. Should we not take the efforts of so many women for community betterment as seriously as they intended them, and, following in the tradition of Tsagigla'lal, realize that the responsibility to be watchful guardians and shapers of the public good remains as essential today as it has been in the past?

Acknowledgments

When I moved to Washington State University in Pullman in 1978, I knew hardly any Pacific Northwest history, and even less about its women. That changed over the next thirty years, as, with WSU's steady support, I researched and taught western women's history. I am deeply grateful to WSU, for the friendship of my colleagues in the Departments of History and Women's Studies, and to the many students who helped me learn over the years. And I might still just be talking about this book had it not been for the opportunity to spend a year as a senior research fellow at Yale's Beinecke Library and Lamar Center. I am grateful to Johnny Faragher, the Lamar Center director, and George Miles of the Beinecke Library, who made it possible. A week at the Imnaha Writers' Retreat hosted by the Fishtrap writers' conference got me going again a few years later.

My next and most overwhelming debt is to all the authors on whose writings this book is based. I frankly had no idea how much has been written about women in the Greater Pacific Northwest—and how little most of that fine work has been acknowledged—until I started collecting titles and reading in earnest.

Although of course I take responsibility for all of the opinions in this book, the truth is that because of the collaborative nature of most of my work I genuinely can't tell where many of my ideas came from. My regional collaborations began with early Women's Studies conferences organized by Corky Bush of the University of Idaho and Diane Sands and Judy Smith of the University of Montana, Missoula. The Washington Women's Heritage Project of the early 1980s, and especially the insights of Kathryn Anderson, Karen Blair, and Margot Knight, was vital, as were the first Women's West conference in 1983, the Coalition for Western Women's History, and my long-lasting collaboration and friendship with Betsy Jameson of the University of Calgary. I have enjoyed shorter collaborations with Ruth Moynihan and Laurie Mercier that made me think about the possibilities and the limitations of manuscript and oral history sources for women's history. Another long-lasting source of ideas, which I hope was as collaborative as I remember, was provided by the graduate students who asked me to direct or serve on their dissertation committees. Katrine Barber, Michelle Conte, Nancy Engle, Patricia Hart, Sandra Haarsager, Linda Hunt, Brenda Jackson, Erika Kuhlman, Tess Rond, Jennifer Ross-Nazzal, Carly Schiffner, and Michelle Tabit, among others, will find traces of their dissertations in this book. Another formative collaboration, instigated by Toni Dewey, was the effort to engage a wide variety of western women's historians in a comprehensive exhibit plan for a proposed Women of the West Museum, a plan that, alas, never came to fruition. Closer to home, for twenty-five years I learned from meeting and hearing writers as they discussed their work at Fishtrap's summer conference at Wallowa Lake, Oregon. At WSU, the opportunity to serve as editor of *Frontiers: A Journal of Women Studies* and to collaborate with Patricia Hart, Karen Weathermon, and the authors whom we published was a gift. Finally, my participation on the board of the Washington Women's History Consortium in the early 1990s taught me how much I did not know about women in politics.

When I began to think about how to organize all the material I had gathered, I had a few role models in mind. I was still teaching at the University of Colorado when Elise Boulding, working with scanty sources, published *The Underside of History* (1976) and showed us all just how much European women's history there was to think and write about. Joan Jensen, as always in the vanguard, was the first to show in *California Women* (published with Gloria Lothrop in 1987) that regional histories could be about more than famous women. Barbara Engel's *Women in Russia 1700-2000* (2004), a favorite with my students, helped me think about how to write in palatable, accessible chapters. And at nearly the opposite extreme, Jean Barman's monumentally readable *The West Beyond the West* (1991) seamlessly incorporated women without making a big fuss about it.

Once I began writing, I continued to need help. At various times I asked many people to read individual sections, including Joanne Mulcahy, Mary Wright, Adele Perry, Jennifer Thigpen, Shannon Applegate, Mary Murphy, Sarah Elbert, Peter Boag, and above all Jackie Peterson-Loomis. I thank them all for their help and advice. For help finding British Columbia sources I thank in particular Nancy Janovicek and also Adele Perry, who generously shared her manuscript about the Douglas family with me. I also thank the many reviewers who saw this manuscript at various times. Even when I disagreed most vehemently with some of them, I still appreciated their time and effort. For editorial guidance, I especially thank Patricia Hart, who got me going, and, at a much later date, my daughter E. V. Armitage, who gave the manuscript a thoughtful and appreciative read. I also want to thank my friends and colleagues Betsy Jameson, Joan Jensen, Mary Murphy, and Susan Wladamor Morgan, who rallied around at a low moment.

I thank Tom Booth and the Oregon State University Press for moving my manuscript slowly but inexorably toward acceptance and publication. And Heather Oriana Petrocelli has my deepest gratitude for navigating the baffling (to me) world of electronic images.

Finally there is my family, who has had to live with this project for a very long time. I thank E.V. for her editorial assistance and Amy for her design sense. And I especially thank my husband Bob, a man of abiding curiosity, who never once said "Haven't you finished that book yet?"

Index